ORIENTAL ARMOUR

ARMS AND ARMOUR SERIES

General Editor: CLAUDE BLAIR

To be published in this Series

HUNTING WEAPONS by Howard Blackmore
ITALIAN FIREARMS by James Lavin
DAGGERS AND KNIVES by Harold L. Peterson
ENGLISH PISTOLS, 1650–1750 by F. Wilkinson and A. Littler
ENGLISH ARMOUR by Claude Blair
REVOLVING ARMS by A. W. F. Taylerson

H. RUSSELL ROBINSON
F.S.A.

ORIENTAL ARMOUR

LONDON: HERBERT JENKINS

First Published by
Herbert Jenkins Ltd
2 Clement's Inn
London WC2

© H. Russell Robinson, F.S.A. 1967

Made and Printed in Great Britain
by W. & J. Mackay & Co Ltd, Chatham, Kent

CONTENTS

List of Illustrations

Author's Preface

The purpose of this book is to provide an introduction to what is generally agreed to be an extremely wide subject. It cannot claim to be comprehensive. Much material is difficult to come by and a great deal of careful research remains to be done. I am only too aware, for example of the scantiness of available information on such subjects as Mamlūk and Turkish armour, Persian and Indian armour before the seventeenth century and many aspects of Chinese military equipment.

However, I hope that, within its scope, this book will adequately serve its purpose. The text is based on my own notes, observations and researches made over the past twenty years and I am, of course, indebted for information from published works and manuscripts.

I wish to express my grateful thanks to my wife Margaret for the typing of the text; my friend and namesake Mr. B. W. Robinson of the Victoria and Albert Museum for help and advice on Persian armour and the loan of many photographs of miniatures for study; Miss Jennifer Scarce of the Royal Scottish Museum, Edinburgh, for assistance in sending photographs and specimens for my examination; Mr. Douglas Barrett of the British Museum for assistance and suggestions concerning India; Mr. R. W. Skelton of the Victoria and Albert Museum for much valuable assistance also in Indian matters; Dr. Ortwin Gamber of the Waffensammlung, Vienna, for suggestions and long hours of valuable discussion; Dr. Alfred Janata of the Museum für Völkerkunde, Vienna, for valuable and generous assistance on the occasion of my visit; and to Mr. Howard L. Blackmore for the loan of a rare book from his library. For kindly supplying photographs, I wish to thank Mr. Randolph Bullock, Curator of the Department of Arms and Armor in the Metropolitan Museum, New York, Miss Cilette Keller of the Bernisches Historisches Museum, Col. Jacques Wemaere of the Musée de l'Armée; and the Director of the British Museum. A special word of thanks is due to Mr. F. Wombwell-Robinson of the Tower of London Armouries staff for photographing many items in the collection.

ORIENTAL ARMOUR

Chapter One

The Origins of Oriental Armour

Oriental armour, whatever its country of origin, developed from one of the basic forms of defence used in the ancient world. All forms of armour are of great antiquity and it is only in degree and material that they changed down the centuries.

Armour of Fabric

Fabric armour was perhaps the oldest and simplest, and it cannot be tied down to any one centre of culture or to any phase of development. It was found in many countries of both eastern and western hemispheres, in primitive and civilized communities, wherever some type of defensive armour was worn. Sometimes it formed the sole defence, particularly for the poorer soldier, and sometimes it was worn in conjunction with another form of armour: beneath the mail to absorb shock, or beneath plate armour to reduce chafing.

We shall see in the following chapters that armour of hides or fabric—either of several or many thicknesses, or of two layers stuffed with wool or fibres—was used extensively in the Orient for all parts of the human anatomy. In India and Asia the cut of the garments had a strong Mongol character; whilst in the Middle East and North Africa, Arab fashions were dominant.

Scale Armour

Scale armour—a defence of very great antiquity—may have begun, as so many aspects of civilization, in the Middle East.

The earliest representation is in the tomb of Kenamon, who lived in Egypt in the reign of Amenhotep II (1436–1411 B.C.). The painting shows a garment constructed of ribbed bronze scales laced to a foundation, with blue bands at neck, sleeve, and bottom edges. A tubular leather neck defence is shown with it.

Another wall painting, in the tomb of Ramesses III (1198–1167 B.C.), in which the scales are clearly rendered with laces connecting them in rows,[1] shows a standing collar and short sleeves. Bronze scales such as those shown in these tomb paintings have been found in Egypt and Cyprus. They have an embossed

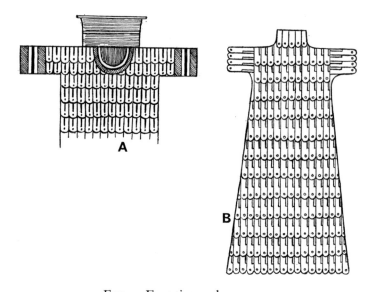

FIG. 1 Egyptian scale armours
A From the wall-paintings in the tomb of Kenamon, 1436–1411 B.C.
B From the wall-paintings in the tomb of Ramesses III, 1198–1167 B.C.

central rib and are laced together rather like lamellar armour in reverse, generally with a leather or fabric lining. Pictorial representations are numerous, as are actual scales from archaeological sites all over the ancient world. Single scales and large portions of armours, such as those from the Roman sites at Newstead[2] and Corbridge,[3] are not unusual finds wherever there has been some form of military occupation.

The graves of people dominated by a warrior class, such as the Scythians, Sarmatians, and Avars, have provided a wealth of military gear for us to study, thanks to their belief that all their earthly practices continued in the next world. Many finds of scale armour of various forms have come from Scythian burials of the fifth to fourth centuries B.C.

The commonest form of scale armour was built up of rect-angular plates with the lower edge rounded or pointed. They were pierced in their upper edges with holes for lacing them to a foundation of leather or fabric, and with pairs of holes at each side for securing them in horizontal rows with a link or twist of wire. Generally, the rows of scales were overlapped in an imbri-cated pattern—like the scales of a fish or the tiles on a roof—but there were instances where they were placed so that one scale overlapped the one immediately beneath it. Some Oriental scales were of a more distinct leaf form, simply sewn in rows to the foundation. Riveting was occasionally employed.

Where scales are represented overlapping upwards—as in the Assyrian reliefs from Nineveh in the British Museum on warriors wearing long scale coats, and on many Chinese clay figurines where the pattern is either painted or modelled—we may perhaps have a convention employed to represent armour of laced lamellae. The possible clue to this theory is the little rib, either carved or modelled, reaching up from the bottom of each scale for about two-thirds of its length, which could well represent the laces connecting the rows of plates together. Also, in such cases the scales are not imbricated, but are placed immediately below each other—a definite feature in lamellar construction.

Scales have been found with a medial rib, but a commoner method of strengthening the thin plates was to emboss the lower ends, which, if not so treated, might quickly have become curled or bent with the movement of the wearer's body. This embossing of scales was taken to extremes in China and in Poland in the seventeenth century, and many fine specimens made in the latter country survive in Polish collections. They were made for the wealthy officers of hussar regiments and display strong Oriental features.

Scales for armour have been made from wood, rawhide, gold, silver, copper, bronze, and iron. Many of the reports upon which we have to rely for our information, written by Greek historians like Herodotus (IX, 22), are rich with descriptions of armours, frequently of scales, as being of gold or silver. Rarely, this may have been the case; but the softness of these metals would have deterred even the most extravagant of monarchs from relying upon them as a protection. Such armours were more likely con-structed of bronze or iron plates gilded or silvered or even simply

of burnished yellow bronze or tinned bronze—both of which could
have been equally impressive and at the same time protective. In
China, under the Han Dynasty, there is some evidence for armour
of jade scales or plates for wear at court.[4]

In ancient Greece scales were fastened to all or part of the rigid
leather cuirasses of the sixth and fifth centuries B.C. Etruscan art

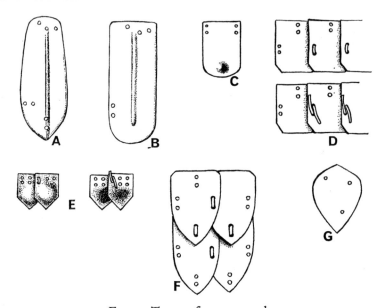

FIG. 2 Types of armour scales
A Egyptian, bronze, seventeenth century B.C., Metropolitan
   Museum, N.Y.
B Syrian, from Nuzi, fifteenth century B.C., Baghdad Museum
C Egyptian with boss, from tomb of Pharaoh Sheshonq, tenth
   century B.C., Brooklyn Museum
D Roman, bronze, from Aventicum, Landesmuseum, Zurich
E Roman, bronze, from Corbridge, Ministry of Public Building
   and Works, London
F Roman, bronze, from Sotin, Zagreb Museum
G Chinese, copper, from Si-ngan, Han dynasty, after Laufer

is also rich in representations of scale-covered cuirasses based
upon the Greek model to be seen on several bronzes in the
British Museum, but it is the flexible Roman *lorica squamata* that
may be the result of direct Syrian or Sarmatian influence on the
Imperial armies.

The reliefs on the Column of Trajan, in the Forum at Rome,
depict scenes from Trajan's Dacian Wars (A.D. 101–102), and in

these the only troops wearing scale armour are the Syrian auxiliary bowmen and the attacking Sarmatian cavalry, allies of the Dacians. The legionaries are shown wearing the laminated *lorica segmentata* and the auxiliary troops, both horse and foot, wear mail shirts called *lorica hamata*.

On the column of Marcus Aurelius at Rome, which carries similar but rather coarsely executed scenes in relief, many of the auxiliary troops wear scale armour—though not to the complete exclusion of mail. The Marcus Aurelius column was erected to celebrate this Emperor's victories against the Germans and Sarmatians in A.D. 175, after six years of war.

We are, of course, mainly concerned with the influence of the Middle East and Asia Minor on the rest of the Orient, and for this we must refer to the scale-clad Sarmatian cavalry on the Trajan Column. They are depicted as wearing built-up conical helmets, and both men and horses are covered with skin-tight armour of scales. The only facts in these sculptures are probably the helmets of the men and the eyeguards of the horses, which are circular and pierced with small holes. The rest, as is now known, is a figment of the sculptor's imagination—no doubt a literal translation of reports that the Sarmatian horsemen were armed, both rider and mount, from head to foot in scale armour. What, then, did the Sarmatians wear? The answer lies in the archaeological finds scattered throughout the Roman world, where Sarmatians later served Rome in the capacity of auxiliary cavalry of the type termed *cataphracti*. From the fort at Newstead,[5] in Roxburghshire, there are leather chamfrons studded with bronze nails, masked parade helmets and what appears to be a piece of laminated bronze armour for a horseman's thigh. From Ribchester,[6] in Lancashire, comes the finest of the masked helmets (British Museum) and a pair of deeply bossed bronze eyeguards from a *chamfron*, probably of leather, while similar finds are recorded from the frontier forts at Mainz and Stuttgart, Germany. The most conclusive evidence available for the method of equipping the *cataphracti* in the Imperial Roman army comes from Dura Europos, two hundred and fifty miles from Damascus on the Euphrates River, where excavations were carried out from 1928 to 1938 by teams from Yale University and the French Academy of Inscriptions and Letters.[7] Dura Europos, a fortified city, had been held by Greeks, Parthians, and Romans, from

whom it was eventually taken by the Sāssānian Persians in
A.D. 256. In a store in one of the towers the excavators brought to
light two complete scale trappers for horses—one of bronze and
one of iron—and a third in a fragmentary condition. The scales
are linked together with loops of wire to form rows which have
then been laced or sewn to a coarse jute fabric and bound at the
edges with red tanned leather. The trappers are open at front and

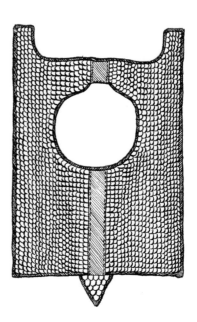

FIG. 3 Scale horse armour from
Dura Europos, third century A.D.,
Higgins Armory, Worcester, Mass.

back, and a hole has been left in the area covered by the saddle or
shabraque. No armour for the horse's head was discovered, but
no doubt it would have been used. For the rider, only two thighguards of lamellar were found—which will be discussed later. A
graffito of a Parthian fully armed horseman, also found at Dura,
shows the complete scale bard in use.

Scale armour was seldom used after this period in such large
quantities, lamellar taking its place to a great extent. The lack of
flexibility in scale armour must have caused a swift decline in its
popularity when other more comfortable types were obtainable.
A large piece of scale armour with links joining the bottoms of
the scales to those in the row beneath was found at Totin and is
now in the Zagreb Museum, Yugoslavia.⁸ Such armour would
hardly require a backing, except as a protection from the ends of

the wire links on the inside, and the lack of movement must have confined this defence to a waist-length sleeveless cuirass.

All scale armour was restricted in flexibility, because the scales cannot turn back on each other. To give adequate protection, they had to be sewn in close-set rows; and in fastening them securely, the backing became taut and puckered, so reducing the movement allowed by the narrow areas between the rows. Lamellar and mail armour, particularly the latter, restricted the wearer's movements only slightly, and in consequence eventually ousted scale armour almost completely.

Lamellar Armour

Lamellar armour in its simplest basic form was constructed of hundreds of small rectangular plates of iron, bronze, or rawhide, pierced with from eight to fourteen holes at top, sides, centre, and bottom, arranged according to the method of lacing employed in the area in which it was produced. The plates, or lamellae, were first laced with leather thongs into horizontal rows, to the length required for whatever part of the armour they were to occupy. These rows of lamellae were then laced together vertically, over-lapping each other upwards—an essential feature of true lamellar construction. The resulting garment could be straight, of any desired length, with or without sleeves. The opening could be at the front or at one or both sides. Long skirts were often split to facilitate riding.

Such armour required little skill to make once a craftsman knew the essential rules of construction. The elaboration in the finish of lamellae, and the complicated techniques employed for lacing them into rows, only came when the armourer could go no further in the improvement of his product. They were not essentials for the strength and durability of the armour. In its simplest form, made from rawhide lamellae and dressed leather thongs, it made a light, efficient and, above all, flexible defence— and one is therefore not surprised that the Mongol hordes, with their great herds of livestock, adapted it to their needs and used it extensively.

Evidence points to the Assyrians as the people responsible for the early development and spread of this form of armour. In the numerous battle scenes depicted in the reliefs from Nineveh and Nimrud,[9] commemorating the victories of Ashurnasirpal and

Ashurbanipal, dating from the eighth and seventh centuries B.C., hundreds of Assyrian soldiers, both foot and mounted infantry—they had no true cavalry—are represented wearing cuirasses constructed of lamellae. These cuirasses reach from shoulder to waist, and in many instances they have short, close sleeves. If we accept the representations as correct and translate the method of construction literally, then we are confronted with a type of lamellar armour quite different from later specimens. A more solid form of construction is suggested, rather than the loosely laced rows of lamellae. Each row of lamellae would appear to be laced down at top and bottom to a substratum of leather or fabric, the same plaited lacing holding the bottom of one row and the top of the next. The convention employed to represent the lacing is a narrow strip of herring-bone lines engraved between the bands of vertical lamellae. The same convention is used on the Etruscan bronze statue of Mars dating from the fourth century B.C., found at Todi and now in the Vatican Museum. Here, a typical rigid hide cuirass made on the Greek model is covered with rows of lamellae laced down at top and bottom. All the edges of the cuirass are bound or piped. There are many similar Etruscan representations of armour made in this way and it is also to be seen in Parthian art when under Hellenistic influence.

As stated in the previous section on scale armour, the Assyrian soldiers wearing ankle-length coats of scales, shown with their rounded ends pointing upwards, each with a rib running for about half of the scales' length, may well represent the more orthodox form of lamellar armour. These heavily armed soldiers are few in number and only represented in one scene, taking part in the siege of a city. Such armour may have been used only for sieges and later adapted by the Persians for their heavy cavalry. The Assyrian soldiers in question wear aventails of the same construction as their body armour attached to the lower edge of their conical helmets, which fit closely round the face and descend to the shoulders. These are the earliest representations of a feature which was to become an integral part of many Oriental helmets.

Fragments of lamellar armours have been found at Etsingol, in south-western Mongolia, on the sites of Chinese watch towers and forts of the late Han Dynasty and dated from the last century B.C. to first century A.D.[10] This is the earliest recorded find in Central Asia, whilst the Mediterranean area can claim far earlier specimens. A Swedish expedition, excavating sites in Cyprus, found lamellae dating from the seventh and sixth centuries B.C.[11]

The continued use of lamellar armour in the Middle East is proved by the finding of the thigh armour at Dura Europos, where it had probably formed part of the equipment of a Parthian auxiliary in the Roman garrison at the time of its destruction by the Sāssānians in A.D. 260. The Parthians and Persians—like the

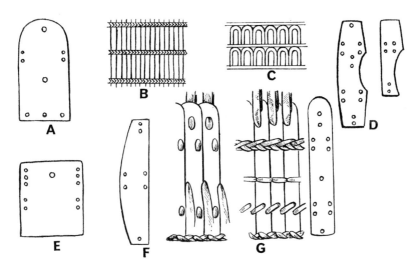

FIG. 4 Types of lamellae
A From Idalion, Cyprus, sixth century B.C.
B Relief from Nineveh, 668–626 B.C.
C Relief from Nimrud, c. 880 B.C.
D Avarian, from Kertsch, fifth century A.D.
E Roman, from Dura Europos, third century A.D.
F From Wisby, Gotland, c. A.D. 1361
G Tibet, face of laced lamellae, back of same, single lamellae

Sarmatians—were noted for their fully armoured cavalry, and it is believed that it is from Iran that the spread of lamellar armour began. Lamellae have been found in Viking graves in Sweden dating from the tenth century A.D., and there is ample pictorial evidence of wide use in eastern Europe: as, for instance, the seals of the fourteenth-century Dukes of Mazovia. In the south, it was brought to Hungary by the Avars and to Italy by the Longobards. The latest evidence for lamellar armour in Europe was the finding of a complete sleeveless coat on a skeleton in the mass graves from the Battle of Wisby, in Gotland, which took place in 1361.

From Central Asia, lamellar armour spread through Mongolia and eastern Russia to the tribes of Siberia. The Chukchies and Koryaks made iron lamellar armours similar to those of Tibet, except that theirs were essentially footmen's armours and were provided with a large wooden shield, covered with leather, to protect the left shoulder and back of the head—possibly as a defence against stones thrown from the slings of their comrades advancing behind them.[12]

Lamellar armour reached China in about the last century B.C. from its nomadic neighbours in the west and north-west, and eventually passed through Korea to Japan in about the fifth century A.D.[13]

Mail

In the course of the world's history, mail—a defence constructed with interlocked rings—was more widely used than any other type of armour.

The Romans are known to have been using mail in the first century B.C.,[14] and referred to it as 'Gallic mail'. The earliest representations from Roman sources show the *lorica hamata* with large shoulder straps of Greco-Etruscan pattern of mail mounted upon a stiffened foundation.[15] But by the beginning of the second century A.D., on the Column of Trajan at Rome, the auxiliary infantry and cavalry wear simple shirts of hip length with short sleeves. From the Aurelius column, and many other sculptures of the second and third centuries, the *lorica hamata* can be followed without change. At Dura Europos, the remains of both Persian and Roman soldiers were found, wearing mail shirts, where they were trapped in the mining operations at Tower 19.[16] A Roman mail shirt in the Saalburg Museum is of the same date (A.D. 260).

The Roman belief that mail was of Gallic origin has been questioned by modern archaeological finds in Scythian and Sarmatian graves. One from Zharovka, near Kiev, is dated to the fifth century B.C. by a Greek kylix found with it. It is, of course, just as likely that the Scythians acquired their mail by trade or by raids on Celtic settlements.

In Sāssānian Persia, mail was widely used—often with an admixture of lamellar. The superb rock carving at Tāq-i-Bōstān, *c*. A.D. 620, which depicts Khusru II in full armour, is carved with such fine and delicate detail that every ring of his mail shirt and aventail are clearly shown. His rounded helmet, with moulded eyebrows and veil-like aventail, is closely related to a helmet found in a Vendel grave at Uppsala in Sweden. The masked helmet from the Sutton Hoo ship burial, now in the British Museum, is also of this family. In this case the aventail is replaced by neckguard and large ear flaps.

For the production of mail it was essential to have a knowledge of wire drawing. And it was necessary to establish settled centres where the armourers, with their teams of apprentices and labourers, could work undisturbed at their exacting and time-consuming task. Mail was always costly and greatly prized, and only the wealthiest of rulers could afford to have their body-guards and standing armies equipped with it. The Mongol hordes had neither the means to produce mail nor, probably, the desire to do so, since it could be taken so easily when raiding civilized communities.

By the fourteenth century Persian miniatures illustrate portions of the armour constructed from a combination of plates connected by mail. The first pieces were defences for the knees—a very vulnerable part of the Oriental horseman, who rode with a short stirrup, so that the knee was prominently exposed to an opponent's weapon. This combination of mail and lamellar developed into complete armour for man and horse—and, in India, even for elephants—by the fifteenth century. Mail had always been slow to construct, and the addition of large plates of overlapping rows of horizontal lamellae into the structure must have speeded up the production of armour—especially when needed in quantity. It would also have considerably reduced the weight and drag on the limbs experienced when wearing mail.

Much Oriental mail was riveted—either every ring or those in every alternate row, the others being punched out from iron sheet.

In Japan, the Philippines, and eighteenth-century India and Persia, much mail was unriveted and—with the exception of the Philippino, which was of brass—this may be put down to the fact that the rings were extremely fine and therefore difficult to rivet.

Some unusual fragments of Etruscan mail in the Musée de l'Armée, Paris, of the fifth to fourth century B.C. are constructed of round and double elliptical links, displaying strong affinities with early Japanese mail of the fourteenth century A.D. and later.

Laminated and Splint Armour

The Greeks and Romans both used laminated armour for the limbs of the cavalryman, as described by Xenophon in his *Art of Horsemanship*[17] and shown among Greek military equipment on the Pergamon reliefs,[18] at Berlin, of 231–228 B.C.

There is also a long-sleeved laminated coat amongst the Dacian and Sarmatian trophies at the base of the Trajan Column, which points to this form of armour already being used by the peoples of eastern Europe and south Russia and, through Greek influence, by the Parthians and Persians.

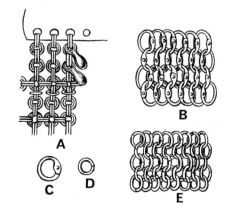

FIG. 5 Types of mail
    A Etruscan mail, Musée de
      l'Armée, Paris
    B Riveted mail
    C Single riveted ring
    D Single butted ring
    E Butted mail

The Roman legionary *lorica segmentata* of the first and second centuries A.D. was a development of this form of armour and may have been evolved from Greco-Etruscan models. The arm defences for the cavalry are shown as of tubular section in the Pergamon reliefs, as are also the sleeves of the coat on the Trajan Column. We must presume that these were of bronze hoops riveted to internal straps of leather, as were portions of laminated Roman armour from Newstead and Carnuntum.

The heavy armed Parthian *cataphractus* of the Dura Europos graffito, and both Parthians and Persians in the rock reliefs of Adashir I at Firuzabad, show arms and legs encased in horizontal laminations. One of the latest examples, dating from the sixth century A.D., is engraved on a silver Sāssānian dish in the Hermitage at Leningrad, showing two warriors in combat with their legs and feet completely covered with laminated defences.

There is, unfortunately, no continuous chain of illustrative material or actual examples to connect us with the fifteenth century, when similar laminations were used by the Mamlūks, Turks, and Indians. These late examples are not, however, mounted upon leathers, but connected by strips of mail at the ends of the laminations.

Armour of straight splints of convex section, laced together to form defences for the forearms or as shinguards, have been found in Scythian graves in the Crimea and south Russia.[19] They were

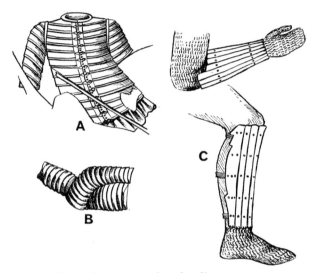

FIG. 6 Laminated and splint armour
A Laminated coat, base of Trajan's Column, second century A.D.
B Laminated vambraces, Pergamon reliefs, third century B.C.
C Splinted vambrace and greave, Swedish, seventh century A.D., after Post

usually backed with leather, which was turned over the sharp edges of the plates.

Similar splint defences have also been unearthed in Vendel graves at Uppsala, in Sweden, and also found with Japanese lamellar armours in burial mounds of the seventh and eighth centuries A.D. Splints for the limbs were also used extensively in Japan from the fifteenth century until 1867, when armour was finally put aside. As in the case of the horizontal laminations, similar splints, connected by mail, were used in Egypt, Turkey, and India from about the late fourteenth century.

It is possible, then, that both of these forms of armour construction remained in use from ancient times until the nineteenth century; but with changing techniques they were adapted to more advanced methods of construction. One may also put forward the argument that the Oriental smith seldom mastered the working of iron in large masses—such as was done in Europe —and that the tools he was accustomed to using confined him to making his armour in segments and joining them together by various means to create a flexible defence which was perhaps comfortable to wear, but never the perfect protection against all weapons of offence. On the other hand, the Oriental smith could, if he wished, have created one-piece helmets of considerable depth and size, and also one-piece shields and cuirasses. No doubt the dictates of his customer and fashion dominated the pattern of his product, as we know was the case in Japan in the Edo Period.

¹ There are several scale armours shown in this painting, in groups of three, probably representing tribute or booty from a defeated neighbour. The rows of scales are in three alternating colours, implying scales of stained hide. If the heads of the scales pointed upwards, these would be excellent examples of lamellar construction.

² J. Curle, *A Roman Frontier Post and its People. The Fort of Newstead in the Parish of Melrose*, 1911.

³ J. W. Anstee, 'Fragments of Roman "Bronze" Scale Armour from Corbridge', *The Museums Journal*, Vol. 53, No. 8, pp. 200–2, Nov. 1953.

⁴ Folke Bergman, 'A note on ancient laminae armour in China', *Ethnos*, Vol. I, No. 5, Sept. 1936.

⁵ Scottish Museum of Antiquities, Edinburgh.

⁶ British Museum, London.

⁷ *The Excavations at Dura-Europos*. Preliminary Report of Sixth Season of Work, October 1932–March 1933, pp. 439–52. Yale University Press, 1936.

⁸ An almost identical piece of scale armour was found in a Roman site at Razgrad, Bulgaria. See Joseph Alfs, 'Der bewegliche Metallpanzer im römischen Heer', *Zeitschrift für Historische Waffen -und Kostümkunde*, Vol. 16, Part 3/4.

⁹ Now in the British Museum, London.

¹⁰ Folke Bergman, 'A note on ancient laminae armour in China', *Ethnos*, Vol. I, No. 5, Sept. 1936.

¹¹ Bengt Thordeman, *Armour from the Battle of Wisby, 1361*, Vol. I, pp. 273–4, Stockholm, 1939,

¹² George Cameron Stone, *A Glossary of the Construction, Decoration and Use of Arms and Armor*, Portland, Maine, 1934.

¹³ J. Edward Kidder, *Japan*, Ancient Peoples and Places Series, London 1959.

¹⁴ Paul Couissin, *Les Armes Romaines*, Ch. VI, pp. 338–46, Paris 1926.

¹⁵ There are many representations of this form of *lorica hamata* on the Arch of Orange and a statue of a Gallo-Roman soldier of the first century A.D. from Vacheres in the Avignon Museum which shows this armour in considerable detail.

[16] *The Excavations at Dura-Europos*, Preliminary Report of Sixth Season of Work, October 1932–March 1933, pp. 188–99. Yale University Press, 1936.

[17] *Art of Horsemanship*, XII, 5, p. 359, Scripta Minora, translated by E. C. Marchant, Loeb Classical Library, 1946.

[18] These are in the victory frieze of Attalus I of Pergamon commemorating his campaign against Antiochus Hierax, Selucid king from north of Taurus and an ally of the Galatians. Now in Pergamon Museum, Berlin.

[19] Greta Arwidsson, 'Armour of the Vendel Period', *Acta Archaeologica*, Vol. X, Fasc. 1–3, 1939.

Persia

―――――――――――――⟫⟪⟫⟪――――――――――――

Mail and Lamellar

The influence of Persian culture on the continent of Asia cannot be too heavily stressed. The neighbouring countries and invaders may all have introduced something into Persia, but always it was absorbed and eventually became an integral part of this great country—just as the Arabs, the Mongols, and Turks all became Persians with strong nationalistic feelings and taste.

The Persians were the armourers of Asia, for they surpassed all others in this important craft. Down the centuries, the demand for Persia's craftsmen was ever increasing and they could be found in Arabia, the Caucasus, India, Turkey, Central Asia, and Russia.

In the ancient world Persia had grown to a great power, her soldiers wearing little or no armour. Herodotus described the great army of Xerxes when, in 480 B.C., he invaded Greece.[1] Of the Medes and Persians as a whole, only a few wore armour. Some had body armour of iron scales and wicker targes and only some of the cavalry wore helmets of bronze or iron. As both Greek mercenaries and Assyrians were amongst the best armed in this great force, one may assume that any armour worn by Persians was inspired by one or the other of these militant peoples.

Xenophon[2] describes Cyrus the younger and his guard of six hundred cavalry, the men armed with breastplates, armour for their thighs, and helmets, and the horses with armour on head and breast. In his *Cyropaedia*, Xenophon describes the troops of Cyrus in greater detail:

'All those who were with him wore the same purple garments, brazen armour and helmets, white crests, short swords and each with a spear made from the timber of the corneil-tree. Their horses were armed with brazen chamfrons, breast-plates and shoulder pieces which also served to protect the riders' thighs.'

Cyropaedia is, strictly speaking, a novel about the young King Cyrus I, and the equipment Xenophon describes is not contemporary with his subject but of his own time (approximately 430–340 B.C.). Xenophon suggests a fairly wide use of heavy armed cavalry when discussing the armies of Artaxerxes, who were worrying the rear of the retreating Greek forces after the Battle of Cunaxa (401 B.C.):

'A Persian army is useless at night since their horses are tethered and usually tied by the feet as well, so that they cannot run away if they are loosed. If, then, there is a disturbance, the horses have to be caparisoned for their Persian riders, and bridled, and then the rider has to put on his armour and mount —all of which is difficult to do by night in the middle of an uproar.'

The brazen chamfrons and breastplates of Xenophon's Persian cavalry may well have followed the Greek model, such as we can see on the Pergamon reliefs at Berlin dating from the first half of the third century B.C. A naturalistic chamfron is shown surmounted by a transverse feather crest, a bridle with similar crest of hair and two peytrals or breastplates. One is of tooled and fringed leather and the other of two rows of long narrow lamellae or splints.

This may, then, give us a period for the development of the fully armoured horseman in Iran and neighbouring countries; but it is not until the first centuries after Christ that evidence, both pictorial and literary, exists in any quantity.

In the Persian mine beneath Tower 19 at Dura Europos was found the body of a Persian soldier, probably killed when a Roman counter-mine broke through and the two forces met.[3] The Persian skeleton wore a hip-length mail shirt with short sleeves, and near by was found a thimble-shaped helmet and the remains of a rectangular cane shield. This soldier died in A.D. 256, when the Sāssānians besieged and took Dura, and had remained undisturbed until the excavations in 1932–3.

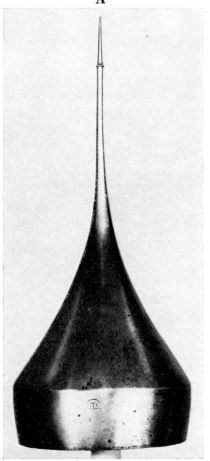

Plate I
Persian Helmets
A Early Sāssānian, from Nineveh, third century A.D., *British Museum*
B Sāssānian, Parthian cap shape, fourth to fifth centuries A.D., *British Museum*
C Fifteenth century, from St Irene, *Tower of London Armouries*
D Fifteenth century, in the Tartar fashion, *Kremlin, Moscow (Not to scale)*

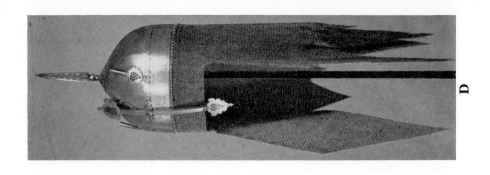

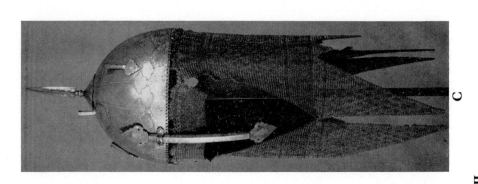

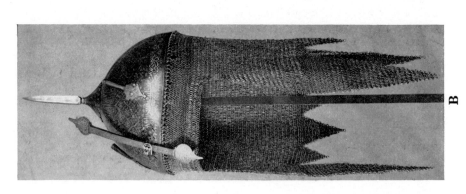

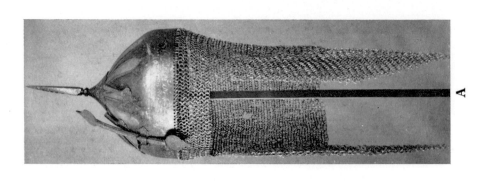

Plate II

Persian Helmets

A and **B** Seventeenth century with rivetted mail   **C** and **D** Eighteenth century with
so-called mail. *Victoria and Albert Museum (Not to scale)*

The Parthians, who by the third century were part of the Persian Empire, are also represented at Dura. Amongst the many graffiti discovered there was one of a Parthian *cataphractus* dating from the second century A.D. It is a crude drawing—probably the work of a child—but still remarkably detailed and informative. The horseman wears a tall conical helmet with little streamers tied

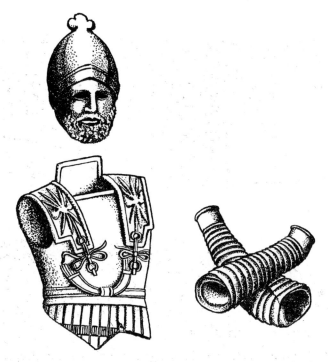

FIG. 7 Greek cavalry armour from the Pergamon reliefs, third century B.C., Pergamon Museum, Berlin

at the point. This would appear to be of segments or lamellae with a hood of mail falling to the shoulders. It has been suggested that the face of the warrior is covered by a mask, but I can see no evidence for this. However, one might say that only his eyes and nose are shown and therefore we may have the forerunner of the veil-like mail faceguard which was soon to become a feature of Persian armour. The warrior's equipment is completed by a defence which later was to become very common in the Middle East and Asia—mail to below the breast and then two rows of vertical splints to the waist, to which is attached a skirt of mail.

His arms and legs are barred with horizontal lines, which represent laminated armour. The horse is armed to its knees with a long scale trapper, open at front and back to permit the free movement of its legs, and what is probably a chamfron covers its face. No stirrups are used, their introduction still being centuries away.

The great reliefs cut in a rocky cliff face at Firuzabad show the

FIG. 8 Parthian *Cataphractus* from a graffito at Dura Europos, second century A.D.

Persian King, Ardashir I (A.D. 224–41), in combat with the Parthian Artabanus V. His son Shapur is unhorsing the Parthian grand vizier and a Persian squire wrestles with an enemy knight. This great frieze depicts these mounted duels with much the same quality as medieval scenes of knights tilting. King Ardashir, who strikes down his opponent with his lance, wears no helmet, but has his tightly curled mass of hair confined with a band tied above his brow, its ends streaming behind. He wears a mail shirt with long sleeves, over which is a tight bodice and crossed straps supporting a circular plate on his breast in the ancient Assyrian manner (see the next section). The King's lower limbs are

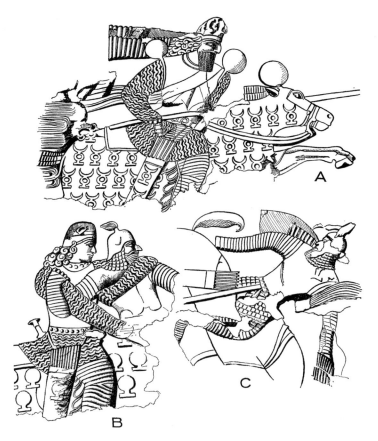

FIG. 9 Rock carvings of Firuzabad, third century A.D.
A Prince Shapur
B Persian squire wrestling with a Parthian knight
C The Parthian Grand Vizier being unhorsed by Prince Shapur

destroyed, but we may assume that they were armed with the same laminated defences that his son and squire are wearing.

Prince Shapur wears a simple rounded helmet and is otherwise armed like his father, except that he has no plate on his breast and has pomegranate-like ornaments standing on stems above the point of each shoulder. The ties of his laminated leg armour are clearly shown. The Persian squire, with his arms wrapped about a Parthian knight, wears a thimble-shaped helmet like that found in the mine at Dura Europos. He wears the sleeveless short surcoat with long mail sleeves and laminated leg armour.

The three Parthians are armed very much alike. They have

rounded helmets with curtains of scale or lamellar attached, scale or lamellar body armour covered by sleeveless surcoats, and both their arms and their legs are completely encased in laminated plates. The sleeves extend over the wrists on to the back of the hands. The similarity with the Dura graffito is very striking although dating from the third century, a hundred years later.

FIG. 10 King Shapur from a third-century cameo, Bibliothèque Nationale, Paris. Note the laminated thigh defence

The Persian royal horses are caparisoned, each one bearing rows of badges or symbols. Such trappers could have been of leather or quilted fabric with the devices applied in precious metals.

A third-century cameo in the Bibliothèque Nationale, Paris, shows Shapur, now King, overpowering the Roman Emperor Valerian (Fig. 10). Here Shapur wears a rounded helmet surmounted by a large pomegranate-like ornament, with smaller ones on each shoulder. The chief interest lies in the fact that he wears laminated thighguards which terminate above the knee and remind one of the piece of bronze armour from Newstead fort.

One of our few sources of information covering Sāssānian military fashions for the next three centuries is the silver dishes decorated with shallow embossed ornament heightened with finely engraved detail. The majority depict monarchs hunting; but a few show sieges and combats in which an admixture of mail and lamellar armour is predominant, as also are tall pointed

FIG. 11 Rock carving of King Khusru II, c. A.D. 620, at Tāq-i-Bōstān
A   Front view of the King's helmet
B   Swedish helmet from Grave XII at Vendel, Uppland, seventh
    century. Compare with the helmet worn by the Persian King

helmets. Perhaps the finest of these is the dish in the Hermitage at Leningrad, with two warriors fighting a duel surrounded by broken swords and discarded shields. They are equipped in identical armour. Tall conical helmets are surmounted by spherical finials, with additional earlike points rising on either side. Aventails of mail are attached to the lower edges of the helmet bowls and the warriors' faces are exposed. They have wrist-length mail sleeves with semicircular guards for the backs of the hands and, over these, a knee-length coat of lamellar armour, opening at the front, with sleeves to the elbows. Their legs and feet are encased in laminated defences. The lamellae show a bi-lobed edge—a form to be seen on several of the stucco figurines found by Stein in Central Asia, those from Kara-shar in Chinese Turkestan and now in the British Museum being the most similar. These figurines also have ornaments attached to the helmet in the region of the ears, a fashion common to China and Japan. In Japan, however, this feature was originally functional (see Chapter VII, p. 177) and only later decorative.

Several Sāssānian helmets have survived, being brought to light in various excavations in the past hundred or so years. The earliest of typical ancient Assyrian form, with mail adhering to its lower edge, is now in the British Museum. It was found at Nineveh and dates from about the third century A.D. The skull is built up of four triangular segments joined at the front, back, and sides with narrow external plates secured with round-headed rivets. The narrow plates have a medial rib and the edges are cusped between the points of riveting. The form of these plates should be compared with helmets found in eastern Europe, south Russia and parts of the Far East. They are particularly like those used in Tibetan helmets still fashionable in the nineteenth century.

Another more usual Sāssānian helmet is that inspired by the tall Parthian felt cap. In profile it is rounded, but from the front it appears to be a tall, sharply tapering cone. Like the helmet previously described, this later type is built up of four main panels—two on each side of the medial crest, joined by narrow external strips and round-headed rivets. The lower edge is wrapped with a horizontal band pierced for the attachment of the aventail. Two specimens in the British Museum have had their iron plates faced with copper, in a similar manner to the conical helmets of Russia and east Europe and the richer helmets found in Japanese burial mounds. Such ornamental plates were frequently gilded or silvered.

The rock carvings at Tāq-i-Bōstān, Persia, include the superbly detailed equestrian figure of Khusru II (c. A.D. 620) as a *clibanarius* of the Sāssānian heavy cavalry, showing the King armed in a mail shirt and a helmet, and his horse Shabdiz with its head, neck, and breast protected by lamellar armour. The King's helmet is rounded and surmounted by a spherical crest, believed to be a bag containing hair drawn up from the top of the head. Whether this is a dummy on top of the helmet or a hole was provided in the crown, as with early Japanese helmets, we cannot tell. A long veil-like aventail of mail is attached to the rim of the helmet, which leaves only the monarch's eyes exposed—a feature shared with contemporary helmets used by the Vendel warriors of Sweden (see Fig. 11B). The King's defensive equipment is completed by a small circular convex shield.

In the seventh century the Arab Caliphate overran the Sāssānian Empire and, as far as we can tell, no great changes took

FIG. 12 Engraving of a Sāssānian warrior from a silver dish, sixth century, Hermitage, Leningrad

place in the Persian equipment then or for a long time afterwards. The invader came under the influence of the remarkable Persian culture and no doubt, in due course, took advantage of the superior craftsmen now at his disposal for the making of his own equipment.

From a century later a fragment of a leather-covered circular wooden shield has survived, bearing a painting of a mounted warrior. This was found in the ruins of the castle of Mug, east of Samarkand, and with it were many documents dating the destruction of the place to the eighth century—when the Persian prince who held it rebelled against the local Arab ruler. Only the central part of the shield remains, so that the warrior is headless and legless. But sufficient of the painting survives to show a long coat of lamellar armour with close-fitting sleevelike shoulder extensions and forearms encased in tubular *bazuband* without handguards, the earliest representation known to the writer.

The dearth of illustrative material for the greater part of six centuries is largely due to the wanton destruction caused by two savage invasions from the east and only such finds as the stucco figures from Kara-shar (Fig. 14) tell us that in all this period there

FIG. 13 Fragment of a circular wooden shield covered with painted leather. Detail of the painting showing a warrior wearing lamellar armour and tubular vambraces (*bazuband*). From the Castle of Mug destroyed in the eighth century. Hermitage, Leningrad

had been little change. These belong to the period of Turkish (1038) and Mongol invasions (1194).

Under Ghāzān Khān (1295–1304), the organization of arms production was brought to a high level of efficiency. There were in each province and town many armourers (*ozan*), both Persians and Mongols, who made bows, arrows, quivers, swords, etc., and who received annually a salary from the State, in return for which they had to furnish a certain number of arms. Every year, ten thousand complete armours were to be supplied. Hitherto, not more than two thousand had been furnished annually. Ghāzān ordered that fifty should be supplied for his own special use.[4] In spite of these large supplies, when Öljeitü decided to invade Syria, in 1315, he had to augment his supplies with one thousand five hundred armours and helmets which he bought from a European merchant.[5]

One of the earliest illustrated Persian manuscripts to survive dates from the early fourteenth century. This is Rashidu'd Din's *History of the World*, produced at Tabrīz between 1306 and 1312. The warriors wear long coats of lamellar armour barred in alternating colours, every other row bearing scroll patterns which could well be a convention to represent rows of lacquered hide lamellae with engraved ornament.

FIG. 14 Stucco figure of a Central Asian warrior, eighth to tenth century A.D., from Kara-shar, British Museum

The helmets are rounded, with a central ornamental spike, and frequently have a turned-up peak or reinforce over the brow. Nape guards are of mail, leather or fabric, as are probably the deep collars of the lamellar coats (Fig. 14).

As will be seen, this form of armour remained popular in Persia, particularly in the north and east, for a very long time, while the alternative—mail—still persisted, it would seem, in central and southern areas. In 1393 we hear of Persian soldiers dressed in mail (*zirih baktah*), with helmets and cuirasses of velvet-covered iron plates—a form of brigandine is suggested—and their horses protected by a kind of cuirass made of quilted silk.[6]

A helmet of rounded conical form, formerly in the collection of Count Krasinski of Poland, dating from the late thirteenth or early fourteenth centuries, retained many features in common with that on the Tāq-i-Bōstān relief. The socket between the eye cut-outs was for a nasal, a feature seldom if ever shown in Persian miniatures. This helmet had a full aventail of mail covering all but the wearer's eyes. It should also be compared with the two Turkish helmets at Istanbul (Pl. XII C, D,) which belong to the same period. This form of helmet is distinctly Persian in origin.

Early-fourteenth-century miniatures depict warriors generally

FIG. 15 Mongol warrior wearing helmet and long coat of lamellar armour, from Rashidu'd Din's *History of the World*, 1306–12

wearing lamellar armour, with aventails of mail attached to their simple helmets of low, rounded, conical form. Earguards are sometimes shown—made up of a pair of circular plates at each side, the upper overlapping the lower. Most of the helmets have a spike or tube at the apex, but no plumes are seen at this date. Occasionally, helmet bowls are ribbed or slightly fluted. As well as the armour described above, there are also warriors armed in the old Sino-Mongolian leather coats with shoulder defences of the same material. Horses are seldom armed, but carry saddles and harness of distinctly Mongol character.

In the late-fourteenth- and early-fifteenth-century miniatures, plate armour for the limbs makes its reappearance in the form of tubular vambraces, consisting of two hinged plates tapered towards the wrist, the lower one extended into a point to protect the elbow. The simple rounded guard—probably of leather or quilted fabric—first seen on the Sāssānian dish in the Hermitage Leningrad (Fig. 11), reappears attached at the wrist of these early vambraces, termed *bazuband*. The late Indian *dastana* is a direct descendant of the early Persian type.

The legs—always vulnerable parts of a horseman's anatomy—were protected with separate knee-plates of 'pot-lid' form, set in mail or mounted upon fabric which extended up the thigh (*rānāpanō*). Usually, boots were worn below these; but sometimes a tubular greave of two plates opening upon hinges encased the shins and calves. These are clearly represented in a miniature painted at Shirāz, *c.* 1433-4, in the Bodleian Library, Oxford.[7] The great Rustam wears his tiger-striped coat over a mail shirt, a fashion which would appear to have gradually superseded armour of lamellar construction fashionable in the north and east, if the evidence provided by the schools of miniaturists is to be relied upon.

In the Library of Gulistan is a copy of the *Shāh-Nāma*, executed by an anonymous artist of the Herāt school in 1429. This work, of a very high artistic standard, presents military equipment in considerable detail and shows warriors wearing lamellar armour over mail with plate vambraces and, in some instances, with thigh and knee defences. The rounded conical helmets all have aventails of mail, with or without earpieces. Some men wear plate greaves with laminated guards for the feet, similar to a boot of mail and plates—probably Mamlūk—in the Tower of London Armouries. The lamellar armour is similar to that worn by the stucco figures from Turkestan, except that the skirt is cut away at the back to facilitate a more comfortable seat on horseback.

The Demotte *Shāh-Nāma* (*c.* 1340), a manuscript now broken up and scattered throughout many European and American collections, illustrates some helmets with aventails covering the warrior's entire face, leaving only small openings for the eyes—a fashion first encountered in the early-seventh-century rock carving at Tāq-i-Bōstān and of which parallels can be found in Russia, eastern Europe, and amongst the helmets from the seventh-century Vendel graves at Uppsala in Sweden. Other fourteenth- and early-fifteenth-century miniatures show the mail aventail (*kūiris*—or, in Pahlavi, *grīvpān*) either hanging to the shoulders,

clear of the face, passing beneath the chin or, as in the Royal
Asiatic Society's *Shāh-Nāma* of *c.* 1440, covering the lower half of
the face. Some are depicted as of lamellar construction with a
border of mail resting on the shoulders.

This *Shāh-Nāma* of *c.* 1440 is rich in the variety of equipment
represented, and it is far less traditional than the majority of
Persian miniatures. Some warriors wear lamellar and some long
coats of fabric over mail, but many appear in laminated armour
with which we first became familiar in Roman and Parthian
times. There are instances where men have plates encircling the
body from armpits to waist, with mail on the upper arms and
shoulders and also below the waist. We are aware of this form of
coat of mail and plates from Mamlūk, Turkish and Indian sources
—but from the last country at least a century later in date. Some
of the armours shown are laminated coats with short sleeves,
whilst in other instances the garment forms a cuirass with
separate shoulder defences. The simplification and stylization of
the equipment has unfortunately meant that any details of construction have been left out.

Many of the helmets retain the crest tube at the apex, the brow
reinforce, and the double disc cheekpieces, described above in
earlier miniatures, created under strong Mongol influence.
Tubular vambraces (*bazuband*) with rounded handguards are
general, but only boots cover the lower limbs.

In the first half of the fifteenth century plumes of coloured hair,
bejewelled feathers, and little pennants began to be attached to the
tall, pointed crowns of the helmets. The little pennants may be of
Mongol origin, for they are to be seen on Chinese helmets and
may also have been used in Russia—where the Persian helmet
seems to have been very popular, if the numbers surviving in
Russian collections are anything to go by. Two examples of tall
Persian helmets, taken by the Turks at the Battle of Chaldirān
(1514) and deposited in their Arsenal of St Irene, are now in the
Tower of London Armouries. One had been altered to Turkish
taste by the addition of a peak with sliding nasal-, ear- and neckguards, at some time in the sixteenth century (Pl. VII, B). A rare
and unusual Persian helmet is that with a complete face mask
embossed to fit the features. In the armoury of the Kremlin in
Moscow is preserved a complete helmet and mask and a detached
mask of similar form and style. In both cases the mask is attached

to the helmet by a turning pin on the brow. Both of these pieces are dated to the fifteenth century by their style and decoration; but one earlier example is known, coming from a *kurgan* at Kreis Kanewsk in the district of Kiev. It appears to be undecorated and was found with a mail shirt. The grave was dated to the tenth century. The masked helmet was copied by the Persians—with other items of cavalry equipment—from the Greeks, and in turn may have been used by the Sarmatians, who could have become familiar with it while serving as auxiliary cavalry in Roman service, where it formed part of their parade armour. Unfortunately, there is no continuity to bear this out and the Kremlin specimens are isolated examples of Persian manufacture, perhaps made to the order of Tartars.

There are two known early Persian helmets with peaks. The earlier, forged in one piece with conical skull and narrow peak, was excavated in Hungary and is now in the National Museum at Budapest. It is engraved with bands of foliate Kufic characters, flying phoenixes confronted in pairs, and an arabesque version of the undulating stem motif closely related to Persian textile design of the fourteenth century. The second helmet, which is dated to the late fourteenth century, is a combination of Turkish and Mongol forms, but is classified as Persian on account of the pair of plume tubes riveted well up on either side of the skull in front. This is in the Military Museum at Istanbul, which is now housed in the old Arsenal of St Irene. The pair of plume tubes are a distinctive feature of Persian helmets, surprisingly never shown in miniature paintings. Their presence on Indian helmets is entirely due to strong Persian influence after the Mughal invasion in the sixteenth century.

Lamellar armour continued to be represented in miniatures into the second half of the fifteenth century, and this is well shown in a manuscript in the F. Cleveland Morgan collection at Montreal (Fig. 19E). Also shown is a scale horse armour which had changed little from those found at Dura Europos.

Mail and Plates

In the previous section the laminated armour is mentioned when it reappeared on the scene in the fifteenth century. Apart from helmets, we cannot state with any degree of certainty whether other items of Persian origin survive from this period. The

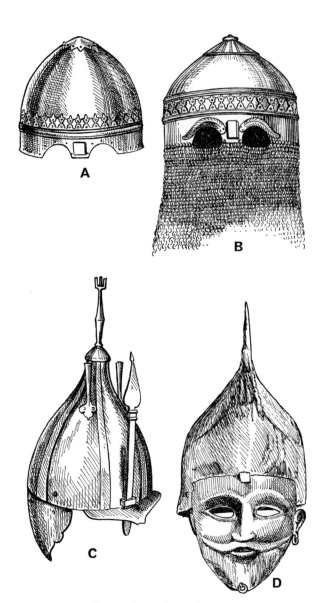

FIG. 16 Persian helmets

A Formerly in the collection of Count Krasinski, thirteenth to
   fourteenth century
B Hermitage, Leningrad, fifteenth century
C Military Museum, Istanbul, engraved and damascened, late fourteenth century
D From kurgan at Kreis Kanewsk, Historical Museum, Moscow,
   tenth century. The mask is a Tartar fashion

FIG. 17 Warriors as represented in Persian miniatures
A Under strong Mongol influence, *c.* 1330, British Museum
B The 'Kevorkian Tabarī,' Mongol influence, early fourteenth century, Freer Gallery, Washington
C *Demotte Shāh-Nāma.* Mongol influence *c.* 1340, Vever Collection
D *c.* 1340, Bodleian Library, Oxford
E Rustam from a *Shāh-Nāma* by the Shiraz School, *c.* 1433-4, Bodleian Library, Oxford
F Detached miniature, *c.* 1420, Victoria and Albert Museum. Note aventail hooked up clear of the face.

armour of the Mamlūks, Turks, and Persians at this time was very alike, and it has been impossible to separate the Persian from the others unless a definitely known type or inscribed piece has been identified.

The simple metal disc worn on the breast and sometimes the back of warriors was one of the oldest forms of body-armour. It was usually supported by crossed straps passing over the shoulders, as in the case of the statue of a seventh- to sixth-century B.C. Italic warrior from Capistrano in the Museo Nazionale, Rome, the Assyrian reliefs from Nineveh of the same period in the British Museum, and the rock carving of Adashir I at Firuzabad. In miniatures the crossed straps are not visible and

FIG. 18 Persian warriors wearing lamellar armour
A Front and B back showing fastening *Shāh-Nāma* by the Herat School dated 1429, Gulistan Library, Tehran

may have been dispensed with in most instances, for usually the disc is worn upon a fabric coat studded with rosette-headed gilt nails—which may simply portray a decorated quilted coat, such as was used in Central India, or could represent a brigandine with a lining of small plates. One of the earliest examples of this 'mirror' is to be seen in the Gulistan *Shāh-Nāma* of 1429, mentioned above, where all the armour—whether studded coat or lamellar—is shown with fastenings down the centre of the back. A detached miniature of *c.* 1540 in the Royal Scottish Museum,

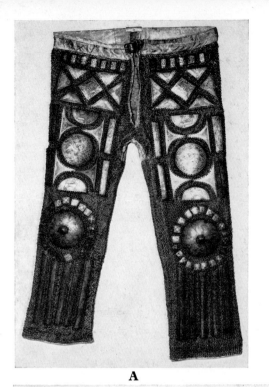

A

B

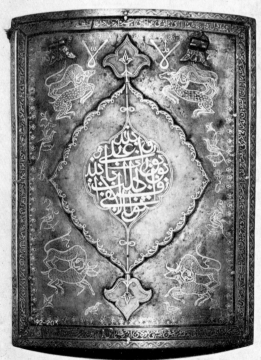

C

Plate III
Persian Armour
A Trousers covered with mail and plates, late seventeenth century
B Boot of mail and plates, Persian or Mamlūk, fifteenth century
C *Char aina* dated 1114H (1702), only two parts shown
A and C *Royal Scottish Museum*   B *Tower of London Armouries*
(*Not to scale*)

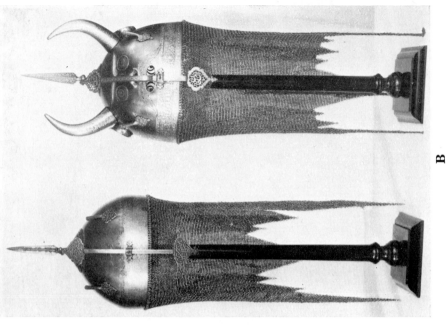

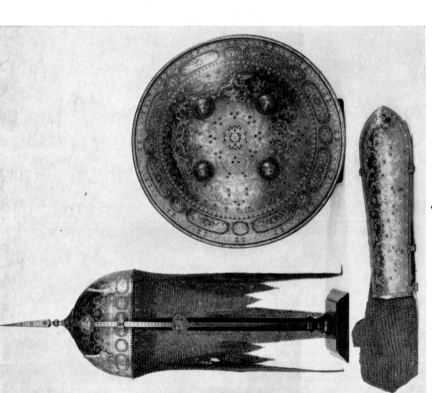

Plate IV
Persian Armour

A Helmet shield and vambrace with overlaid silver ornament set with turquoise, early nineteenth century

B Typical late Persian Helmets. The demon head example at right has a fixed nasal, early nineteenth century

Edinburgh, exhibits slightly larger plates on the front and back; and from then examples begin to become fairly common and continue throughout the sixteenth century.

In the second half of the fifteenth century and the whole of the sixteenth, miniatures show a marked decline—for, apart from minor features of the equipment, one warrior is like another and it is obvious in many that stylization and simplification had begun to completely dominate the miniaturist's art. With few exceptions, the Persian warrior is shown in rounded conical helmet with tall central spike or plume-tube, mail aventail falling to the shoulders clear of the face, and generally with earguards as well, now almost always of blunt, angular, pointed shape. The helmets are fluted and decorated with engraved or gold damascened geometric and floral patterns in a deep band around the bowl. The body and arms are usually devoid of visible mail—but we must assume that the rich coats, with short sleeves and frogged fastenings down the front, cover the body armour. The forearms are encased in tubular *bazuband*, with or without extensions for the hands. Over the high-heeled, knee-length, leather riding-boots are worn greaves, covering only the front of the leg and fastened with ties or straps. If no greaves are worn, long extensions to the knee and thigh defences take their place. The thigh armour shown is usually constructed of vertical rows of small horizontal plates set side by side and, as we know from surviving examples, connected by mail, with a circular dished plate for the knee-cap. The extensions attached to the lower edge of the knee-plates are either pointed curtains of mail or a long pointed piece built up as the thigh portion from small plates and mail.

A *Shah-Nāmā*, dated 1028[H] (1618–19), in the Walters Art Gallery, Baltimore, shows warriors wearing square plates on their breasts over mail and fabric coats. Several of the helmets are of distinctly late form, but the general lack of detail and the poor standard of the work deter one from putting too much faith in the little evidence it contains.

The cuirasses in European collections from the Turkish Arsenal of St Irene—referred to as 'pot-lid' or 'jannisary'—were probably as much Persian as Turkish, for one breastplate, richly damascened with gold inscriptions in Persian, is in the collection of Topkapu Sarayi at Istanbul. It belongs to the sixteenth century —a period when circular plates are quite common as a breast

FIG. 19 Warriors as represented in Persian miniatures
A *Khamsa* of Nizami dated 1439, Uppsala University Library
B and C *Shāh-Nāma*, *c.* 1440, Royal Asiatic Society
D *Shāh-Nāma*, *c.* 1440–50, Collection of Dr Hakim, Bombay
E Late lamellar armour, second half fifteenth century, F. Cleveland
   Morgan Collection, Montreal
F *Shāh-Nāma*, *c.* 1490, British Museum

defence in Persian miniatures. These cuirasses consisted of large
circular convex plates, with horizontal breast- and shoulderpieces, and vertical side-sections all joined with mail. The opening
was at the right side, and small shield-shaped shoulder-plates were
linked to the main shoulder- and neck-piece. These were the
principal Turkish body armour worn over a mail shirt throughout the sixteenth century, and this could also have been the case
in Persia.

In the Stone Collection in the Metropolitan Museum in New
York there is a Persian *char aina* (four mirrors) of the late sixteenth

FIG. 20 Warriors as represented in Persian miniatures
A Detached miniature, *c.* 1540, Royal Scottish Museum
B *Shāh-Nāma*, dated 1582, Biblioteca Laurenziana, Florence
C *Shāh-Nāma*, *c.* 1618–19, Walters Art Gallery, Baltimore
D *Shāh-Nāma*, dated 1648, Royal Library, Windsor Castle

or early seventeenth century which could be a direct descendant of these cuirasses (Stone, Fig. 56, 2). The breast- and back-plates are hexagonal with a central boss and radiating flutes, while the side-sections are rectangular with cut-outs to fit beneath the arms connected with straps. I believe this to be a transitional type between the heavier cuirass connected by mail and the later rectangular 'four mirrors' joined with straps or hinges with removable pins. I consider the circular plate shown in sixteenth-century miniatures to be a convention representing the central plate of the cuirass, just as seventeenth-century miniatures show a single rectangular or hexagonal plate without other attachments, when we know full well that four plates were actually in use.

The helmet and vambrace of Shāh Abbās the Great, now in the British Museum, are of the type normally forming part of an

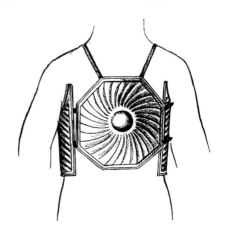

FIG. 21 Fluted *char aina*, late sixteenth or early seventeenth century, Stone Collection, Metropolitan Museum of Art, New York

armour consisting of helmet (*kulah khud*) with quadrangular spike at the apex, sliding nasal and mail aventail, a pair of vambraces with mail-covered fabric guards for the backs of the hands (*bazuband*), cuirass of four rectangular plates joined by hinges or straps (*char aina*), and a matching circular steel shield (*sipar*). The helmet is dated 1035^H (A.D. 1625–6) and is enriched with verses from Sa'di's *Bustan* in praise of Shāh Abbās. The surface of the bowl is yellow watered steel with burnished frames to the diamond-shaped cartouche on four sides, each containing an inscription in gold.

Abbās I dethroned his father in 1587, defeated the Turks in 1590 and 1618, retook Baghdad in 1622 and died in 1628. Such a warrior king would have had the most modern of equipment and may have set new fashions himself. The British Museum pieces, by their exceptional quality, are proclaimed as being made for a person of the highest rank. It has been argued that the fine butted mail of steel and brass rings is of the late eighteenth and early nineteenth centuries and that therefore these pieces are not what the inscription claims. In defence, I would point out that amongst the many rich armours made for the Archduke Ferdinand of Tyrol in the second half of the sixteenth century, preserved in the Waffensammlung at Vienna, there is a parade armour for man and horse inspired by the strong Classical influence of the Renaissance. It is, in fact, the equipment of a Roman *cataphractus*; but instead of scale armour, a shirt of mail is provided for the man and a complete mail trapper for the horse. This mail is of fine butted or jumped iron rings with elaborate arabesque patterns worked in brass rings. Indeed, an armour inspired by Persian models which were without doubt known to and acquired by European collectors such as the Archduke himself. This fine mail, in the best examples, is very close and smooth to the touch. The fact that the maker did not have the long and wearisome task of flattening, punching, and riveting the rings must have also cut costs considerably. No doubt, in time, the rich appearance compensated for the decreased defensive quality of the mail—for by the early eighteenth century little, if any, was riveted.

The earliest dated *char aina* known to the writer is in the Royal Scottish Museum, Edinburgh—the breast- and one side-plate of which is shown in Pl. III, C. It is dated 1114[H] (1702) and is decorated with tigers attacking deer and cattle, with borders and large central cartouche carrying inscriptions from the Sura of Victory from the *Qur'an* in gold false damascene. Most of the buckle and strap fastenings have been broken or removed. *Char aina* are joined—either by straps and buckles in pairs, crossed or horizontal, or by hinges with removable pins—in a similar manner to the old tubular armguards. *Char aina* joined by hinges are larger, on the whole, than those connected by straps, so that the edges meet easily, and they occasionally have the breastplate divided down the centre fastened with a fifth hinge and thus opening like a waistcoat.

Also in the Royal Scottish Museum is a pair of fabric trousers covered with mail, with splints and plates set into the rings covering the front. Spiked bosses are provided for the knee-caps and the decoration, partly engraved, is very similar to that on the *char aina* described above. They probably date from the late seventeenth or early eighteenth century, and come from an armour very

like those made in Sind, in western India.[8] The mail is riveted and
constructed with rings made from round iron wire.

In the same collection are two good examples of early *bazuband*
or vambraces. One is of the seventeenth century, chiselled with
pairs of eye-shaped motifs and set down the medial ridge of the
main armplate with garnets. The fabric handguard is covered
with mail, each alternate row of rings being of the type punched
out of sheet iron with a bar across the centre. The other is dated
1123[H] (1711) and is decorated with verses from the Sura of Victory at the borders and in cartouches applied in gold false

FIG. 22 Detail of mail with punched barred
rings in alternate rows

damascene. The brass and iron butted mail of the handguard is
extremely close and fine, and what is also interesting is that the
mail connecting the small splints which fasten round the inner
side of the arm is riveted. This is no doubt because when the
vambrace was worn the mail would be under constant tension
and butted rings would pull open. Two or three splints connected
by mail replace the solid plate for the inner arm in most vambraces
made after the sixteenth century. Almost all those surviving with
the hinged solid inner plate are of Indian manufacture. Fastening
is generally by strap and buckle.

The Persian helmet, in its later form, has a distinct character of
its own. The bowl is rounded and quite deep when compared
with Indian examples. The central point—usually forged in one
with the bowl in earlier helmets—is applied, and into this is
screwed a long quadrangular spike. It is fitted with a curved nasal
of square section with foliate terminals, which passes through a
socket on the brow part of the bowl fitted with a set-screw for
securing it in the raised or lowered position. When lowered, the
bottom finial would come to below the level of the wearer's chin,
so giving reasonable protection against a sweeping cut with a

sword. On either side are riveted small plume-tubes into which were set ornaments of tinsel, gimp, and feathers, sometimes one much larger than or of different character from the other. The mail curtain, for which we have used the European medieval term 'aventail', is attached to the lower edge of the helmet bowl with close-set rings passing through holes drilled in the metal. The curtain is quite long, reaching the wearer's shoulders, with a point in the front at each corner and with another two in the centre of the back. The front edges come well forward on either side of the face and are connected by a fringe which passes across the brow section. This acts as a screen for the eyes and may, in fact, have covered them in many cases, for they are deep enough for this purpose. In portraits of men in armour, the artist always left out this feature, so that his sitter's face was fully exposed. From the seventeenth century miniatures show warriors with rich scarves, or *pagris*, tied over their helmets. This fashion may have been introduced through the closeness of the new helmet, which meant that the lining was insufficiently padded to keep the heat of the sun from the head. The helmets in fashion up to the sixteenth century were certainly larger and a small headcloth or cap may have been worn inside as well as the lining, similar to the Japanese custom of wearing a headcloth beneath the helmet to give greater comfort and a more secure fit. This wrapping of the helmet obscured the greater part of the bowl and, therefore, much of its decoration; but no doubt a colourful silk scarf, richly sewn with pearls and with gold fringes at the ends, compensated for this to some extent.

The seventeenth-century helmets in the Victoria and Albert Museum differ very little from the later specimens of the late eighteenth and early nineteenth centuries in the Wallace Collection (Pl. IV), except that the mail of their aventails is riveted and therefore the rings are of large diameter. It should be noted, too, that the decoration is more simple and generally in better taste.

The wire used for Persian mail was of rounded section. Mail shirts generally had half-length sleeves and were either put on over the head, with the corners of the neck-opening made to overlap each other, or were like coats opening down the front and fastening on the chest with buttons or ties. Quilted collars— sometimes of velvet studded with gilt nails, or more usually of rich brocade bound with gimp braid—were sewn to the mail. An additional mail cape or standard was normally attached permanently at the neck. Its lower edge was finished in a series of long points. One should add that this was more common on later shirts of butted mail. Trousers of mail mounted upon fabric do not appear to have been worn in Persia as frequently as in India. The Portrait of Fath 'Alī Shāh by Ghulām Ahmad, dated 1234^H (1819) and now on loan to the Victoria and Albert Museum (Pl. V, A) from the Hon. Mrs Yvonne Rodd, shows the King wearing richly studded mail shirt and trousers, the latter tucked into high riding-boots over which are deeply bossed knee-plates and greaves for the front of the leg only. The powdering of studs and the decorated borders of the mail coat are shown as precious stones and pearls. The shield shown in this portrait is still kept in the Royal Treasury at Tehran. The King wears no *char aina*, but the jewelled plumes and rich scarf tied around the helmet are clearly shown.

In the Wallace Collection there is a handsome *char aina*, made to open down the centre of the breastplate and decorated with tasteful gold damascened scroll ornament which bears the name of Fath 'Ali Shāh Qajar and the date 1224^H (1809) (Pl. V, B).

The decorating of mail with applied dangles and studs may be of considerable antiquity and was certainly popular in Russia and Turkey and, through the latter, in Hungary in the sixteenth century. A shirt with three bosses on the breast, one of which bears the name of Shāh Abbās the Great, is preserved in the Topkapu Sarayi at Istanbul. This applied ornament enhanced the normally plain mail shirt when no cloth covering or *char aina* was worn. When the custom began, pendants of coral, brass or silver were hooked or riveted into the rings of the mail—to be followed by bosses and stars and, later, by rich stones in gold mounts.

Persian armour generally encountered in Western countries today consists of a helmet, a single vambrace for the right arm, and a circular steel shield. Their decoration varies considerably, one from another, and often the very finest are lined with a cheap red cotton fabric stuck in with a pitchlike adhesive.

These sets were often bought in great quantity by wealthy collectors, but were more frequently acquired by dealers and tourists in the bazaars of Persia and the Middle East—and one wonders what happened to the *char aina* and the vambrace for the left arm, for in the case of the finer specimens they must certainly have existed at the time of their manufacture. It would appear that the traders decided to make up convenient sets—and when the stocks of genuine pieces came to an end, new ones—generally rather poor copies—were produced. These included the badly shaped helmet-bowls and skimped mail curtains of quite large butted rings. The chiselled decoration deteriorated into crude and automatic copies of older specimens and eventually led to the very worst imitations of all, which were etched with acid and never gilded. Of the gold and silver decoration applied to these pieces, one can only say that it varies in quality as much as the chiselled ornament. As the chiselling becomes debased so does the gold and silver become thinner, with many of the inscriptions applied therewith becoming meaningless through the illiteracy of the forgers.

Padded clothing worn beneath the armour seldom survived. An Indian quilted jacket for wear with armour of Persian fashion is in the Tower collection. It is of green silk and only lightly quilted with rows of vertical stitching. In the Fath 'Ali Shāh portrait described above, a long skirted coat is shown beneath the mail, but it does not appear to be quilted. Several of the Persian armours in the Moser-Charlottenfels Collection at Bern have large padded collars which cover the leather shoulder-straps of the *char aina* and are also held in position by them passing through specially prepared holes. They project well out over the points of the shoulders and have an additional standing padded defence of conventional leaf form for the chest.

Amongst the armours in the Moser-Charlottenfels Collection is one of special interest, as it forms a link between Persia and the peoples of Central Asia. It consists of a shirt of riveted mail with long sleeves and skirt, a *char aina* connected by crossed straps, a mail cape with long pendant points lined with fabric, and a low, rounded, conical helmet surmounted by a blunt spike with an aventail of large riveted mail. To the brow portion of the bowl is riveted a small peak with deep flanged edge, such as one finds on Chinese, Mongolian, and Bhutanese helmets. It is, in fact, almost identical to the Bhutanese helmet form, with mail replacing the quilted Chinese-type ear and neck flaps. This armour (No. 419–422) comes from Bochara in Turkestan.

The Shield

From ancient times the peoples of Persia favoured a light, tough shield made of withies or cane. As remarked on at the beginning of this chapter, Herodotus describes the soldiers of Xerxes who carry targes of wicker. Large and deeply convex shields built up of concentric rings of cane or withies are carried by the Sacae (Scythian) guards in the reliefs from the great staircase of the

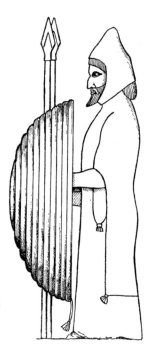

FIG. 23 Scythian guardsman of the Persian Kings, from a relief on the great staircase, Persepolis, third century B.C.

Achaemenid, from the Palace of Persepolis, now in the Berlin Museum. All but the caps of these guards are in the Persian fashion. The large shields are not those of nomadic horsemen, but are a foot soldier's defence.

The Persian cavalry, it would appear, did not always carry shields, and it is not until Sāssānian times that warriors, particularly the heavily armed horsemen, are shown carrying small convex circular shields. The material from which they were made is unknown, for they are represented in sculpture or embossed on silver dishes. The remains of a rectangular shield found in the mine at Dura Europos, although near a possibly Persian corpse, could have belonged to a Roman auxiliary. It was made of vertical

canes held together by being passed through a series of holes
made in the leather backing.

Many of the early Persian miniatures, particularly those under
Mongol influence of the late thirteenth and early fourteenth
centuries, seldom illustrate shields. When they do the shields
would seem to be of stout hide—small, circular, and convex, with
applied metal bosses. By the late fourteenth century many more
shields are represented and often clearly depict concentric rings of

FIG. 24 Section of a Persian cane shield with steel
boss in position

cane woven with silk thread into a light but firm convex defence,
usually fitted with a central steel boss. Several colours of silk
thread were used and remarkable geometric patterns produced.
They were lined with fabric and had a leather cushion behind the
central boss, over which was braced a plaited leather grip, the
ends of which were secured to four iron rings riveted through to
four ornamental washers. On Indian shields these washers are
replaced by four bosses.

This excellent horseman's shield was used in Persia and also in
Turkey until the eighteenth century, although with the wider use
of firearms from the sixteenth century the steel shield tended to
replace it in Persia.

The circular steel shield was usually produced *en suite* with the rest of the plate armour and was more rounded than the cane shield, which tended to be of flattened conical section. The characteristic of the Persian steel shield was the pronounced lip at the edge, which may have been copied from the hide shield of India and Central Asia. The edge was generally reinforced with an applied semicircular moulding of iron or brass, frequently gilded. There was no central boss, but four small ones were attached over the points where the grip rings were riveted. To the surface of the Persian steel shield was applied every technique of the skilful metalworker. Real and false damascene in gold and silver, chiselling, engraving, and piercing, and a wide variety of

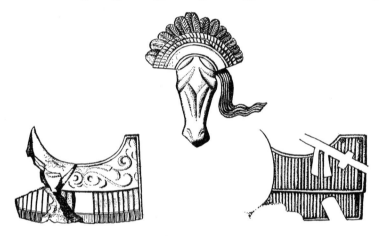

FIG. 25 Greek horse armour. Crested chamfron and two types of peytral from the Pergamon reliefs, third century B.C., Pergamon Museum, Berlin

contrasting colours were employed—ranging from straw to black —for the watered surface of the steel. It may be true to say that the pattern applied to the shield set the design for the rest of the armour.

A number of hide shields to be seen in private and national collections are painted in the Persian manner, but usually their bosses and fittings are of Indian make from Sind or Bhuj-Kach. A favourite subject is hunting, with scenes of handsome young men wearing tall black caps, armed with sword, spear, or gun, on foot or on horseback, chasing rather small and not unfriendly animals. The quality of the painting suggests that in many cases they were the work of a skilled miniaturist. Some inferior work is encountered, particularly on sets of helmet, vambrace, and shield of late bazaar quality—all of which are complete forgeries.

Horse Armour

Xenophon's description of the Persian cavalry of his time (fifth–fourth century B.C.) tells us of armour for the horse's head

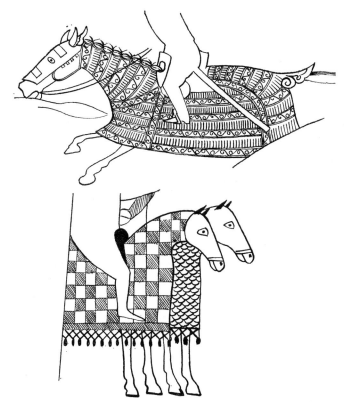

FIG. 26 Horse armours from Persian miniatures
A Lamellar armour, detached miniature, *c.* 1420, Victoria and Albert Museum
B Chequered and scale armours from a manuscript, dated 1439, Uppsala University Library

(chamfron) and a breastplate which also covered the rider's thighs. He repeats this description in his treatise on horsemanship for the Greek cavalry, and the Pergamon reliefs in the Pergamon Museum at Berlin can assist us therefore to visualize contemporary Persian equipment.

The Dura Europos graffito of a Parthian *cataphractus* illustrates the complete bard where the bronze or iron scales were secured in rows to a fabric foundation. The Firuzabad rock carvings show only the fabric or leather caparison a century later (third century A.D.), but the Tāq-i-Bōstān figure of Khusru II (*c.* A.D. 620) shows a return to the arming of Xenophon's time. The whole of the horse's head, neck, and breast is covered with lamellar armour hung with ornamental tassels. The lamellar, carved with great care and attention to detail, shows clearly the form of the lamellae and the method of lacing employed as the same as the coat of plates from the Battle of Wisby in 1361. The vertical edges of the plates exposed are convex (see Fig. 26).

Horse armour could have continued to be used in Persia, but it is seldom, if ever, shown in miniatures painted before the early fifteenth century. Johannes de Plano Carpini describes the manu-facture of lamellar armour for both man and horse by Mongols in the thirteenth century (see p. 138) at a time when Persia was ruled over by Kublai Khan. It could be that, due to the comparative peace of the period, little horse armour was seen by the artists. By the early fifteenth century, however, some fifty per cent of horsemen painted in miniatures are shown as riding barded horses. These bards are complete and very definitely defensive. Their construction varies considerably, there being three or four, and sometimes more, different types of horse armour shown in one tiny picture.

A battle scene of *c.* 1420 in the Victoria and Albert Museum, probably from a manuscript of the *History of Hafiz i Abru*, in which all the soldiers wear lamellar armour, shows only the two leading warriors on barded horses. One bard is clearly of lamellar, while the other would appear to be quilted and faced with a chequered fabric. The horses' heads are guarded with simple plate chamfrons and the throat armour is distinctly tied across the top of their necks, over their manes. A breastpiece (peytral), large side-panels (flanchards), and croup-piece with tailguard (crupper) complete the armour, and only the beasts' noses and legs below the knees are exposed. A miniature in a manuscript dated 1439, in Uppsala University Library, shows four armed horses, two of which have bards of imbricated scales and two of large square plates or lamellar. The lower edges are fringed.

The remarkable *Shāh-Nāma* in the Royal Asiatic Society

Library, discussed earlier in this chapter, shows a great many barded horses, many of which bards are represented as of lamellar of iron, while others are of lacquered leather lamellar banded in two colours. As in the case of the men's armours shown in this work, some of the horses are wearing armour built up of iron laminations either mounted upon leather straps or joined with panels of mail. The following passage from the journal of Joseph Barbaro, Ambassador to Persia from the Signoria of Venice in 1474, describes similar horse armour being used by the army of Shāh Ismā'īl I.

> 'Of the which (horses of service) there were II ml (2000) covered with certain armure of yron, made in little squares and wrought with gold and sylver, tacked together with small mayle, which hanged downe in maner to the grounde, and under the gold (edge) it had a frynge.'[9]

Barbaro also describes Shāh Ismā'īl's army as being almost destitute of armour when first organized, but after remaining at Shirāz several months:

> 'they now begin to wear very beautiful and rich armour so that whoever beheld them found and adjudged them marvellous and delightful'.

After capturing Herāt his army included:

> '100,000 horsemen with complete armour for both man and horse'.

The remarkable horse armours taken by the Turks from the Mamlūks and acquired by European collections from the Arsenal of St Irene fit the above description perfectly, as does also the horse armour from Sind in the Tower Armouries. We may therefore accept the fact that this became a common Asiatic form of defence for the warrior's all-important mount—probably originating in Persia, from whence it spread to other centres of Muslim culture.

Miniatures of the second half of the fifteenth century and into the first half of the sixteenth century continue to illustrate bards of scale and lamellar, the former closely resembling the armour of Roman *cataphractus* found at Dura Europos, while the chamfrons

FIG. 27 Horse armours from Persian miniatures
A Laminated armour, *c.* 1440, from a *Shāh-Nāma*, Royal Asiatic
  Society
B Armour of large plates, probably leather, *c.* 1505, from a *Shāh-Nāma* formerly in the Kunstgewerbe Museum, Leipzig

still have much in common with the leather ones from Newstead
Fort.

There is some evidence that in the sixteenth century there was
a lightening of horse armour, just as there was in man's armour.
Studded fabric, and fabric alone, of a rich kind—very likely
padded—replaces the metal; and armours built up of large rectangular plates, richly painted with gold and colours, suggest

armour of leather. Only the chamfrons appear to be of metal. After 1600, no armour for the horse is in evidence—although no doubt, like other Orientals, the Persians used large embroidered saddle-cloths or shabraques as well as complete trappers for display.

Centres of Manufacture
The main centres of arms manufacture in Persia were Khorasan and Ispahan. When Timur took Damascus in 1401 he is said to have moved all the finest workers in steel to Khorasan; but Ispahan, famed as the home of the great swordsmith Assad Ullah, did not reach importance until the time of Abbās the Great.

Those wishing to learn the armourer's trade went as pupils to the masters of these centres and, when they had learned, moved to other cities in Persia or beyond her boundaries to Egypt, Syria, India, and Russia, where the demand for skilled Persian armourers and smiths was ever at a premium.

Few names of these makers have been recorded and genealogies do not seem to have been kept.

A typical signature is that on an enamelled copper *char-aina* in the Tower Armouries, which reads thus:

'The noble Ghulam Alī Khan. Made by the humble Alī of Ispahan in the month of Sha'ban in the year 1213^H (1798)'.

This inscription certainly gives the name of the patron and the armourer's place of residence—but unfortunately, as is so often the case, Alī is a very common name and hundreds must have been living in Ispahan at the time this cuirass was made.

CHAPTER TWO

[1] *Herodotus*, VII, 61–88, ed. Harry Carter, London, 1962.

[2] *Anabasis*, VIII, 6, 7.

[3] *The Excavations at Dura-Europos*, Preliminary Report of Sixth Season of Work, October 1932–March 1933, pp. 188–99. Yale University Press, 1936.

[4] H. H. Howarth, *History of the Mongols*, III, p. 515. London, 1888.

[5] Ibid., p. 565.

[6] Ibid., p. 712.

[7] Onseley Add., 176.

[8] A similar pair with engraved plates, though not of such good quality, are illustrated in the catalogue of the Count of Nesselrode; see Plate 20, *Armes et Armures de la Collection du Comte de Nesselrode au Château de Tzarevtchina*, Gouvernement de Saratov, Russie, 1904.

[9] J. Rota, *La vita del Sophi*, Venice, 1508, cited in appendix of R. du Mans, *Estat de la Perse en 1660*, pp. 272, 274. Paris, 1890.

Chapter Three

Turkey

'Spangenhelm', Lamellar, and Mail

The Tu Kiue (Turks), a Central Asian tribe, were subject to the Jwen-Jwen in the early sixth century A.D. They were established at the foot of the Great Altai, on the western border of present-day Mongolia, where they worked in metals for their masters. Eventually, one of their chieftains—Bu-Min—led his people in revolt and routed the Jwen-Jwen, scattering the remnants, some going east to north China and others to the west across the steppes.

The Turks also divided, some against China and others against Bactria, India, and Persia. Led by Bu-Min's brother Istemi, the western bands were soon in possession of Turkmenistan and by A.D. 568 a new barbarian upheaval was well under way.

In China, the tide was not stemmed until 590; but in the west the restless Turks were seldom quiet for very long, their wars and conquests lasting until the end of the seventeenth century. They made an alliance with the Greeks of Asia Minor and attacked Persia simultaneously in 572. King Khusru I held out until 574 and in that year ceded Armenia to the Turks and Bactria to the Greeks. So the Turks were established in Asia Minor, from whence they were able to dominate Asia and south Russia. The Byzantine diplomats now had an empire to deal with, and no longer the *khans* or chieftains of scattered tribes.

The western group of Jwen-Jwen and the Ephthalites, driven out of Sogdiana by the Turks, fled to the Ukraine, absorbing on their way the remnants of Attila's Huns. The combined peoples became the Avars, who drove out the Lombards and Gepidae from the Hungarian plains and occupied the Danube region. These wandering peoples had similar cultures and, influenced by

the people they conquered, developed a distinctive cavalry equipment which could have been seen from eastern Europe across the
steppes to central Asia.

The earliest representations of Turkish warriors are the stone
grave figures found at Kertsch in the Crimea.[1] They are shown as
wearing typical conical helmets built up in segments, of similar
character to those worn by Syrian bowmen and Sarmatian horsemen on the Trajan Column. Three examples are given in Fig. 28,

FIG. 28 Turkish stone figures from Kertsch, fifth to sixth century A.D.,
Historical Museum, Moscow

all in the Historical Museum, Moscow. One warrior has a narrow,
pointed neckguard hanging at the back, and another has a short
nasal made by a continuation of the front strap of the helmet
frame. These two do not show body armour, but they wear
shoulder-straps connected by rings or discs to a horizontal
breast-strap, suggesting an attempt to copy the harness worn by
Roman centurions to carry their *phalerae* or medals. The third
figure has a helmet of four plates, the front and back with cusped
borders overlapping the side-plates. It has a scaled chin-strap, like
those on nineteenth-century military headdresses, and the front
of the throat is protected by a band of vertical lamellae. The
cuirass is of distinctly Roman pattern, vaguely following the form
of the torso, with pendant leather straps over the shoulders and
forming a skirt about the hips.

It is not impossible at this date for the Turks to have seen a form of Roman armour still being worn by soldiers of the Byzantine Empire, and Dr Ortwin Gamber has only recently pointed out to me how the shoulder-clasps and belt-mounts found

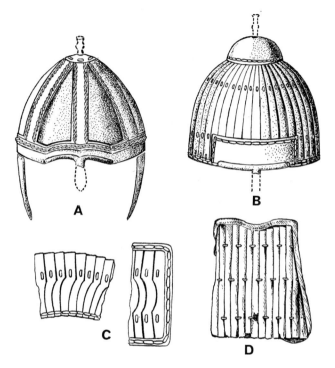

FIG. 29 Avarian armour from graves at Kertsch in the Crimea, second half of fifth century A.D.
    A Conical helmet with plates laced together with wire
    B Helmet of Mongolian shape with the plates joined with wire
    C Portions of laced lamellar armour backed with leather
    D Vambrace or shinguard of splints lined with leather

in the royal ship burial at Sutton Hoo may form part of a Roman-type parade costume made for a seventh-century Saxon king. Amongst the tribes who caused the destruction of Rome there was nothing to represent power, dignity, and authority like the uniform of a Roman general.

From Avarian graves at Kertsch have come interesting pieces of military equipment dating from the fifth to sixth centuries. Perhaps the most important of these is a typical Mongolian helmet built up of radial segments wired together, with an inverted cup on the top and a brow-plate originally furnished with a nasal. Another, now with the above in the Historical Museum, Moscow, is a more usual 'Spangenhelm'—but instead of the plates being riveted they, too, are laced tightly and neatly together with wire. A plume-tube is attached to the apex, the brow is

FIG. 30 Horseman wearing conical helmet and mail with splints on forearms and shins, *c.* A.D. 860, from a golden pot forming part of the Treasure of Nagyszentmiklos, Budapest Museum

cusped over the eyes, and originally there was a nasal. Like many of these helmets, cheek-pieces in the Roman manner are attached.

In these graves, and in others found across south Russia, have been discovered many fragments of splint armour laced to leather, used as shinguards or as vambraces for the forearms. Also with these have been found curious pieces of body armour made up of closely laced lamellae with a leather backing, which could have formed part of a cuirass such as that found at Pasterskaja near Cigirin, Kiev (Fig. 29C). The famous Proto-Hungarian gold jug found at Nagyszentmiklos in Hungary, and now in the Budapest Museum, is embossed on one side with a mounted warrior

wearing a conical helmet with an aventail and shirt of mail. On
his forearms and shins are similar splinted guards. This warrior of
the ninth century may be a Turk; but even if not, the representation is of the type of equipment used by the Turks and their
neighbours in Asia Minor and eastern Europe in the eighth to
tenth century.

When the Turkish and Hunnic tribes were attacking China in
the time of the Han Dynasty, they were already trained to fight as
disciplined cavalry and all were fully armed in the manner of the
Iranians, from whom they had copied their armour and tactics.[2]
This armour was lamellar, and thus we find the majority of the
Asian nomads equipped. A rock carving at Suljek in Siberia,
probably representing an armed Avarian horseman, shows the
conical helmet with Roman cheekguards and a long coat of
lamellar armour with short sleeves. The lamellae are represented
by rows of short vertical lines, the same convention as that used
on a silver dish in the Hermitage at Leningrad showing an eighth-
century Turkish horseman (Fig. 31B). Here the warrior is either
turning his face away or is represented as wearing a veil of mail
covering it. The mail is shown by a scale-like convention frequently met with in art, particularly in Persian and later Mughal
miniatures. Like some Sāssānian warriors, this one wears a short
sleeved mail shirt beneath his long coat of lamellar. Two other
interesting features are in evidence on this dish. They are the
large hair throat-plume attached to the throat-strap of the horse's
bridle—an ornament that was to be copied in eighteenth-century
Europe with Polish and Hungarian uniforms, both under strong
Turkish influence—and an early representation of the stirrup.

The conical helmets of this period were frequently richly ornamented.[3] The iron plates or segments were often wrapped in
heavily gilded copper sheet, and thin strips of punched silver were
laid behind the edges of the plates at the line of overlap. Applied
ornaments—such as small plates and studs, and the spatulate
strips attached to the brow area of many of these helmets with the
point upwards—usually had the same silver borders. The taller
and more elegant of these helmets had long points or plume-tubes
at the apex, which also received embellishment in the form of
gilding or punched decoration. Punched ornament was applied to
the finest of the 'Spangenhelm' in geometric patterns, scales, or
representations of animals scattered over the surface of the helmet

FIG. 31

A Rock carving of an Avarian(?) horseman wearing conical helmet
   and lamellar armour, Suljek, Siberia

B Turkish horseman wearing mail and lamellar engraved on a silver
   dish of the eighth century, Hermitage, Leningrad

Plate V

A Portrait of Fath' Ali Shāh by Ghulām Ahmad, dated 1234H
(1819) loan to *Victoria and Albert Museum from Mrs Yvonne
Rodd*

B *Char aina* of Fath' Ali Shāh dated 1224H (1809), *Wallace
Collection, London*

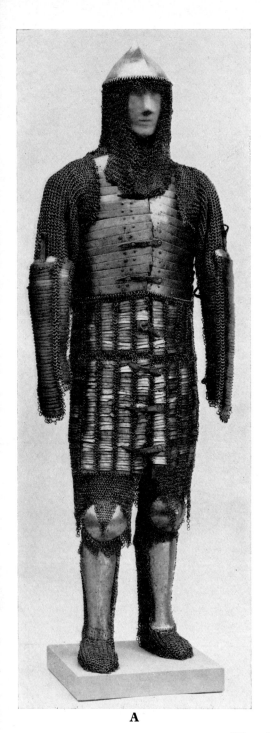 

A   B

Plate VI
Complete Turkish armour, fifteenth century.   A front.   B back
Metropolitan Museum of Art, New York

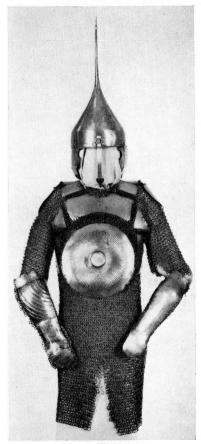

A

B

C

Plate VII
Turkish and Mamlūk Armour

A Mamlūk shirt of mail and plates, late fifteenth century
B Turkish armour of plates and mail, early sixteenth century. The helmet is a converted Persian one, the vambraces not a pair
C Turkish body armour of mail and small plates bearing inscriptions in silver, late fifteenth or sixteenth centuries
Tower of London Armouries (*Not to scale*)

Plate VIII

Turkish Armour

A Helmet and cuirass entirely
engraved and gilt signed Ali,
early sixteenth century, *Waffensammlung, Vienna*

B Mail shirt enclosed in fabric
(Arab. *kazaghand*), sixteenth
century ? *Topkapu Sarayi
Muzesi, Istanbul*

A

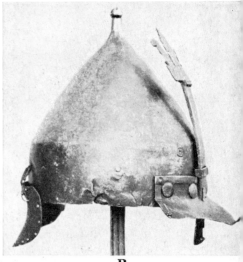

B

C

Plate IX

Turkish and Mamlūk Helmets

A *Muwa'ama* of Governor
Khayrbak of Aleppo, Mamlūk
c. 1515
B *Kawnas*, Mamlūk, second half
fifteenth century
C *Chichak*, Turkish, first half
sixteenth century. It retains its
original lining of red cloth
D *Chichak*, Turkish, late sixteenth
century
E *Chichak*, of raw-hide covered
with velvet and mounted with
copper-gilt, Turkish, seventeenth
century

A and B *Topkapu Sarayi, Istanbul*
C, D and E *Tower of London
Armouries*

D

E

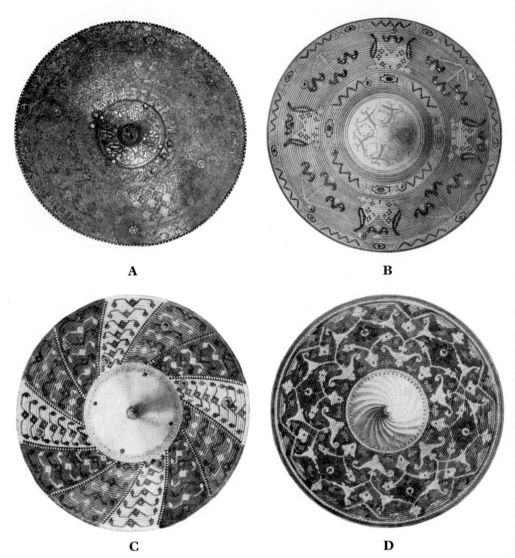

A

B

C

D

Plate X
Shields

A Engraved and damascened steel, Mamlūk or Turkish, late fifteenth century. *Tower of London Armouries*

B Cane wrapped with silk with steel boss, Persian, eighteenth century. *Hermitage, Leningrad*

C and **D** Cane wrapped with silk with steel bosses, Turkish, sixteenth century. *Real Armeria, Madrid*

Plate XI

Horse Armours of Mail and
Plate
A Turkish or Mamlūk,
fifteenth to sixteenth
century. The man's armour
is Turkish. *Bernisches
Historisches Museum*

B Sindian, iron brass
mounted, late seventeenth
century. *Tower of
London Armouries*

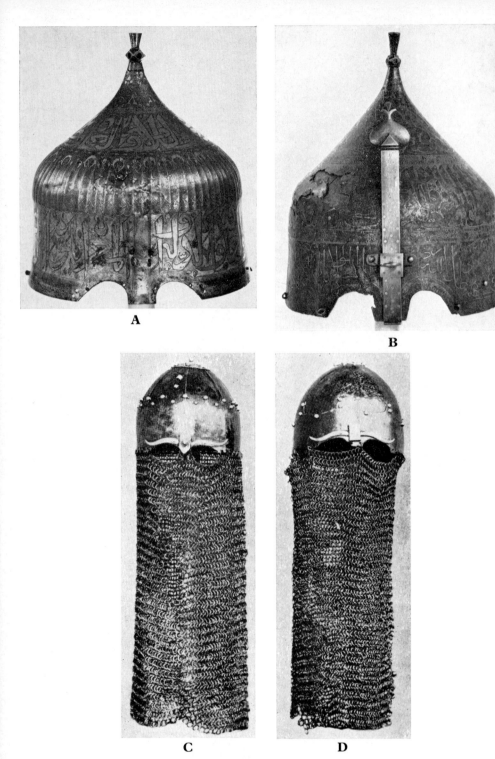

Plate XII

Mamlūk and Turkish Helmets

A Mamlūk 'Turban' helmet engraved and damascened in gold and silver, fifteenth century
B Turkish 'Turban' helmet damascened in brass, late fifteenth or early sixteenth century
C and **D** Two Turkish helmets with aventails, late thirteenth or early fourteenth century
   A and B *Tower of London Armouries*   C and D   *Topkapu Sarayi Muzesi, Istanbul*
   (*Not to scale*)

panels. Gilded helmets found in Japanese burial mounds of the
sixth and seventh centuries also carry punched decoration—one,
in the Tokyo National Museum, with animals and reptiles strik-
ingly like those on eastern European examples.⁴ (Fig. 89).

The Turks who had stayed between the Caspian Sea and the
Pamirs had become Muslims and were therefore allowed to hold
positions of rank by the Persians. There was also a considerable

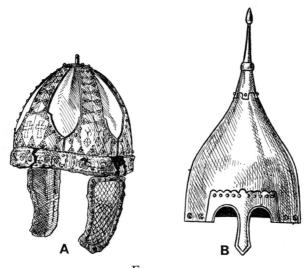

FIG. 32
A Decorated Spangenhelm with cheekpieces from
    the battlefield of Tolbiacum, A.D. 496, Städtisches
    Altertumsmuseum, Mainz
B Typical tall conical helmet with nasal of the steppe
    peoples, from the grave of a Varangian or Slav
    prince, tenth century, Army Museum, Warsaw

amount of infiltration of Turks into Persia through Kashgar,
where the Emirs were themselves Muslim Turks. In A.D. 999 a
Turk named Mahmud—the son of a slave in central Afghanistan
—started a revolt which brought about the downfall of the
Samanid dynasty and founded the Gaznawid dynasty. He then
invaded India through the Kabul passes, took Peshawar, crossed
the Indus and, in 1005, took Lahore. Although the Turkish
power soon waned in this part of India, the Muslim faith was
imposed on the people permanently. The Seljuk Turks, who had
served the Persians well, now revolted against the Gaznawids and
took the whole of the Persian plateau in 1038–40. This brought

all the Turks eager for war and plunder under the Seljuk leader Tughril Beg and his successor Alp Arslan, so that by 1076 Baghdad, Antioch, Damascus, and Jerusalem had been added to their empire.

This brief résumé of Turkish movement will assist the reader to understand how these Muslim Turks became, in time, Indian, Persian, and Mamlūk. Their arms and equipment were those of the country in which they were given office by their rulers and, generally speaking, most was of Persian fashion.

FIG. 33 Turkish soldier wearing coat of lamellar, twelfth century, Çinili Köşk, Istanbul

The relief of two warriors in the Çinili Köşk at Istanbul shows Turkish soldiers in short coats of lamellar armour with simple conical helmets, carrying short straight swords. They are of the twelfth century and may represent foot soldiers of an emir's body-guard.

Mail and Plates

The Istanbul Museum in Topkapu Sarayi contains a very large collection of Turkish arms and armour and also hundreds of Mamlūk and Persian pieces captured by Turkish armies in the fifteenth and sixteenth centuries. The earliest pieces of armour of Turkish origin are two rounded conical helmets with their skulls built up of segments. They closely resemble the Persian helmet formerly in the collection of Count Krasinski of Poland, with cut-outs over the eyes and broad flat sockets for nasals. They have applied eyebrows and retain their long veil-like aventails of mail. They date from the late thirteenth or early fourteenth century and represent the early development of the 'turban' helmet.

The Turkish 'turban' helmet reached its fullest development and most characteristic form in the fifteenth century (see Ch. IV, p. 78). It is evolved from the Persian rounded helmet, which we

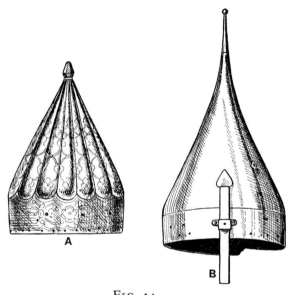

FIG. 34
A Ribbed and engraved Turkish helmet, mid-fifteenth century
B Tall conical helmet with nasal, Turkish, first half fifteenth century; both in British Museum, from the Arsenal of St Irene

are first acquainted with on the rock carving of King Khusru II in the first quarter of the seventh century A.D., with the mail aventail encircling the entire head and covering the face from the eyes down. In the course of the fourteenth and fifteenth centuries this type of helmet was given a tall, conical skull, to which it was usual to attach a small pennant. The tall skull was being made by armourers in south Russia and eastern Europe from the fifth to tenth centuries, usually in conjunction with a fixed nasal and browplate cusped to clear the eyes, a mail aventail also being a characteristic of this style.

There is in the British Museum a good example of an early-fifteenth-century Turkish helmet of this pattern which is too small in diameter for anything larger than a normal padded lining. But as the century progressed the larger variety developed. Although Turkish 'turban' helmets were fine examples of a high technical ability in the working of iron, they were frequently inferior to those of Mamlūk make.

Mail shirts of the thirteenth and fourteenth centuries may also survive, but without some definite means of identification, such as an inscription, they can never be recognized for what they are.

Laminated plates worked into a mail shirt, or forming the main body of a garment in conjunction with mail, became increasingly popular throughout the whole of Islam. In Turkey and India they were used to a greater extent than anywhere else.

One of the earliest existing complete Turkish armours, dating from the fifteenth century, is in the Metropolitan Museum of Art, New York (Pl. VI). The construction of the body armour is very close to those shown in the Royal Asiatic Society's *Shāh Nāma*, with laminations from neck to waist on breast and back, those in front being divided down the centre and joining the back ones with links of mail at the sides. Below the waist is a very deep skirt, built up of about twenty vertical rows of small horizontal lamellae connected with strips of mail. The front of the coat is closed by eight straps and buckles, and the mail sleeves are of three-quarter length. Covering the forearms and back of the hand are defences of horizontal splints in three rows, joined with mail and fastening with straps. The leg armour consists of three main plates: one for the thigh, a circular conical knee-cap and a well-shaped greave for the shin, set in mail and fastening at the back of the legs with straps. Mail coverings for the feet, which could have originally been sewn to leather shoes, are provided. The helmet has a shallow bowl with medial ridge drawn to a sharp central point. The aventail, which meets across the throat, is attached to the bowl with small loops riveted to the edge. (Similar loops are used to secure a curtain of mail to the back of a peaked sixteenth-century helmet in the Tower Armouries.) The very long skirt of this armour would be very impracticable on horseback, even with the high-pitched Turkish saddle, and it is therefore possible that it was made for an officer of janissaries.

The regular Turkish helmet was called *chichak*, from which the German name *Zischägge* is derived. The helmet of the Metropolitan Museum armour, with its shallow bowl, is probably an early form of *missiourka*—a type of head defence better known as Caucasian because of its popularity in that part of the Turkish Empire. It was worn by the lighter-armed Turkish troops and also used in Hungary, Poland, and Russia. It consisted of a shallow bowl which just covered the top of the head, to which was attached a deep aventail of mail. It was worn over a cap or *fez*, about which a small turban was wrapped. Georgian *missiourka* were generally handsomely decorated with silver and niello.

As in the Middle East, coats of mail containing vertical rows of small horizontal lamellae were favoured by the Turks and in the fifteenth century formed the principal body armour of the beys and emirs. This type of defence was sometimes made with larger plates at the front and smaller ones at the back. A pattern found in Turkey and Russia, generally opening at the right side, was more in the form of a cuirass to be put on over a mail shirt. There are examples in the Kremlin, Topkapu Sarayi, and the Tower Armouries, and all display a very high standard of quality. They are entirely built up of horizontal plates connected by narrow strips of mail. Although heavy, they display great strength and suppleness.

Throughout the whole history of Turkish armour mail shirts held their place in the ranks of the *spahis* and were about the last item of armour to be discarded in the Turkish Empire, with the exception, perhaps, of the shield. Turkish mail was generally constructed of large rings made from round or flat wire, with every link riveted. The attachment of brass stars, studs, and mounted jewels was a not uncommon means employed to embellish the plain undecorated mail shirt in the sixteenth century —a custom also found in Russia and eastern Europe, and no doubt a survival from the habit of attaching protective amulets to the vital areas of the mail. In the Caucasus—where mail shirts, worn with *missiourka* and a pair of *bazuband*, were being used by warriors well into the second half of the nineteenth century—we find the same thin and fatigued mail shirts as in the Sudan. The long period of use without a means of replacement or competent repairs has meant that what they had was worn out. Caucasian shirts can be recognized by little brass hooks attached to the corners of the neck opening and used for closing it. The same hooks are also to be seen on the forward edges of the aventails attached to the steel caps.

A rich body defence worn under ordinary clothes—of which an example survives in the Topkapu Sarayi Müzesi—is the *kazar-ghand*, to use its Arabic appellation. This is a mail shirt covered inside and out with fabric; and because it could be both rich in appearance and comfortable to wear, it must have been a popular form of light arming. Many of the mail shirts and coats surviving today may have originally been mounted in this manner, but all traces of the fabric have rotted away. The Topkapu Sarayi speci-man has long sleeves, with mittenlike extensions for the backs of the hands, and small ball buttons and loops to close the front and the wrists of the sleeves. There are also five buttons on each breast across the top of two pocketlike patches for the attachment of containers for cartridge-bottles, such as one associates with Georgian and later Cossack dress. This example is said to be of the sixteenth century (Pl. VIII, B). Another, covered with yellow silk and without attachment for cartouche pouches, is in the British Museum and is probably of the late seventeenth century.

At the close of the fifteenth century the peaked *chichak* took over as the headpiece *par excellence* of the Turkish cavalry. In its earlier form it had a tall, conical, generally fluted, skull—a pattern which remained popular with the higher ranks and with Euro-pean nobility, who had it copied. The later and more common style had a rounded skull, either plain or closely fluted and with or without engraving. An early example in the Tower Armouries, mentioned above, has a rounded skull, a small flat peak and a heavy mail curtain for the back of the neck. It has had cheekpieces attached by leathers, but these and the sliding nasal are now lost. The helmets of this pattern usually had a fixed peak through which the nasal passes, with a broad, flat socket above it which grips the nasal by friction. A late plain helmet in the Tower has a set-screw to hold the nasal and belongs to the second half of the sixteenth century.

The neckguard was generally small and concave, attached to the back of the bowl by three short double links which permitted considerable freedom of movement. Like a tall crowned helmet in the Armoury of the Palace of Valetta, Malta, some Turkish *chichak* have their peaks attached, hanging slightly below the forward edge, by three similar links. Others have the peak secured by turning-pins, so that it can be removed. The large cheekpieces are the chief characteristic of this form of helmet.

They are built up of four plates on earlier examples and of three in later ones—the earlier having the sections attached to the padded extensions from the helmet lining, the later ones having their pieces riveted firmly together (see Pl. IX). The central plate is always embossed with a 'kite' shape, pierced for hearing, and the forward edge generally cusped and flanged so as not to impede the vision to the side.

A specimen with fluted skull, in the Tower collection, retains

FIG. 35 Engraved Turkish helmet with sliding nasal and peak attached by means of four links, first half sixteenth century; Armoury of the Palace of Valetta, Malta

its original quilted red cloth lining, which extends to the edge of the peak and, originally, to that of the neckguard. It is held by small round-headed copper rivets.

The Tower also possesses an interesting tall crowned helmet of rawhide, covered with crimson velvet and mounted in copper gilt. The conical cap at the top, the peak, the plume-tube, and ornamental plates placed around the sides are thin and ornamental. It was probably only used for parade.

As the double plume-tubes became a characteristic feature of Persian helmets, so did a large single tube mounted above the left eye become a distinctive element of Turkish helmets of the late fifteenth and sixteenth centuries. Plumes were built up with small feathers in several stages and, as with the janissaries, very large plumes were removed for action.

Vambraces for the forearms were of several forms. Those of horizontal lamellae connected with mail; the rigid ones of a single large plate for the front of the forearm and back of the hand, sometimes handsomely fluted and engraved, with additional splints connected with mail; and the Persian type, coming to a point under the elbow with a mail-covered fabric extension for the hand, attached around the arm with splints connected by strips of mail.

The late fifteenth and early sixteenth centuries are richly represented by armours commonly termed 'janissary', after the famous Turkish infantry, which were acquired in quantity from St Irene in the last century and dispersed throughout Europe.

The janissaries were formed by Sultan Amurath I in 1360, in the first instance as a bodyguard made up of converted Christian captives. They were highly privileged and richly rewarded and, like most proselytes, more fanatical than the genuine Osmanli (hereditary Turkish warriors). Their numbers grew, so that in time they formed a permanent standing army and a terror to neighbouring Christian states. Eventually, they became the makers and breakers of sultans and a menace to their own country. But it was not until 1826 that they were finally destroyed by Sultan Mahmud II.

The so-called 'janissary' armours were, however, for the cavalry (*spahis*) and consisted of large circular convex plates for breast and back, with a series of plates attached with mail for the shoulders and neck, the chest, and sides of the body. They were decorated with radiating flutes and embossed and engraved ornament and the edges were always trimmed with silk fringes. One of the finest specimens of this type of Turkish armour is that bearing the signature of one Alī—probably an Egyptian, for the links of the mail are stamped with a pattern of concentric rings (see Ch. IV). The rounded bowl of the helmet is closely fluted and all other surfaces of helmet plates and cuirass are engraved with arabesque strapwork and *Qur'anic* texts and entirely gilded. This armour is in the Waffensammlung at Vienna, where also are to be seen splendid examples of sixteenth-century helmets in the Turkish fashion made for eastern European rulers either in

Turkey or by south German armourers. They are of the tall, conical, crowned type and in most cases fluted.

The Turkish mail and plate cuirasses (*korazin*) were completed with *bazuband* or vambraces and worn over a mail shirt—and not infrequently with complete leg armour, consisting of small plates

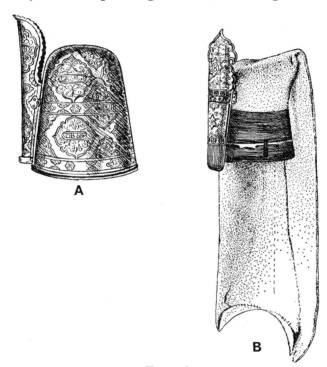

FIG. 36

A Etched janissary helmet, sixteenth century, Bayerisches National-museum, Munich

B Felt cap of a janissary with chiselled and damascened plume-tube, dated 1691, Badischen Landesmuseum, Karlsruhe

and mail for the thighs with circular knee-plates, splint and mail greaves for the lower leg, and mail or mail and plate shoes. Good examples of complete Turkish armours of the sixteenth century can be seen at Turin, Florence (Museo Stibbert), Bern, Paris (Musée de l'Armée), London (Tower of London), New York (Metropolitan Museum of Art), and Toronto (Royal Ontario Museum), whilst elements of armours are dispersed widely in public and private collections.

The janissaries had almost completely discarded armour by the sixteenth century and wore a characteristic uniform by which they were recognized throughout the East and Europe alike. It consisted of a tall felt cap with a transverse fold several inches above the head, so that the upper part came down to the shoulders at the back. To the centre of the front was attached a broad tapering tube with rounded base to carry the large plumes worn on parade. These tubes, which closely resemble Turkish vambraces, were frequently richly chiselled, fluted, and damascened and, by their quality, proclaimed the wealth of the wearer. The dress was completed with a skirted coat and full Turkish breeches of the type that fitted the leg closely from knee to ankle.

An unusual janissary helmet, probably for an officer of a body-guard of the sixteenth century, is in the Bayerisches National-museum, Munich. It is of tall thimble shape, with a large plume-tube attached to the front. The surface is decorated with bands and lobated diamond-shaped panels containing inscriptions and scrolled foliage—not engraved, as one would expect, but etched with acid in the European manner. In the sixteenth century the Turkish infantry were largely equipped as musketeers and by the mid-seventeenth century the cavalry had practically discarded all of their armour. Contemporary paintings in the Historisches Museum der Stadt Wien of the siege of Vienna in 1683 show that Turkish cavalry had only the shield for defence and carried a long pennanted lance and a curved sabre (*kilig*).

The Shield

We do not know what form or construction was used for the earliest Turkish shields or, in fact, if any were carried at all. It seems very possible, however, that like other Central Asian people they were familiar with and usually carried a small circular shield of hide or of wood covered with leather.

In their wars against the Christians in the Holy Land the Turks were acquainted with and used the kite-shaped shield; but the circular form predominated, and the most usual kind was the Persian cane variety. This light and resilient defence, with its large steel boss, was ideal for mounted warfare—and with its woven patterns in coloured silks it had added appeal to the Oriental warrior.

There are many such shields in the Topkapu Sarayi Müsezi, and also some of the flattened conical iron shields with engraved decoration which may be of Mamlūk origin but used by the Turks after capture. Indeed, it is very likely that most of the arms and armour captured by the Turks in their wars of expansion were constantly reissued for use, whatever their origin or style, until they were damaged or until eventually armour was completely discarded.

The shields carried by the cavalry of the Turkish army besieging Vienna in the late seventeenth century were of the cane variety. Amongst the booty taken after the relief of the city in 1683—and now in the Historisches Museum der Stadt Wien—there are a number of cane shields which are faced with painted leather, whilst some woven with silk are also to be seen.

Horse Armour

Turkish horse armour follows the fashions described for Persia in the previous chapter. Hans Stöcklein,[5] when writing on the development of Persian armour, suggests by his statement that the horse armour G.717 in the Musée de l'Armée, Paris, is Mamlūk, that all the others in European collections are the same —for in construction they are identical, except for minor details. It is not impossible that horse armours of an almost standard pattern had been developed in the Islamic world by the second half of the fifteenth century and that, unless makers' marks or dates were put on them, it would be difficult to tell a Persian one from a Turkish one and vice versa. The armours in question all come from the Arsenal of St Irene and it is therefore unlikely that their origin could ever be positively traced.

In the Castle of Forchtenstein, in eastern Austria, there are two Turkish caparisons for horses captured when the Turks were on their way to Vienna in the late seventeenth century. They are of several layers of fabric, faced with velvet and set with ornaments of copper gilt. At the time of their manufacture they would have been of little protective value.

Amongst the detached pieces of armour from St Irene there were a considerable number of chamfrons of the fifteenth and sixteenth centuries and several interesting examples are now in the Armeria Reale, Turin, and in the Tower Armouries. At Turin there are two excellent specimens of the type built up of vertical rows of horizontal lamellae connected with mail (D.31) and another containing larger areas of mail linking plates and borders to form a complete hood for a horse's head (D.30). The edges all carry silk fringes.

In very few cases are earguards present, and in the case of the horse armours at Paris and Bern they have been added in the nineteenth century. A more rigid chamfron, consisting of a solid plate

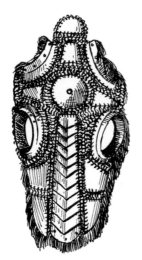

FIG. 37 Turkish chamfrons built up of small plates connected with mail and bordered with silk fringe, early sixteenth century; Armeria Reale, Turin

to fit the front of the horse's face, with embossed eyeguards and flanges for the ears, more closely resembles early-sixteenth-century European examples. In fact, except for the lack of earguards, they are exactly like a series made, probably in Flanders, for the arsenal of King Henry VIII. The Turkish chamfrons of this pattern generally had cheekpieces attached by mail.

CHAPTER THREE

[1] Wsewolod Arendt, 'Ein Alttürkischer Waffenfund aus Kertsch', *Zeitschrift fur Historische Waffenkunde*, Vol. XIII, pp. 49–55, July 1932.

[2] Berthold Laufer, *Chinese Clay Figures*, Part I, *Prolegomena on the History of Defensive Armour*, Ch. III, p. 222, Chicago, 1914.

[3] Paul Post, 'Der kupferne Spangenhelm', *Sonderdruck aus 34. Bericht der Romisch-Germanischen Kommission 1951–1953* (1954).

[4] Suenaga Masao, *Nippon Jodai no Katchū*, Tokyo, 1934, Plates 8–12.

[5] Hans Stöcklein, 'Persian Arms and Armour', Vol. III, pp. 2555–85, A. U. Pope, *Survey of Persian Art*, Oxford, 1939.

Chapter Four

The Middle East

'Spangenhelm' and Scales

The Syrian bowmen shown on the Trajan Column wear helmets of similar character to those worn by the Romans whom they served as auxiliaries, but the skulls are taller and, in all cases, built up of segments. This is, in fact, an almost identical helmet to the barbarian 'Spangenhelm' so widely used in Europe from the fourth to the early twelfth centuries.

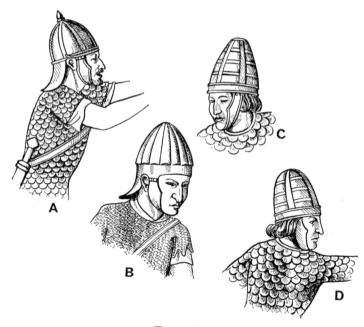

FIG. 38
A and B Syrian auxiliary archers
C and D Sarmatian horsemen
Trajan's Column, second century A.D.

The peoples of the Middle East served Rome in the capacity of archers and cavalry. Whether on horse or foot, they wore the conical helmet and scale body armour, both either of bronze or iron. For pageants and parades, the cavalry adopted from the Greeks, during Alexander's occupation of their country, the helmet with a close-fitting face mask. Other peoples serving in the Roman cavalry also followed their custom—and so from camp and fort sites all over the Roman Empire have come these remarkable helmets and masks, some of yellow bronze, poorly

FIG. 39 Romano-Syrian helmet with iron skull and silver mask, first century A.D., from Homs, Damascus Museum

designed and worked, or of rich dark bronze or iron superbly forged and skilfully engraved, closely vying with the armour made for the gladiators in the depth of their relief.

This is, of course, Roman equipment; but the conical helmet and scale *lorica* is traditional, surviving from the days of Egyptian and Assyrian conquests. Two Romano-Egyptian helmets have survived (Fig. 40). Both have rounded conical skulls built up of four iron segments riveted into a frame of crossed strips, encircled by a band forming the lower edge. To this are attached hinged cheekpieces of typical Roman type. One of these is preserved at Leiden, in the Rijksmuseum, and the second, found at Der-el-Medineh, is now in the Cairo Museum. The only difference is that the latter has cut-outs over the eyes, with an applied brow-plate and nasal, giving it the same character as many found in eastern Europe and south Russia. Both examples date from the late third or early fourth centuries A.D. Mail—also a part of Romano-Celtic culture—passed to the Middle East, where its production became a flourishing craft for which the city of Damascus was later renowned.

Mail and Lamellar
The simple mail shirt as used by Roman auxiliaries in the second century A.D. became a standard defence of the Middle East and remained a constant favourite with the Arabs to within living

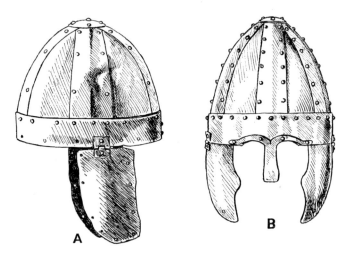

FIG. 40 Romano-Egyptian helmets, *c.* A.D. 300
A Leiden Rijksmuseum
B Cairo Museum

memory, with very little change in fashion and construction. The mail shirt (*dir'*) was a valued possession and an important heir-loom, handed down from one generation to another and, as may be seen from surviving Sudanese examples, used until the rings were worn to breaking-point.

The nomadic desert Arabs had long been known to the peoples of Syria and Persia as fierce and warlike. They had little or no armour at all, but carried hide shields for defence and were armed with the spear, straight sword, and bow and arrows. They were hit-and-run raiders, mounted upon fast horses or dro-medaries, and much of their equipment—particularly armour—would be acquired by looting settlements and forts on the northern borders of their wild domain. The Greeks of Syria and

the Persians, who held the *limes* along this frontier, had occasionally taken Arabs into their service and found them to be stout
warriors—and one is not surprised that when Muhammad went
into the desert to gather the tribes for his unification of Arabia in
the faith of Allah he began the formation of a remarkable force
which was, in time, to dominate much of the world. The Prophet
died in 632 and the leadership was taken over by his father-in-
law, Abu Bekr, who continued the campaign for another two
years until his death. Omar, a more vital personality who inspired
the now united Arabs to join him in a *jihad* or holy war, began the
conversion of the 'whole world' to Islām by taking Persia in 635.
This was followed by Syria, Palestine, and Egypt; and when the
vast Empire had settled down under its new rulers, the primitive
Arab became a citizen in towns and cities far from his homeland,
and in time also took to being a tiller of the soil. Under the
influences of Persian culture, and Greco-Roman Syria and Egypt,
he changed. Absorption into new societies often meant the Arab
element disappearing from responsible posts, even Jews and
Christians being acceptable at this time for their exceptional
abilities. It was such people as the Zoroastrians, with their images,
who felt the lash of persecution.

For the sake of clarity, this chapter concerns itself mainly with
the Muslims of the Middle East and North Africa. Initially, they
were influenced by the military equipment of Greco-Roman
Syria; and after the founding of the Umayyad dynasty in 661, with
Damascus as the seat of the Caliphate, Persian culture and techniques began to spread to all parts of the Arab world. Unfortunately, there is little material evidence concerning the
equipment of Muslim warriors at the height of their power.
The devout Muslim, following the code of the *Hadith*, refrained
from creating or being responsible for the creation of any human
or animal likeness—and so we are deprived of much valuable
material for a considerable period of time.

The conical helmet continued, but by Umayyad times it was
forged in one piece. A rare piece of sculpture—from the Umayyad
Palace of Khirbat-al-Mafdjir—now in a very fragmentary state,
represents two warriors of about the twelfth century (Fig. 41).
They wear deep helmets with fluted conical skulls over close-
fitting hoods. The detail of their body armour may have been
applied in gesso or paint, the only sculptured detail being a belt

passing over the right shoulder from the left side and another round the waist.

Lamellar armour probably came with the Turkish invasion in 1163–91, for a contemporary relief now in the Çinili Köşk, Istanbul, represents Turkish warriors with conical helmets and short coats of lamellar, armed with straight swords. Supporting this evidence is a drawing made in the eighteenth century of a circular window of the twelfth century formerly in the Church of St Denis, Paris (Fig. 42A), showing mail-clad crusaders in

FIG. 41 Stone figure of a soldier, twelfth century, Umayyad Palace of Khirbat al-Mafdjir

combat with Saracens who wear conical skull caps, coats of lamellar and carry round shields. Also of the twelfth century is a fragmentary painting on paper from Fostat, Egypt, and now in the British Museum (Fig. 42B), showing a battle between Christian knights and Muslims. The Saracenic warriors wear rounded helmets or turbans and long-sleeved mail shirts. Their shields, like those of the Crusaders, are kite-shaped. Their arms are recurved bows and long straight swords, while their infantry are carrying spears and shields and wear no body armour.

Mail and Plates

The Mamlūks were Turkish slaves formed into bodyguards by the successors of Salah-ed-deen, the Ayyubid dynasty, who seized power in 1250. In their time steady progress was made in the con-

struction of armour. Usama b. Munkidh, a Saracenic contemporary of King Richard I of England, describes in his memoirs[1]
the equipment of an emir in Ayyubid times. It consisted of a
helmet (*khawdha*), mail shirt (*dir'*), leggings (*sāk al-mūza*), boots
(*khuff*), and spurs (*mihmaz*). His arms were a sword (*saif*), lance
(*rumh*), dagger (*sīkh* or *nimdja*), javelin (*harba*), and shield (*turs* or
daraka). Padded or quilted and studded jerkins were used as a sole

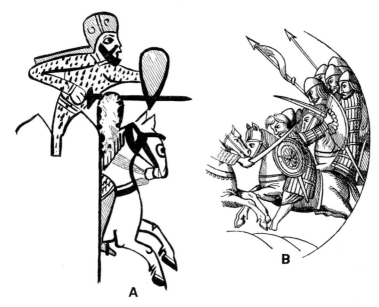

FIG. 42 Saracenic warriors of the twelfth century
A From a painting on paper from Fostat, Egypt, British Museum
B After an eighteenth-century engraving of a window formerly in
the Church of St Denis, Paris

defence for the body or worn over the mail shirt, as we have seen
was also a Persian fashion. Usama also describes a type of mail
much used by the Saracens. This was the *kazaghand*, a mail shirt
sewn between two layers of fabric, the outer one a rich material.
This defence was also used by the Turks, as discussed in Ch. III,
p. 64.

Under the Mamlūks, there was a steady increase in the use of
small plates linked into the mail or applied over it with straps and
buckles. The mail shirt with the addition of small plates is referred
to as *djawshan*. Mamlūk mail can be identified by its flat rings
doubly or singly riveted in each alternate row, the intermediate

rows made without a join, having been punched out of sheet iron. These rings were then stamped with a pattern of concentric rings, dots or scriptural texts. A fine specimen of the second half of the fifteenth century in the Tower Armouries has the rings on the shoulders, upper breast and back stamped with *Qur'anic* inscriptions, changing in the half-length sleeves to rings stamped with lines. The skirt portion is made up of plain rings, and between the breast and skirt are vertical rows of horizontal lamellae connected by narrow strips of mail. These plates are engraved with arabesques and foliate ornament, originally silvered. The garment, which opens down the front as a coat, is fastened with six straps and buckles (see Pl. VII, A). Another mail shirt, in the author's collection, entirely of large links punched with concentric rings, has a short opening at the neck and would be put on over the head.

Armour for the limbs was of the Perso-Turkish type, consisting of rigid plate vambraces for the forearm with an extension for the back of the hand forged in one with the rest and strapped around the inside of the arm with small, mail-connected splints. The thighs were armed with vertical runs of horizontal lamellae connected with mail and attached to a circular dished knee-plate. Leather boots were probably the more usual covering for the lower leg; but amongst the armour from Constantinople, now in the Tower, is a boot of plates and mail which could be either Mamlūk or Persian, judging by the engraved ornament. This is but one problem with which we are confronted when attempting to discover the origin of the hundreds of pieces housed in Topkapu Sarayi Müzesi and dispersed amongst the museums of Europe and America.

The Mamlūk helmet continued to be of conical form with or without an aventail or nasal. During the fifteenth century, if not earlier—due, possibly, to Turkish and Persian influence—the deep helmet cut-out for the eyes and fitted with a veil of mail over the face was developed to its most perfect conclusion by the Mamlūk armourers. This we now classify as the 'turban' helmet, because its size implies that it was worn over a turban or a heavy padded cap wrapped with a headcloth. The bowls are frequently boldly fluted in bands, vertically, diagonally, or spirally at the apex. The surface is often richly engraved with foliate arabesques and superbly ornamental inscriptions, damascened with gold and silver. A flat nasal reinforces the defence of the face. No plume-tubes are provided, but a hook is attached well up on the front, slightly to one side, for hitching up the aventail clear of the face when not in action. The aventail is attached to a series of vervelles or loops on the outside of the lower edge, in the same manner as was employed on European bascinets in the second half of the fourteenth century—which may, indeed, have directly influenced this feature in the Middle East.

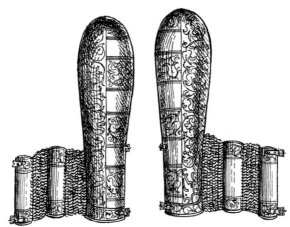

FIG. 43 Pair of vambraces of Kānsūh al-Ghūrī, Mamlūk, fifteenth century, Topkapu Sarayi, Istanbul

Warfare between southern Europeans and Islam brought about many interchanges of ideas, amongst which are types of Mamlūk armour which could have been developed from Venetian originals taken in actions at sea. The first of these is the mail coat with plate reinforcements discussed above. In the fourteenth century the European soldier wore a cuirass of small plates riveted within a fabric garment. The plates were mounted horizontally, overlapping upwards, and attached to the fabric by their upper edges. By the late fourteenth century the plates were small, the nail-heads gilt and many in number, and the outside faced with rich velvet. It was, in fact, a brigandine and was so classified until the sixteenth century. I would suggest that from the coat of plates, normally worn over the mail shirt by Europeans, the Islamic armourers devised the combined mail shirt and coat of plates in their *djawshan*. The possible alternative origin is that, to overcome the weakness of lamellar armour, the easily cut and torn connecting laces were replaced by mail—joining the plates by being passed through holes drilled in the edges. To accomplish this, however, the plates had to be mounted horizontally instead of vertically, completely changing the character of the defence.

A form of body armour, particularly popular in Italy, was the brigandine mentioned above—a defence both comfortable to wear and colourful to look upon. At the beginning of the fifteenth century brigandines were used by the Mamlūks and called *karkal*. They are clearly defined by Kalkashandī[2] as being made of iron lamellae covered with red or yellow *dībādj* (brocade). Rich coats worn over the armour are shown frequently in Persian miniatures of the fourteenth and fifteenth centuries, but studded coats in the manner of brigandines are not in evidence until early in the latter century, coinciding with their use by the Mamlūks. We may then consider, with some reason, the possibility that the *karkal* of the Mamlūks and Persians was derived from the European brigandine.

In the course of the fifteenth century, under the Circassian Mamlūks, the peaked helmet with sliding nasal, large cheekpieces, and small plate neckguard began to replace other kinds. In the writer's opinion, this helmet was evolved from Mongol forms and was developed mainly by the Turks, from whom the Arabs, Hungarians, Poles, and Russians copied it. In the sixteenth century south German and Austrian armourers began copying this helmet for use in the Hungarian tournaments, so popular at the European courts; and later in the early seventeenth century it was developed into the *Zischägge* or 'lobster-tailed' horseman's pot evolved for the arming of the new dragoons.

The late Professor L. A. Mayer called these helmets 'the Muhammad-ibn-Kulaun type', no doubt because they were introduced at the time of this Sultan (1293–4).[3] At least the tall conical, often fluted skull is of that period, and, under the Circassian Mamlūks, the Turkish features were added. Sultan Barsbay's (d. 1438) helmet in the Louvre, Paris (Fig. 44) has a very tall skull (38 cm) with the finial of the nasal of fleur-de-lis form. This tall shape was called *kawnas*.

In the late fifteenth century rounded bowls began to replace the taller conical type. Of existing specimens, many are plain, sometimes completely gilded or silvered, whereas others are decorated

with engraved ornament, including scroll foliage and inscriptions.
The peaks of these helmets are small and flat, with the forward
edge cut to a point and the rear edge flanged upwards for riveting
to the bowl. It is slotted at the centre, for the flat nasal to pass
through, and above it—on the bowl itself—is riveted a rectangular socket which grips the nasal firmly. It is held in the raised
or lowered position only by friction. The cheek- or, more cor-
rectly speaking, earguards are attached by two short leathers to
the inside of the bowl at each side. They are built up of four
plates: a wide central one embossed with a kite-shaped panel,

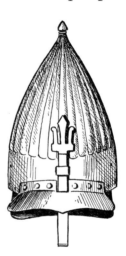

FIG. 44 Helmet of the Mamlūk Sultan
Barsbay, d. 1438, height 38 cm.; Louvre,
Paris

sometimes pierced for hearing; a semicircular piece on either side;
and that coming closest to the wearer's face with a cut-out on a
level with the eye to give visual clearance for a sideways glance.
The last segment is a small pointed plate to which the chin-strap
is attached. All of these cheekpieces (Fig. 45) were originally
mounted upon extensions from the helmet lining, but as these
were generally of fabric they have rotted and the smaller pieces
have been lost. Whilst kept at St Irene, some helmets have fortunately had the pieces riveted together solidly and so they have
been preserved.

A good example of a late Mamlūk helmet, now in the Topkapu
Sarayi Müzesi, is that which belonged to the last Governor of
Aleppo, Khayrbak, who betrayed his country to Selim I in 1515.
It is of the low, rounded type called *muwa'ama* and is, for a man
of rank, a very simple headpiece.

Many pieces of Mamlūk armour have been recognized for their excellence of quality, finish, and decoration. Although often of pure Turkish fashion, they can be detected by certain features even if no distinguishing inscription has been engraved upon them. The firm, unfaltering, engraved arabesques and scroll foliage—which, although carefully executed, do not suffer from the stiffness of so many repeated patterns to be met with on Oriental metalwork—and the flat decorated rings of the mail are two of the main points of recognition. On the earlier pieces the

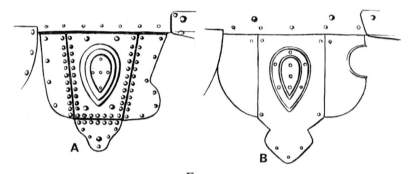

FIG. 45

A Cheekpiece of a Mamlūk or Turkish helmet with the sections mounted upon the fabric of the lining, fifteenth and early sixteenth centuries

B Cheekpiece with the sections riveted together and attached to the helmet by leathers, sixteenth to seventeenth centuries

leaves of the scroll foliage are engraved with a marked thickening at the butt and a turn over at the tip—features which do not survive the first quarter of the fifteenth century.

The Shield

The shield (*turs*) was generally round, with a binding or border reinforcing the edge. It was equipped with a simple horizontal hand-grip at the centre and one or more bosses on the face side. The material used was either wood, metal, or hide. If made of hide, it was called *daraka*—the original shield of the desert tribesmen. The wooden shields were laminated. Sometimes various types of wood were used in the same shield, and the laminations were sewn together with cotton thread.

No actual specimens survive, but they are clearly represented on the Bab an-Nasr of Cairo (Gate of Victory), dated 1087, and the gate of Kal'at al-Guindi in Syria, dated 1187. These shields are slightly convex, but some of the bronzes made in Cairo of armed men show small round shields which are distinctly conical.

The 'Norman' kite-shaped shield was not only known to but also used by the Saracens, as we have already seen on the fragmentary painting from Fostat. It survived until the fourteenth century as a means of displaying Arab heraldic devices if not as a defensive shield.

A good specimen of a Mamlūk iron shield from the Arsenal of St Irene is in the Tower Armouries. It is of low conical section, with an applied concave central boss to which has been fitted a central finial or spike. The hand-grip is a tubular iron loop secured by two ornamental rivets at each end, and there are six other rivets secured over petalled washers on the face of the shield for arm-straps and a guige or neck-strap. The whole of the outer surface is engraved with arabesques and foliate strapwork, with inscriptions encircling the boss and the outer edge, which is also pierced by close-set round-headed brass rivets for the lining. They may also have held a silk fringe, a very popular decoration for both Arab and Turkish armour.

Horse Armour
The earliest reference to Arab horse armour is of the time of Muhammad, when they began to copy the Persian cavalry and develop the fully armed horseman (*mudjaffaf*) using felt horse armour (*tidjfaf*)—presumably somewhat similar to that shown in the reliefs of Ardashir I at Firuzabad.

It is conceivable that the Arabs continued to copy Persian models when horse armours were made, but it would appear—if our scanty evidence is to be relied upon—that no horse armour was used during early Saracenic times. Neither the window formerly in the Church of St Denis in Paris nor the painting from Fostat in the British Museum show any form of horse armour being used by either Christian or Muslim. It was certainly never used in Europe before the thirteenth century.

Amongst the armour removed from the Arsenal of St Irene, and now to be seen in European national collections, are several fine horse armours constructed of columns of horizontal lamellae of iron connected by narrow strips of mail. These were for a long time classified as Turkish—simply, no doubt, because they had come from St Irene at Istanbul—but they are now believed to be of Mamlūk origin.⁴ The best specimens are to be seen at Dresden (1), Turin (1), Florence, Museo Stibbert (2), Bern (2), and Paris, Musée de l'Armée (1). With the exception of one at Bern, which is partly Mamlūk and includes a fine 'turban' helmet with its aventail, they have fully armed Turkish riders seated on them.

These horse armours should be compared with many of those shown in the *Shāh-Nāma* in the Royal Asiatic Society Library of *c*. 1440. In the miniatures the plates tend to be considerably larger; but the principle of construction and the overall general effect is the same.

The chamfrons usually consist of a rigid central face-plate without earguards, flanged for the eyes and nose, with double or single cheek-plates attached with strips of mail. The cheek-plates are also sometimes built up of horizontal lamellae.

African Peoples under Arab Influences
Through traders in North Africa and the Red Sea ports—and, no doubt, largely through the slave trade—many African peoples were converted to Islam, and were to a considerable extent influenced in dress and general way of life by the Arabs.

Foremost amongst these were the more settled communities of the Sudan and northern Nigeria, where the quilted coat and the mail shirt remained in use longer than anywhere else in the world.

The Sudanese equipment became quite commonplace in Britain due to the quantities of arms and armour brought home by soldiers who fought against the Mahdi and his fanatical supporters in the campaign which ended with the Battle of Omdurman in 1898.

The better-armed emirs wore rounded helmets, with an aventail of riveted mail and a heavy fixed nasal, over a quilted lining which spread out over the shoulders and could also be secured across the face below the eyes. Over the body, they wore a long, quilted *jibbah*, either with or without a mail shirt over it.

The mail shirts were all made on the same pattern: short sleeves, round neck opening, and long skirt split to the level of the fork at front and back (Fig. 46). These splits were broad and squared at the top, with the skirt sections tending to be narrow, although giving reasonable protection to a horseman's legs. All examples of these shirts show very considerable wear and much

patching with crude links of wire or split rings of modern European manufacture. I would suggest that these are generally of old
Arab make. All the rings are riveted, except in the case of later
repairs, and many are so worn with use that they could be broken
with the fingers without effort.

The quilted coats were usually simple long-skirted, long-
sleeved garments, split fore and aft to the fork and to the breast at
the neck. The material was usually coarse white cotton with a

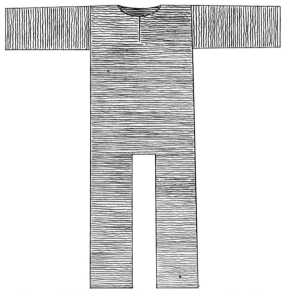

FIG. 46 'Cut' of a typical Sudanese mail shirt

coloured edge binding and stuffing—seldom thick—of cotton
wool. The lines of stitching were vertical and horizontal, spaced
about half an inch to one inch apart. The patched garments of the
dervishes were often copies of the richer coats with panels of fine
brocade, as on the splendid coat taken from the Mahdi's tent and
now in the Tower Collection—the helmet shown with which is
one of many made in Birmingham for the Khedive of Egypt's
regiment of 'Iron Men'. The equipment was completed with a
mail shirt made of split rings—and when the mail was struck by
Sudanese bullets the brittle rings shattered and caused appalling
wounds. The Sudanese, it would appear, only used the helmets
they captured from the Egyptians, preferring the old shirts they
had to these new ones fraught with so much risk.

An unusual armour in the Tower Collection has a typical Sudanese helmet sewn to a thickly quilted lining which extends to the shoulders, across the lower face, and then down to form a cuirass which laces up under the left arm.

When a Sudanese metalworker was recently asked if he knew how to make mail, he offered to make a sample shirt. With the aid of his two sons, he produced a typical example of the old 'cut', but with one main difference: the rings were butted and not riveted.[5]

In Nigeria there are two neighbouring tribes who have warred with each other constantly down the centuries. Both have retained troops armed as mounted spearmen in the old Arab fashion; and both have continued to wear armour.

The first are the Bornu, who have long been famous for their exciting charge for the benefit of royalty and eminent personages who visit their King. They wear long quilted coats, with a high collar rising to a point at the back, long sleeves, and an opening down the front. This is worn either under or over the mail shirt. A coat from Bornu in the Tower Collection, London, has rust stains from mail in the white cotton lining across the shoulders and at the sides. The wearing of mail under the clothes was a not uncommon custom amongst the Saracens, and Ibn Taghribirdi tells us of how Emir Tatar died of an illness brought on through wearing cold mail next to his skin.[6] The mail shirts vary much in quality and all appear to be of Arab make. A shirt now in the Lagos Museum is Mamlūk, with Qur'anic inscriptions stamped upon the rings.

Few helmets of Nigerian make are known, but a recently acquired specimen in the Tower made of tinned copper is of typical conical form, with a curiously fixed nasal and the remains of an aventail attached through holes in the lower edge. The few surviving rings are of iron wire butted.

The Begharmi—the other tribe mentioned above—have specialized in the making of quilted armour for both rider and horse and, in consequence, have been likened by modern writers to medieval knights and even Crusaders, with the suggestion that they may have been acquainted at some vague period in history. The romantic has long seen a Crusader origin in mail shirts and cross-hilted straight swords from the Sudan—two of the latter having been placed upon altars in a famous London church as a symbol of the Crusader spirit of the movement it represents. We know now that this notion is nonsense, but one can easily see how romantics were impressed with this view.

The Begharmi warrior wears a long stiffly quilted coat, and his horse has a complete trapper reaching to its knees. On his head the man wears a quilted cap or hood surmounted by a brass helmet like an inverted bucket, with crossed hoops and central

FIG. 47 Quilted cap (A) and helmets (B, C, D and E) of brass and copper with trimmings of cloth and feather crests of the Begharmi, Nigeria, after Zeller

plume-tube with a crest of feathers (Fig. 47). The horse is provided with a leather-lined brass chamfron with an odd transverse ridge at the level of its eyes. The front is ornamented with bosses, and small cheek-plates are attached with leathers.

This type of chamfron is also used by the Bornu, but instead of armour they rely more on elaborate breast-straps, collars, and cruppers for display.

The quilting of Begharmi armour is either carried out in a close set series of concentric rings of stitching or, as with the Sudanese and Bornu, in small squares. The outer fabric is sometimes built up like a patchwork quilt in geometric patterns with two colours.

CHAPTER FOUR

[1] P. K. Hitti, *Usāmah's Memoirs Entitled Kitāb al-I'tibār*, Princeton, 1930.

[2] Kalkashandī, *Subh al-A'shā*, Cairo, 1331–38H, IV, II, ult.

[3] L. A. Mayer, 'Saracenic Arms and Armour', *Ars Islamica*, Vol. X, 1943. Much of the material in this chapter is based upon this article, the only reliable study yet written on the subject.

[4] Hans Stöcklein, 'Persian Arms and Armour', in Vol. III, pp. 2555–85, A. U. Pope, *Survey of Persian Art*, Oxford, 1939.

[5] A. J. Arkell, 'The Making of Mail at Omdurman', *Kush*, Vol. IV, pp. 83–85, 1956.

[6] *An-Nujum az-Zahira*, VI, p. 506/7, s.a. 824; or Muksid, Ms. Paris, Ar. fo. 122ᵛ; *SM.* Iᵇ, p. 113, n. 13b.

India, Ceylon, Philippine Islands

When Alexander the Great invaded India from the north-west in 327 B.C. he was confronted by large armies, with great numbers of elephants and chariots, which at first appeared very formidable. The Greeks, well disciplined and experienced, quickly overcame their fear of the elephants and soon turned the Indian forces in demoralized retreat.

As far as we can judge, the Indians were without defensive armour except for the shield, which for many centuries is the only protection shown in Hindu sculpture.

From the first centuries A.D. we have the remarkable sculptures of Gandhara, in north-west India, where strong Hellenistic or Roman feeling dominated the arts.[1] The people were largely Scytho-Parthians and Kushans—the latter, from Central Asia, who invaded the territory in about 90 B.C. and established contacts with Augustan Rome.

When represented in their sculpture, warriors wear turbans on their heads, long-sleeved tunics and full trousers tucked into ankle-boots, such as the ancient Scythians, Persians, and Parthians are always represented as wearing. Over the tunic they wear close-fitting cuirasses carved with a trellis pattern which, at first glance, looks like a convention for imbricated pointed scales. But as true scales are in some instances carved on the shoulder and breast area of cuirasses, with the trellis pattern below, it obviously represents some other form of defence—perhaps quilting. From the shoulders and waist hang pendant straps in Greco-Roman fashion, the skirt in several layers—as seen on the statues of Roman emperors and the gravestones of legionary officers. The God of War is shown in Fig. 48 from a small piece of sculpture of the first or second century A.D. in the British Museum. The straight sword, carried by the God at his left side, is similar to the *spatha* of the Roman auxiliary cavalry.

The Romans are also known to have traded with the peoples of the Deccan, the Satakarni, and the Sacae—an Indo-Scythian

FIG. 48 Karttikeya, the God of War, Gandhara School, second to third century A.D., British Museum

people from the north who fought for the possession of this coastal strip for the very sake of this trade. Douglas Barrett, of the British Museum, has brought to my notice a fairly recent discovery of a series of man-made caves at Pitalkhora in the Deccan.[2] The rock face is richly carved in native Indian style, with little or no outside influence at first glance. With closer study, however, one becomes aware of a foreign element in the case of two *dvarapalas* or guardians at one of the entrances. They stand holding spears, are naked to the waist, except for collars and coiled bangles, and round their waists wear simple *dhoti* or skirts. Over the *dhoti*, however, each wears a deep belt mounted with metal plaques from which depends a skirt made up of three layers of square-ended straps with a fourth layer with pointed ends showing below. The part of the *dhoti* which could be brought around the upper body is hanging neatly over the top edge of the belt, in front and to one side. This belt and skirt of straps would appear to be an attempt to copy the *cingulum militare* and the lower half of Roman military equipment. These rock carvings are believed to date from the first century B.C. to the second century A.D.

Under the Persian Sāssānids, the first real Persian influence began to infiltrate into the art of north-west India. But it is doubtful whether any great cultural changes took place elsewhere in the continent, then united under the Guptas. The ancient Hindu[3] armies were built up of troops divided into six categories: hereditary soldiers who formed the backbone of the army; mercenaries; troops provided by corporations (*sreni*); troops supplied by subordinate allies; enemy deserters; and wild tribesmen used for guerrilla warfare. The majority of hereditary warriors were of the *ksatriya* class, but all classes served in the army and some writers on national polity considered even outcasts might serve as generals.

The divisions of Indian armies were four in number: elephants, cavalry, chariots, and infantry. The chariot was not very much used in war after the commencement of the Christian era, but the elephant—so easily panicked to trample and rout one's own forces —was retained until the eighteenth century. By the second half of the fifth century, however, there were the great Hunnic movements taking place in Central Asia, with one branch of the tribe pouring down over the Indus into Kashmir. Its leader Mehiragula, 'the Attila of India', slaughtered and destroyed everything in sight. But by 520 it halted, making no further progress southward—probably due to being unable to cope with the tropical climate.

A further invasion came with the Turks, who took Peshawar in 1005 and crossed the Indus, taking Lahore in 1010. They were Muslims, and although they soon lost their power they imposed their faith on the inhabitants permanently.

The Arabs having taken Kabul with a well-equipped force in

711, Muhammad Kasim marched across the mountains of Balu-
chistan, reached the lower Indus and invaded Sind, from whence
he turned north to the Punjab.

The Turks were persistent in their attempts to take India, and
another invasion followed in the late twelfth century. It was led
by Kutbuddīn Aibak, who extended Muslim rule over the whole
of Hindostan and founded the 'Slave' dynasty with his court in
Delhi.

Unfortunately, throughout this long period of active history
there was nothing to illustrate a development of armour. The
Indian peoples had probably not developed armour of defence to
any great extent, apart from the shield, and it was not until they
were confronted by armoured Arabs, Turks, and Mongols that
they possibly realized how important it could be. We must assume
that the Arabs came armed in mail with conical helmets and that
the Turks and Mongol tribes brought mail and lamellar, although
there is no later evidence for the use of the latter in India. Mongolian leather and scale armour was probably also introduced.

The Mongols' presence in the north-west in the thirteenth and
fourteenth centuries kept the Emperors of Delhi strong; but in
1397 Timur marched into India over the Indus, eventually taking
Delhi and destroying all before him. Timur turned back, leaving
a weakened north. It was Baber, a descendant of Timur, and his
successors who eventually took and held India—so founding the
Mongol or Mughal Empire in the sixteenth century.

Throughout the fifteenth and sixteenth centuries Indian armour
must have followed the fashions brought in from Central Asia
and Persia in the north-west and via the sea trade from the Red
Sea ports to western Muhammadan ports of India.

Some of the pieces of armour which now survive in the
armouries of the old Indian states and in European and American
collections may date from the sixteenth century, the period when
the Mughal Emperors were fighting to establish themselves.
Countless years of neglect, with monsoon rains and humidity,
have no doubt in many instances rapidly advanced the appearance
of great age on pieces little more than a hundred to two hundred
years old. It must also be borne in mind that rich armour and
jewelled weapons were regarded as a royal gift long after they
were no longer required for use. Finely damascened armour was
still obtainable late in the last century in the bazaars of India.

The ever-present problem of unchanging Oriental fashions is a very real one where Indian arms are concerned, particularly during the three hundred years that India and the West have been closely associated. Today we can only endeavour to trace the place of manufacture for a piece of armour; and, if this is possible, we may have some idea of how this particular type of defence came to be used in that part of the Indian continent. Some armour is characteristic of one particular state, such as that of Sind, whilst many states used armour of Persian fashion and it is impossible to distinguish one from another.

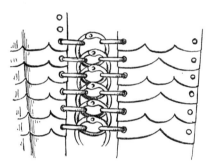

FIG. 49 Detail of mail and plate construction

Mail and Plates

The oldest surviving Indian armours are those consisting of a mail shirt reinforced with splints, plates and lamellae of iron. These armours, of Indian manufacture, were directly influenced by those made in Turkey and Persia and also in Egypt under the Mamlūks. Those with long mail skirts are probably the result of Egyptian influence through trade from the Red Sea ports.

Indian mail-and-plate coats seldom have more than six plates at the front of the body. More generally, they have only four large rectangular ones carrying the straps and buckles, with loops and buttons above connecting the mail on the chest. The back usually contains five rows of closely overlapping horizontal plates, and four smaller vertical plates are set in at each side—two to the front and two to the back (see Pl. XIV, A,B). Lamellae sometimes form standing collars, but quilted and studded fabric tends to be the more usual material. The mail sleeves vary from half to full length, and the skirts—always divided to the height of the fork— can reach from mid-thigh to mid-calf. The rings are of round-sectioned wire, entirely riveted, and must have originally been strong and reliable defences.

These armours usually display much wear, indicating constant use over a long period. They are decorated by the addition of fretted borders of brass or iron riveted to the edges of the larger plates, and with pierced terminals for the buckle and strap fastenings. When brass is used for applied borders, every alternate lamellae of the back could be of brass. The edges of the back

FIG. 50 Examples of patterns worked in *Ganga-Jamni* type of mail
A Aventail of a helmet, brass and iron, Lahore
B Shirt and trousers, brass and iron, Lahore
C Aventail of a helmet, brass and iron, Hyderabad
D Shirt and trousers, brass copper and iron, Lahore

lamellae are frequently engrailed, cusped, and fretted, adding much to the decorative quality of the garment.

Lord Egerton of Tatton[4] lists armours removed after the siege of Seringapatam, in Mysore, in 1799. They include many coats resembling those described above, such as *Zirah baktar*. Fifteen rows plain narrow scales with chain skirt. Worn by officers of high rank.'

From the armoury of the Maharaja of Datia there is a coat of this pattern with gilded plates, now in the Tower Armouries, which was given to Viscount Hardinge, the British Governor-General of India (1844–7). With it is a helmet (*tōp*) built up of mail and plates, originally mounted upon a quilted cap. It consists of a central boss with a plume-tube, ten vertical gores for the crown, and six horizontal strips round the base—the front two having once held a socket for a nasal. There are earguards of rather Turco-Mamlūk form but joined with mail, and a long pointed mail neckguard. On either side, at the front, are two further plume-tubes. All three plume-tubes contain the remains of silver-gilt tinsel ornaments. Had the nasal survived, it would certainly have had large terminals to protect the lower half of the wearer's face. This helmet may be classed as typical of Indo-Muslim helmets of the earlier type.

Two large helmets of similar character, coming from Seringa-patam and said to have been worn by Hyder Ali's heavy cavalry, are in the British Museum and Tower Armouries. The British Museum specimen retains all of its large squared neckguard, the lower half of the Tower example having been broken away. The gores of the crown are all made with a medial ridge for added strength, and both examples retain their heavy nasals (see Pl. XIX, B). These helmets have both been exposed to great heat in a fire, possibly at Seringapatam during the siege.

In the Stone collection in the Metropolitan Museum, New York, there is a rare example of a pair of vambraces for the forearms (*dastana*) built up of splints and mail, the edges of the splints being decorated with applied fretted and engrailed borders. The main plate of the right one carries a transverse curved blade just above the wrist, to make a blow with the forearm more effective, while the left is equipped with a stout cabled bar for the same purpose. This feature survives in later *dastana* as an elliptical embossed ridge.

Armour of mail and plates was developed to a remarkable degree in Sind and neighbouring Kuch. Two of the finest speci-mens are in the Museum für Völkerkunde, Vienna (Pl. XIII), one entirely of plates and mail and the other largely mail with re-inforcing plates on the body. The plate armour—with its built-up helmet with flat grotesque mask and throat, ear and neck defences —was an extremely efficient defence, except that some restriction in vision must have been experienced. This same problem would also have arisen with the other Sindian hoods and helmets, which have a padded triangular flap of mail over the face pierced only with two small eye-holes.

The arrangement of the plates varies, but the number and the area covered is usually greater than on other armours of similar construction—the chest also included instead of simply being protected by mail, as on Turkish and Mamlūk coats. The fastening is by means of pairs of rings riveted to the plates from neck to waist, drawn together with a cord and tied.

The leg armour is in the form of trousers, with the seat and back of the legs to below the knees left free for a more comfortable seat in the saddle. All the linings are well quilted and, although undoubtedly extremely hot, must have made this one of the more comfortable types of armour to wear. The feet were provided with leather shoes with curled toes, over which mail and plates or—as in the case of the armour at Vienna—rigid plates were applied.

Sindian vambraces are of the tubular type, being opened and closed by means of long removable hinge-pins. They are not generally cupped to fit up behind the point of the elbow, as in Indo-Persian *dastana*, but are straight like sections of guttering. Two forms of handguard are encountered: those of mail on fabric, and a more usual variety built up of narrow rows of pointed scale-like lamellae joined with mail, three for the back of the hand and a shorter fourth row for the thumb. In the case of the mail armour at Vienna, the long sleeves are extended to rounded points to defend the hand.

The decoration of these armours consists of applied brass enrichments—either simple borders and bosses attached to the plates or complete overlaid panels of embossed, pierced and engraved decoration. On most of the armours the smaller lamellae are alternately of brass and iron, the brass ones embossed *en suite* with the applied mounts.

The Indian practice of making helmets from segments of iron plate and connecting them with mail led to a wide diversity in the formation and size of the plates and in the areas of mail employed.

Amongst the few pieces of armour remaining in the Red Fort, Delhi, are two helmets of a northern pattern—now rather incomplete—which have their skulls constructed with three main plates. Two semicircular plates, worked to a shallow dished form, are joined to a curved central strip with large riveted mail. Other specimens—in the Stone collection at New York and in the Indian Section of the Victoria and Albert Museum—are more complete, retaining their long mail aventails and nasals with large terminals. These helmets are of munition quality and probably date from the sixteenth or very early seventeenth century.

Other helmets go to the opposite extreme, being composed of hundreds of small lamellae placed in concentric rings, linked by narrow bands of mail and mounted upon quilted fabric. Two such specimens in the Tower Armouries are very typical of their kind with ear flaps and broad squared neckguard hanging on to the shoulders. The older specimen, retaining its quilted cap, comes from Mysore and was taken at Seringapatam. In form, it closely resembles the quilted helmets of Tippoo Sultan previously described.

The *Ain-i-Akbarī*, written by Abul Fazl under the direction of Akbar to record all that had been achieved in the Empire in his time, describes the contents of the great arsenal. The original illustrations reproduced by Egerton are not very enlightening and but few pieces of armour are given. They include the mail shirt (*zirih*) and the *angirk'hah*, or long fabric coat, worn over the armour and shown in a great many Persian and Mughal miniatures.

The *bhanju*, described as a 'coat with gorget', and the *g'hug'hwah*, 'mail coat for head and body in one piece', are interesting, but the drawings tell us nothing of their true appearance. The 'gorget or neckpiece' called *kant'hah sobha* suggests the front plate of a European collar of the sixteenth or seventeenth century although the sketch resembles more the European officers' gorgets of the eighteenth century.

Mail was ever a popular defence on its own, worn over a quilted coat (*kubcha*). The older mail was always riveted and the wire round in section. A hood, shirt, and trousers, and sometimes leather shoes with mail sewn over the uppers, formed a common equipment for the lighter of the armed cavalry of northern India and the Deccan. The hoods, like those from Sind usually had a triangular flap for the face, but were not pierced with holes for vision. The mail, being unlined, was like a veil which could be seen through. A turban formed the padded lining and, with the outer mail, formed an excellent defence against a sword. The heavy-bladed and spiked maces of India took a lot of stopping anyway, and few helmets could possibly withstand them. Fine

examples of hoods and suits of mail made in Lahore—one of the
greatest centres for armour-making under the Mughals—can be
seen in the Tower and Victoria and Albert collections.

The older mail shirts of riveted links were usually of shirt
form, put on over the head; but later, from the seventeenth
century, under Persian influence, they were generally made to
open down the front like a coat. With the flow of Persian culture
through the Mughal court came the fine butted mail with patterns
worked in brass and copper rings. In the manufacture of this
mail the Indian armourers, frequently trained by Persians,
excelled themselves—even decorating suits with large *Qur'anic*
texts as well as elaborate and more automatic geometric trellis and
diapered patterns. The silvery iron rings combined with the
yellow brass were called *Ganga-Jamni*, being likened to the meeting
of the dark waters of the Jamna and the muddy ones of the Ganges.

Riveted mail shirts had standing collars stiffened by having
strips of leather laced through each row of rings, a practice found
in Nepal and Bhutan as well as in the Arab countries. On fine
butted mail coats a different technique was required, and so we find
the quilted brocade or velvet collar with matching facings on the
chest with gimp buttons and loops for fastening. Attached under
the fabric collar a cape of mail, which fell over the shoulders in
series of long points, was worn in the Persian manner. The lower
part of the coat, without fastenings, was confined round the waist
with a colourful sash, generally a cashmere shawl folded and
wrapped round and into which daggers could be thrust. Swords
were usually carried on a shoulder sling, with the exception of
Persian *shamsher*, which had waist belts with double slings.

An interesting form of mail, probably of Persian origin, has
every alternate row of rings punched out of sheet metal. These
rings have two semicircular openings with a central crossbar, and
the rings connecting them are riveted. The purpose of this feature
is in some doubt, but one theory suggests that the rings—being
unable to turn—reduced wear. One can argue, however, that, if
the rings did not turn, the wear was confined to a smaller area and
not spread around the complete circumference, and they were
therefore likely to break more quickly from weakening. The rings
of mail have been known to stretch under tension and the bar
could have been a reinforcing brace to reduce the possibility of
stretch, at least in every other row.

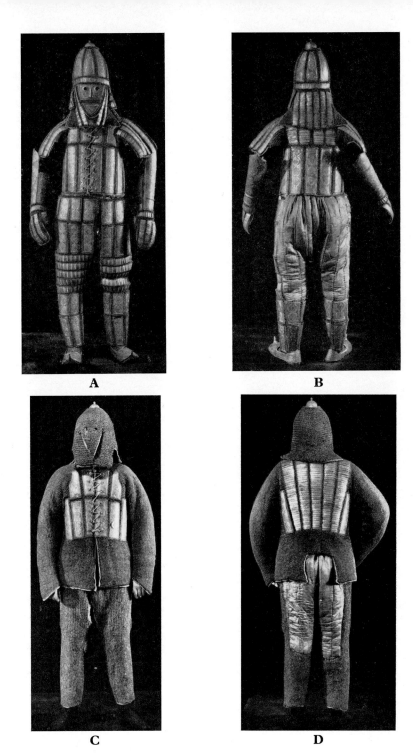

A B

C D

Plate XIII
Sindian Armours

A and **B** Complete armour of mail and plates overlaid with
embossed brass ornament, late eighteenth or early nineteenth
century

C and **D** Complete armour of mail with plates on the upper part
of the torso only, late eighteenth or early nineteenth century
Museum für Völkerkunde, Vienna

A   B

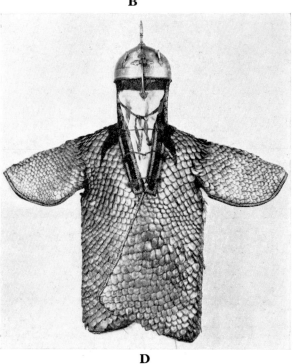

C   D

Plate XIV
Indian Armour
A and **B** Helmet and body armour of mail and plates, North Indian, seventeenth to
eighteenth century
C Studded coat faced with black velvet and reinforced with rectangular plates,
Rajput, eighteenth century
D Coat of pangolin scales decorated with gold leaf, Datia, nineteenth century
Tower of London Armouries (Not to scale)

Makers of Indian mail sometimes signed their work by pouring a small quantity of molten brass on to an area of rings on the breast and smoothing the outer surface to receive an engraved inscription.

Mail coats were generally made with long sleeves, and the average length of skirt reached mid-thigh. The trousers, like the lower part of modern pyjamas, were of fabric with a tubular seam at the waist for a belt or draw-cord, the latter finished with elaborate gimp tassels. The mail was sewn to the fabric and usually left the seat and inside of the legs to the knees free, to provide a comfortable seat on horseback. In some cases they had mail all round the leg, from fork to ankle.

Leather and Fabric
It is unlikely that the medieval Indians began making mail for themselves the moment they saw their enemies wearing it. Some may have been acquired by trade and some made by Turkish, Persian, or Arab armourers brought in for the purpose; but it would be a long time before thousands of shirts and helmets could be made to equip regiments of heavy cavalry and infantry. Quite early in Indian history some attempt may have been made to create simple cuirasses such as primitive peoples have often devised for themselves without outside influence. The Indians had plenty of outside influence, and a simple leather cuirass on the lines of a waistcoat with shoulder-straps may have been evolved.

The Nepalese *kukri* and the Muhammadan and Hindu forms of sword termed *sosun pattah* (willow leaf) are direct descendants of the Greek and Persian sword called *machaira*, which, in its turn, was evolved from the Egyptian and Babylonian *kopis*. Efficient forms of arms and tools have always survived through changing cultures and, in the conservative East, I would submit the possibility of Greco-Roman influence surviving in the simple leather and fabric cuirasses of central India.

Two good examples—one from Indore and the other from Mysore, both of eighteenth-century date—are in the Indian collection of the Victoria and Albert Museum. The specimen from Indore (Fig. 51) is composed of stout hide covered with crimson and green velvet and studded with a pattern in gilt-headed nails, consisting of a scaled ground with borders and circular central panel of conventional floral ornament. The shoulder-straps, with scalloped extensions for the points of the shoulders and the tall extension for the back of the neck, are decorated with the same studded decoration. The fastening is down the centre of the front.

The second example, once a personal armour of the Sultan Tippoo of Mysore, was taken at the fall of Seringapatam in 1799. The cuirass is nearly an inch in thickness and is composed of many layers of coarse cotton fabric covered on the outside with

FIG. 51 Cuirass (*peti*) of hide covered with crimson and green velvet with a pattern in gilt nails, eighteenth century, from Indore, Victoria and Albert Museum

green velvet. The shoulder-straps, of the same thickness as the rest, are made in the form of conventional blossoms with leaves spread to connect the upper corners of the breast and back. The fastening of the front is by laces and is set to the left of centre. The helmet with this armour is of the same material as the cuirass and a little thinner. It is of deep rounded shape, with divided cheek and ear flaps and a broad neckguard. The outer green velvet covering has now worn away to expose an under-layer of printed fabric. Inside the lining at the back is embroidered an inscription stating that the helmet has been dipped in the holy well of Zam-Zam at Mecca and is therefore impenetrable. This form of cuirass was termed *peti*.

Amongst other quilted armours made for Tippoo Sultan are two in the Royal Collection at Windsor Castle. They consist of crimson velvet padded coats, skirted and long-sleeved, with broad embroidered quilted belts and helmets. One helmet is like the Tower specimen, with peak, double ear flap, and squared neck flap bound with a green *pagri* and having a large iron nasal fastened in front with spreading terminals. The other is quite similar, but has a broad, very thick brim surrounding the crown. It also has a large nasal. The Tower helmet has no nasal, and ties beneath the chin with soft lengths of *pagri* cloth (Pl. XVIII, B). The embroidery of all these specimens is in gold orris thread, in floral patterns executed on crimson velvet.

From central India and Rajputana came a more common form of fabric armour which, in many instances, bore a strong similarity to the clothing and armour of the steppe peoples of Mongolia and Central Asia. There were two main patterns. Those entirely of quilted fabric consisted of a hoodlike cap made up from four segments, with large rounded ear and neck flaps, sometimes fitted with a metal nasal, a long straight and full coat with scalloped flaps over the shoulders and upper arms, and high matching riding-boots. The padding generally consisted of layers of soft material and a thin one of cotton wool, faced with crimson or green velvet and lined with silk or satin. The surface of the whole was decorated with nails in a scale or diamond pattern, with repeat floral or herringbone design at the borders. In some cases a layer of thin leather was laid beneath the velvet to give a firmer seating to the little nails, which were simply bent over at the back. To protect the front opening of the coat, from neck to waist, a long bib-like strip was tied at the back of the wearer's neck before the coat was put on. The fastening was by gold or silver lace buttons and loops, seven or eight being about the average number. A good example from Indore in the Tower Armouries is shown in Pl. XV, A. These studded and padded coats were a continuation of the old Arab, Turkish, and Persian military garments described by Usama and Kalkashandi of Saracenic Egypt. It was only in cut that they differed.

A rich and often handsome variant of this class of armour was that with damascened plates added to the centre of each of the main areas. The coat was made in two sections, fastening over the shoulders and at the sides as far as the waist with buttons and loops, the skirt split to the waist at the centre of front and back. In the centre of the breast and back were fastened with nails large convex circular plates with a horizontal plate above them and one

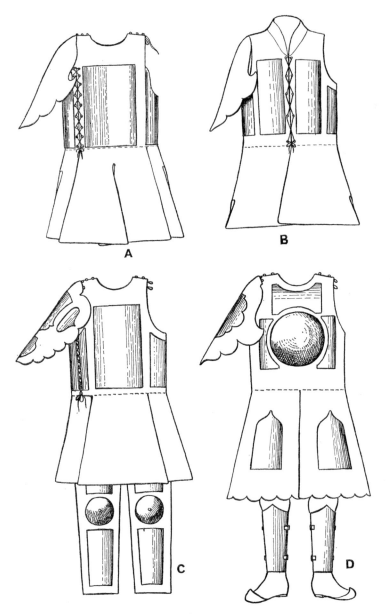

FIG. 52 Types of 'Coat of a Thousand Nails' with plate reinforcements
A From Gujerat, formerly in Meyrick collection
B From Rajputana, Tower of London Armouries
C Hermitage, Leningrad
D Hermitage, Leningrad

at each side—of a similar design to the Perso-Turkish cuirass, but without the connecting mail. To the centre of the skirt sections, in front of the thighs, were fastened convex plates with pointed tops and squared bases. The large shoulder flaps, which were separate and attached by loops and buttons, each had a central plate following the pointed and lobated outline of the fabric. All the exposed areas of velvet between and around the plates were studded with patterns as described above. The back section could be distinguished from the front by a vertical central flute running through the upper and central circular plates. These equipments were completed with an Indo-Persian helmet (*tōp*), a pair of vambraces (*dastana*) with matching studded velvet handguards, and a pair of high boots, also of matching pattern.

In the Tower Armouries there is an armour of the type just described which has become associated with the Burmese General Maha Bandula, who died at the Battle of Donabyu in 1825—an unlikely story, for which there is no supporting evidence. Another variant of this studded armour is a short-skirted coat, opening at the front, with a series of rectangular plates attached vertically to the upper part—one on each breast, one under each arm and two at the back. An example in the Tower Armouries has applied gilt borders to the plates instead of gold damascene (Pl. XIV, C). The Rajputs called these armours *chihal'ta hazar māshā* ('coat of a thousand nails').

In the Hermitage, Leningrad, are two very fine studded armours with reinforcing plates; but, unfortunately, it is not recorded from whence they came. One has studded trousers with plates for the front of the thighs, knees, and shins, and the other has boots with straight shinguards attached.

Other variants were combinations of plate cuirasses with additions of studded fabric—such as the Rajput cuirass of European pattern in the Metropolitan Museum of Art, which has shoulder flaps and four sections of skirt of studded velvet, and a *char aina* in the British Museum mounted upon padded fabric with strips of studded crimson velvet between the plates. Straps and buckles were also provided in the usual manner, so that the plates could be tightened round the body.

Although most surviving examples of this form of armour were made to the north of central India, it must have been very common and fairly widespread—for from Mysore, in the south, there is Tippoo Sultan's brown velvet horse trapper in the Royal Collection at Windsor Castle, powered with gilt nails and with a handsome gilded iron chamfron. The *chihal'ta* or 'forty-fold coat', sometimes corrupted to *chiltah*, was a common defensive garment worn by soldiers and may be of considerable antiquity in India and Central Asia.

Scale Armour

Armour of leather or fabric covered with imbricated scales of metal, horn or leather, may have been quite common in Hindu India and also to some extent after the Turkish, Mongol, and Arab invasions. Scale armour of one form or another would seem to have been used at some period in the history of most civilizations. It was used by both Greek and Roman troops, and we know from the sculptures of Gandhara that it had already been used in north-west India.

Another suggestion for its wide use in India comes from the oft-repeated scale pattern worked in gilt nails on fabric armour and on the fabric handguards of vambraces—which could imply that, in earlier times, scales had been employed for these parts of the armour.

The State of Datia has provided two very remarkable scale armours (*baktar zillo*), both of which were presented to members of the British Royal Family in the nineteenth century. One, still in the Royal Collection at Sandringham House,[5] consists of a rounded helmet of horn scales of the armoured ant-eater or pangolin, with a narrow peak over the brow and three plume-tubes, and a large coat of the same scales. This coat spreads from the shoulders to a wide skirt and has broad flaps to cover the upper arms. It opens at the front and is fastened with gilt buttons and gimp loops on the breast. Each scale is decorated with gold leaf, varnished and sewn to a strong fabric base. The edges are bound with velvet embellished with gilt nails and small precious stones. The second example, now in the Tower Armouries, is the same, except that the helmet is lacking and the borders do not carry any jewels (Pl. XIV, D).

Another specimen in the Tower collection, now in a very bad state of repair, is only illustrated by a detail in Pl. XXVII, C. It comes from Lahore, in the Punjab, and is of small size. The scales are of iron, polished bright, and each is riveted to a leather base lined with green velvet, with canvas between. The edgings are of gold orris braid. In certain positions the scales were sewn down by their upper corners and, at the edges, even riveted to each other. The shoulders carry straight strips with scales hinged down the sides and at the ends, so that the upper edges of both front and back are concealed where they come together, and would, if not so covered, be unsightly as well as vulnerable. Hinged scales also border the neck. The cut and style of these coats suggest strong central Asian influence, which have already been noted in armours of fabric.

Plate Armour
When plate armour is mentioned in connexion with India it immediately calls to mind the Indo-Persian *char aina*—the hemispherical helmets and vambraces, of which there are a great many to be seen. There is, however, a much rarer form which may have been evolved about a century earlier, in the late sixteenth or early seventeenth century, through European influence.

The Portuguese were the first European settlers to arrive and they founded a settlement at Cochin, on the south-west tip of the Indian continent—the Dutch establishing an East India Company post a century later, in 1602. The English and French did not really enter the scene until the eighteenth century, so that whatever European influence is to be seen in Indian armour must have come from either the Portuguese or Dutch settlements.

An early-seventeenth-century helmet in the British Museum (Fig. 53A) has the skull copied from a Portuguese helmet of cabacete or Spanish morion type. It is a superbly made piece, with a large backward-curving stalk at the apex. A short concave neck-guard is fixed rigidly at the back and at the front is riveted a small peak, a little above the edge of the bowl, through which passes a large nasal in the fashion of Arab and Turkish helmets. The last feature was probably derived from Arab models familiar to the Indians through the Red Sea traders. The lower part of the nasal is, however, of pure south Indian form, being of deep crescentic shape to protect most of the wearer's face. The nasal has chiselled borders with pearled edges and a peculiar hinge at its centre, the purpose of which is not at all clear. There are the remains of hinges at each side for the attachment of cheekpieces. The whole has been silver gilt.

A helmet also from south India, in the Stone Collection at New York (Fig. 53B), is embossed in the shape of a small turban. It has the same narrow peak, large nasal spreading to guard the face, and hinged ear- and neckpieces.

This large nasal is almost certainly a feature of southern Indian armour and a means of identification. Mail hoods for the cavalry were sometimes equipped with them, held by a socket riveted to the mail in the centre of the brow.

The cuirasses of European character are not of any definite

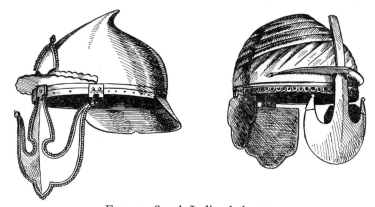

FIG. 53 South Indian helmets
A Silver gilt iron with morion-shaped skull, seventeenth century, British Museum
B Turban-shaped, c. 1700, Stone Collection, Metropolitan Museum, New York

type, being a mixture of both native and foreign styles. Only the example in the Stone Collection, mentioned above in connexion with fabric elements, is more in line with true European models, being of simple rounded form with a medial ridge to the breast-plate. All others known to the writer have the breast-muscles embossed on the breastplate—and, in one case, the shoulder-blades on the back. All the breasts have a medial ridge with a gentle curved profile; but none have the waist flange of European cuirasses, nor do they have the bold turned edges at neck and arm openings. Instead, there are usually applied semicircular borders laid over a further applied strip with fretted edges and gold dama-scened ornament. The cuirass of this type in the Tower Collection does not have these borders, but has gilt nails passing through gimp braid, used to secure the lining. The fastening was usually by strap and buckle; but in the case of the fine cuirass in the Museum für Völkerkunde, Vienna, both shoulders and sides are secured by means of hinges with removable pins. This example— which has been heavily scaled through being in a fire—with its standing guard at the back of the neck, and with its stylized breasts and shoulder-blades, has a remarkably Classical look, for it has much in common with a Greek bronze cuirass of the eighth to sixth centuries B.C.

Two breastplates, in the Wallace Collection, with applied borders and central ornament are probably from Gujrat or Sailkot in the Punjab and of eighteenth-century make. One bears the inscription 'Allah Muhammad Ali'. There is a cuirass of very similar type in the Palace Museum at Alwar, in Rajputana, of the same period.

The Tower specimen forms part of an armour which came from Hyderabad in the Deccan, and it is interesting because both breast and back are made up of four main plates riveted to internal strips and polished smooth. The joins were originally covered by bands of false damascene—now almost entirely removed, except at the borders.

Another form of cuirass of not very common pattern, also in the Tower Collection, is built up of vertical panels of heavily silvered iron joined by their longest edges with hinges, one pin of which is removable so that the cuirass could be put round the body. To the upper edge of three of the splints are attached half-hinges—two to the front and one in the centre of the back—to which other sections of hinges could be attached with pins. These probably formed the terminals of V-shaped shoulder-straps of riveted mail. Small holes are provided in upper and lower edges for the attachment of a padded lining.

The Indo-Persian armour—consisting of helmet (*tōp*), cuirass in four sections (*char aina*), vambraces (*dastana*), mail shirt (*zirih*), and sometimes mail trousers—was introduced with the flood of Persian culture into India under the Mughal Emperors. It was probably not until the late seventeenth century that it was made in quantity. But from the north-west to the Deccan it had spread to most states by the late eighteenth century and was found even in Tippoo Sultan's armoury in the south.

There were two distinct differences between these armours and those of Persian make. The helmets were much lower in the bowl;

and the vambraces were always tubular, being fastened round the forearms with hinges with removable pins or with straps and buckles.

The earlier form of tall conical Persian helmet was found in seventeenth-century India. There is a fine specimen of this type at Alwar and another at Vienna. The latter has no provision for an aventail of mail and may have had fabric ear- and neckpieces attached to the lining. It is decorated with *Qur'anic* inscriptions in gold false damascene and fitted with a long slender nasal with leaf-shaped terminals. It dates from between 1600 and 1650 (Pl. XX, A).

Also of the seventeenth century, and very much in the fashion of Persia in the sixteenth century, were helmets of Indian make decorated with bands of superbly executed floral chiselling, probably made for Mahratta warriors. They were of low conical form, surmounted by an ornamental knob stemming from the large chiselled conical cap. The lower edge of the bowl had a broad band of decoration and a moulded beading below this, probably to protect the rings of an aventail fastened through holes in the lower edge of the bowl. A good example, in the Tower, has hinged earguards and a socket for a nasal. On the centre of the bowl, in front, is an inlaid trident—a symbol of the God Siva.

The average Indo-Persian helmet was fitted with a nasal, but rarely with a set-screw fastening. The Indian used nothing to secure the nasal in the lowered position; but to hold it up he had a swivel loop attached to the bracket, which could be engaged with a hook on the lower end of the nasal just above the terminal. Following Persian fashion, there were always pairs of plume-tubes on the front of the bowl, and frequently a third screwed into the top in place of the alternative quadrangular spike. When spikes were fitted, they were usually much shorter than Persian ones. Only in the earlier specimens was riveted mail used for the aventails. They were almost always of fine butted mail, with a pattern worked in brass, or brass and copper rings. It was most usual for this to match the shirt and trousers worn with it. The mail passed across the brow and descended to the shoulders, finishing with points on either side at the front and with one or two in the centre of the back. Linings were of quilted fabric and, in some instances, had a curtain hanging down at back and sides to keep the mail away from the head. Ties of braid with tinsel tassels were provided for securing the helmet under the chin.

Some helmets were of oval form—so fitting the head better than the normal form, which was perfectly round. The Sikhs used oval helmets so that their long hair could hang more easily at the back of the head. Or if they wished to keep their hair in a bun on top of the head, they wore a helmet with a broad, raised crest shaped like a French 'Cap of Liberty' to house it. These oval

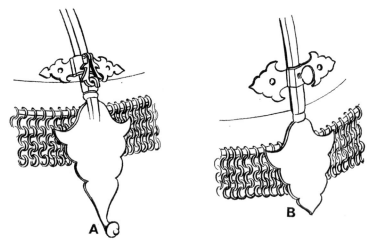

FIG. 54 Methods of securing nasals in the raised position on Indo-Persian helmets
A The more common link and hook
B The less common set-screw, the Persian fashion

helmets rarely had nasals—but one quite common type with oval fluted bowls, plume-tubes at front and on top, nasal and short curtain of mail was made in Lahore in the second half of the nineteenth century. The decoration was in gold and silver false damascene, and very thin.

The Indian *char aina* were usually of rectangular shape, slightly transversely curved to fit against the body. The side-plates were normally cut out on the upper edge to fit beneath the wearer's arms. The plates varied considerably in size, sometimes meeting easily at the edges and sometimes showing a considerable amount of mail between. The edges of the plates were generally fitted with an applied semicircular moulding, the actual edges never being turned over as with European armour. Separate padded linings were attached with glue or sewn to each plate. The most usual fastening was by pairs of straps and buckles. Shoulder-straps showed a little variety—for though most were straight, narrow straps of leather or webbing, some were embroidered leather or fabric, made wide at the centre and tapering to pass through the buckles at the ends. A fine, large *char aina* in the Red Fort at Delhi has mail shoulder-straps permanently fastened to the backplate and fastening to the breast with gold damascened clasps which hook into slots in the breastplate.

The vambraces or *dastana* were, as described above, of tubular type like the older Persian style. They were always lined with rich *kincob* (brocade) or velvet, handsomely finished with braids and gimps at the edges. The extensions for the hands were provided with loops for the fingers and thumb. Their outer surface was covered with fine mail, richly embroidered with gold, silver, and spangles or patterned with gilt nails. As it was quite common for mail shirts to have studded velvet collar and facings, the studding of the handguards and the velvet would be matching.

The plumes worn in Indian helmets were of feathers or tinsel, sometimes of both. The greatest favourites were those made from slender black heron feathers mounted on sticks, with gold gimp in circular sprays, and called *bagtakalghi*. Large tufts of silver gilt tinsel ribbon, like pompons, mounted upon gimp-wrapped sticks were also used extensively, or sprays of soft white feathers tipped with little bunches of gold tinsel. In the south, and to the west in Sind, plumes were seldom if ever used. No existing helmets from these parts of India are fitted with plume-tubes, unless they have been acquired from further north.

The most remarkable Indian armour that exists is the chiselled, pierced, and engraved set in the Hermitage at Leningrad. It consists of helmet, four mirrors, and vambraces. The helmet, in the form of a Mahratta cap, with backward-curling point and surrounded by a coronet of outward-curling petal shapes, has a large recurved nasal, hinged plate guards for cheeks and neck, and a detachable guard for the lower part of the face which can be put behind the nasal. The panels of this helmet are pierced like the finest lace with trellised strapwork and blossoms, with Hindu deities on brow and nasal. The *char aina* and *dastana* have the same patterns chiselled in the surface, but are not pierced.

Another Mahratta helmet of this shape but of more solid construction is in the Victoria and Albert Museum. It is of dark Damascus steel, with bands and panels of scrollwork in low relief, heavily gilded. There are no ear- or neckpieces, which may have been of quilted fabric or replaced by a mail aventail in this instance. A similar, cap-shaped helmet (Fig. 55), but with forward-curving crown—a Rajput form—in the State Armoury at Jaipur is little more than a framework of engraved and damascened iron, built up of leaf-formed strips springing from a band

FIG. 55 Cap-shaped framework helmet, chiselled, pierced and damascened, Rajput, eighteenth century; State Armoury, Jaipur

containing pierced panels with figures of gods from the Hindu pantheon. The tapering nasal is fixed with a single plume-tube above. It would have been lined with rich quilted fabric, extended to cover the ears and neck. There is another similar pierced Rajput cap helmet surrounded by a metal *pagri* in the Stone Collection at New York. Both of these examples are of the late eighteenth or early nineteenth centuries.

Decoration
Indian armour was normally decorated with gold *koftgari*—a pattern laid on to the surface of the iron by hammering gold wire into areas of closely hatched cuts made with a draw-knife—commonly called false damascene. Armour was seldom ornamented with true damascene—which was gold hammered into the pattern cut into the surface of the iron, as was the practice with the best Persian work and on Indian arms.

The patterns were confined to borders, central and corner panels, and sprays. They consisted of bands of scrolled floral and foliate ornament between narrower borders of sprigs, petals, conventional buds, leaves, and pellets. Low-relief scrollwork, conventional blossoms, and trees were usually entirely gilded, standing out against the dark watered iron of the unornamented panels between.

The influence of Iran, though considerable, seldom included the decorative inscriptions in bands and cartouches so loved by the Persian embellishers of armour. Only occasionally did a religious text appear on even Muhammadan armour, and then it was applied to a small area—such as a finial of a nasal, or within a cartouche in the centre of each of a set of four mirrors.

In Lahore work, Persian motifs sometimes occur in the form of birds and beasts, the sun and peacocks. The crescent was common on Muhammadan shields, usually offset from the bosses to one side and, like them, made in relief and applied.

Precious or semi-precious stones, usually uncut, were sometimes set into armour, backed with bright tinsel to give them brilliance. When applied to armour they were in simple floral settings, and it was only on shield-bosses that they approached the extravagance of sword- and dagger-hilts.

The rich chiselled decoration of central and southern India was frequently gilded or silvered and gilt which, although conveying an impression of overall richness, actually tended to mask the fineness of the chiselled detail.

The Shield

The earliest representations of shields are to be seen in the sculptures of Sanchi, where they are shown as rectangular with a rounded top—like those used in ancient Egypt—and decorated with double crosses (Fig. 56). Cavalry shields were small and bell-shaped, with the broad, rounded base carried downwards. The material from which they were made is unknown, but wood faced with leather seems the most likely construction. These examples date from the first century A.D., and rectangular shields continued to be shown on sculpture for about another three hundred years.

The Gandhara sculptures of the first to second centuries show round shields and suggest a convex surface. It may be that these circular shields were already of buffalo or rhinoceros hide—the chief materials for Indian shields until the seventeenth century, when the iron shield was probably made to complete Indo-Persian equipments.

The average Indian hide shields were from two to three feet in diameter and of demi-elliptical section. They were made with a lip at the edge—a means of strengthening and a precaution against warping—which varied considerably in size. Some shields had no lip at all and, consequently, twisted with age. Hide shields were made in smaller sizes, varying from approximately nine inches in diameter, with a marked lip to catch the point of an opponent's

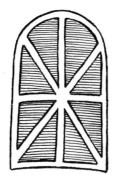 

FIG. 56 Infantry and cavalry shields from the Sanchi reliefs, first century A.D.

weapon, to twelve or twenty inches. The small, nine-inch fist-shields were used in the same manner as the buckler in Europe to catch and parry blows.

The four bosses, common to all Indian shields, acted as washers for the riveting of the hand-loop rings on the inside. These rings secured the corners of a square cushion of padded cloth or velvet for the hand, the two short, narrow straps being held together at the centre of the shield. A guige or suspension strap was passed through the hand-loops and could be easily removed if not required. In many examples the guige is a silk scarf with silk or tinsel fringes at the ends. Some of the central or southern shields approached the conical, with a lip at the edge.

The shield, whether of hide or steel, was called *dhal*. Rhinoceros hide, when obtainable, was the most desired for hide shields because of its great strength and durability. It was occasionally left with a natural surface on the outside which was given a coat of brownish lacquer; or both the inside and outside were smoothed completely and given a highly polished brown or black lacquered surface. The defensive quality of this thick rawhide—for such it actually was—was judged on its clarity when held up to the light. The nearer the hide was to being transparent the higher it was regarded—and many a richly decorated lacquered shield had a small circular window left in the ornament so that the quality of the hide might still be seen.

The handsomest of decorated hide shields were made in Hyderabad in the Deccan, in Sind, in neighbouring Bhuj-Kach, and in Udaipur. Some existing ones of those made in Sind have the entire surface covered with floral patterns cut out in flat relief, lacquered in rich colours, with the details picked out in gold. Others have richly painted floral panels and borders on a yellow ground, while the more common have enriched borders and centre, with the remaining surfaces—both external and internal—coated with a translucent brown varnish.

In some cases, these shields are equipped with an arm-strap in addition to the double hand-loops, secured through two extra bosses which are spaced a little further apart than the usual four. The bosses are all *en suite*.

Shield bosses are of iron decorated with false damascene, or of gilded copper or brass, cast or engraved with floral motifs. A favourite form used on Sindian shields is a gilded flower of nine pointed petals as seen from the underside.

The majority of Indian shields are light, but there are exceptions which are extremely rare. One of these is a shield made from a large turtle shell, now in the Museum für Völkerkunde, Vienna. It is made to be carried like a kite-shaped shield, with the pointed tail end of the shell downwards, and is fitted with the normal double straps and square cushion with four bosses on the face side. The surface is varnished brown, with painted circular centre panel and border. It is from central western India, and was probably made to be carried by a shield-bearer before a prince.

The common black or brown shields, with their damascened steel bosses, were used by most Indian peoples and states. Several examples in the Tower Armouries are Mahratta, and others—similar except in details of finish and decoration—are Rajput or Punjabi. One large, black, hide shield from Rajputana has per-cussion pistols concealed in the four bosses. The barrels of these

A

B

Plate XV
'Coats of a Thousand Nails'

A Quilted and studded armour, Indore, eighteenth to nineteenth century
B Studded armour reinforced with plates, Rajput, eighteenth to nineteenth century
A *Tower of London Armouries*   B *Wallace Collection, London*

Plate XVI

Indo-Persian Armours

A Complete armour with rectangular
char aina, Lahore, late eighteenth
century

B Complete armour with octagonal *char
aina*, Lahore, late eighteenth or early
nineteenth century
Tower of London Armouries

pistols, being extremely short, would not have carried a ball straight for more than a few feet.

The small fist-shields, sometimes made from plaited rattan, were carried by Indian night-watchmen until quite recent times in conjunction with a lathe or baton; and the Sikh holimen, to this day, wear *chakra* or quoits on their turbans and carry sword, spear, and hide shield of moderate size.

The steel shield in India was made in similar sizes to those of hide and, with the exception of a few types, did not have a lip or edging. The degree of convexity varied considerably—some smaller examples being almost flat, while others, mainly from the Deccan, approach the conical. Sometimes an applied border of semicircular section was added, and in rare instances the edge was turned over a wire.

The decoration of steel shields was by several methods, mainly *koftgari* (false damascene) or by chiselling in low relief. The raised ornament was gilded, and the background of chiselled or engraved borders and central panels was often blackened to heighten the detail.

A shield in the Tower Collection, from Hyderabad in the Deccan (Pl. XXI, A), is of deep form with a flanged rim. The surface of the steel is spirally fluted and the bosses and wide decorative border are of pierced and gilded copper applied over a red tinsel, with a crescent of silver on a gilded mount. The lining is of crimson velvet, with diapered pattern applied in gilt nails.

Linings of many shields were of plain velvet with a narrow embroidered edge, and others were embroidered all over with floral designs in gold or silver orris thread.

The *madu* or *maru* was a small fist-shield mounted upon a pair of roebuck horns with steel tips. It was primarily for parrying, and in some instances a pair of flamboyant blades replaced the horns. The shields were of steel, chiselled and gilt, with four small bosses. Pairs of horns were also used, without a shield, for the same purpose. Their use was mainly confined to northern and central India.

Horse Armour

The arming of horses for war in India was probably never as common as in Persia and Turkey. Certainly, under the Mughal, horse armours are represented in miniatures, particularly in illustrations for historical works and such books as the *Shāh-Nāma*; but they are following a pattern set by the Persian miniaturists, with but minor modifications to Indian fashions.

Heavy armed cavalry was maintained by many state rulers, but 'heavy armed' may apply only to the rider. We may assume that at least some of these bodies of cavalry rode barded or armed horses, and that the armour generally used was constructed of mail and plates—or even simply a trapper of mail or fabric.

A recently published manuscript, the *Kitāb-i Chinghīz-nāma* (*Book*

FIG. 57 Quilted and studded horse armour from the *Kitab-i Chinghīz-nāma*, dated 1596; Gulistan Library, Tehran

of Jenghiz Khān)[6] in the Imperial Library, Tehran, completed in Akbar's studio on May 25th, 1596, shows many armed riders and horses (Fig. 57), the majority in the late stylized Persian equipment. However, here and there throughout the work an Indian feature stands out to show that this is not a slavish copy of the Persian. These details are mainly confined to swords, daggers, and body armour which, because of the greater detail put into them, show that they have been observed by the draughtsman and not just copied from a copy of a copy—as must often have been the case both in Persia and India.

The *Ain-i Akbari*, which describes the military equipment used in Akbar's time, lists the following armour for the horses of Mughal commanders: a thick quilted trapper which hung low on each side, protecting the beasts' bellies, called *artak-i kajam*; a triangular iron mesh (mail) caparison, *kajam*, placed over this; and the horse's head encased in an iron mask, *kashka* (chamfron). That the mail caparison should be 'triangular' can be seen from the specimen at Sandringham described below. A piece of horse armour not included in the above description, but illustrated and listed in the *Ain-i Akbarī*, is the *gardani* or neck armour, also common in miniatures of the period.

The *Book of Jenghiz Khan* shows the armour we have been familiar with from Persian and Turkish sources—that of mail and plates—as well as the quilted caparisons. The horizontal lamellae in vertical columns, linked with narrow bands of mail, are the same; but the artist has taken the trouble to show alternate rows of plain lamellae, and lamellae with ornamental edges—a very Indian characteristic.

In the Tower Armouries there is a horse armour of this type, from western India, retaining most of its original padded lining. It is built up of vertical rows of horizontal lamellae connected by mail with circular bosses, surrounded by radiating lamellar, on either side of the neck, breast, and crupper defences. The chamfron consists of a rigid central face-plate, with nose- and cheek-pieces of lamellar and mail. Two short spines are riveted to the base of the face-plate, and a tail of black horsehair is attached to the tailguard extended from the centre of the crupper. The bosses and face-plate are edged with brass, and the lamellae of the cheek-pieces are alternately brass and iron. In the nineteenth century this armour was used on an equestrian figure representing a 'Norman Crusader'—the rider wearing mostly Indian mail. This amusing anachronism, once one of many, formed part of the display connected with the famous 'Line of Kings' in the Tower Armouries; and later, when removed under Hewitt to the Oriental Gallery, it was labelled Persian. It is, without doubt, of Indian make and of the seventeenth century.

Mughal miniatures show part, if not all, of some horse armours as made of studded fabric. At Windsor Castle the complete housing for a horse, referred to above, is made of brown velvet, powdered with a pattern of gilt nails. Completing this bard is a gilded iron chamfron of Turkish pattern, with fluted face-plate and cheekpieces of studded black velvet. This armour came from Seringapatam, where it had formed part of Tippoo Sultan's personal armoury.

Mail trappers were used in thirteenth-century Europe, but only in India were they used in the Orient. Mail in large pieces was heavy and dragging; and even when laid over quilted fabric, it moved—particularly on a horse's crupper, where it was difficult to fasten it securely.

A large mail trapper presented to King Edward VII by the Maharaja Rana of Dholpur is in the collection at Sandringham House (No. 528). It is composed of large, flat, riveted rings of iron and brass in a chevron pattern and is edged with braid. There is no lining, and therefore it was possibly put over a quilted *artak-i kajam*—and the mail, when spread out, does almost resemble a triangle, but with a rather blunt point. With this mail is a chamfron with broad plain face-plate and wide hinged cheek-plates. The eye-holes are small and cut out from the edges of both face- and cheek-plates. A line of spear-shaped jingles hang across the upper and lower edges, with tubes for pendent tails of hair on each side of the nose, and a plume-tube riveted on the brow. Although presented in the nineteenth century, I believe this armour to be of much earlier date.

A late example of horse mail made in two sections is in the Tower of London. The mail is butted and of round wire, with a trellis pattern in brass links. It consists of a hood with eye- and ear-holes, with a central hole for a head-plume which would be attached to the bridle beneath, and a crupper. The hood has a bold chevron pattern worked in the mail to lie on the centre of the mane, and the sides hang down to defend the shoulders. Both sections are mounted upon red cloth edged with crimson velvet and a green silk fringe, with a lining of printed chintz calico. It is of the late eighteenth or early nineteenth century and was made in Lahore.

Elephant Armour

The Indians, rather unfortunately, placed great reliance on elephants. But though at first they might strike terror into an enemy unfamiliar with them, they were by no means invincible. The Romans found means to disperse the elephants of the Carthaginians and, in turn, the Greeks and the Turks soon lost their fear of these towering beasts—in spite of the large numbers sent against them. Fire quickly brought panic to the ranks of the best-trained war elephants—and when demoralized, trumpeting and screaming with terror, they would stampede from the battle, throwing the soldiers and drivers from their backs, and trample the troops advancing in closed ranks to follow up the expected slaughter of the foe.

The Muslim conquerors of India, who had themselves defeated Hindu armies and their hosts of elephants, were soon under the spell of this living 'tank'—and in consequence they, too, suffered

FIG. 58 Armoured war elephant from the *Kitab-i Chinghīz-nāma*, dated 1596; Gulistan Library, Tehran

many defeats at the hands of invaders not equipped with elephants. Indian armies are variously reported as having contained from three to six thousand elephants.

Armour for elephants is described as being of leather, and the tusks of the beasts were tipped with metal points. The average complement of men riding on an elephant was a *mahout* and two or three fighting-men armed with bows, javelins, and long spears which enabled them to attack the enemy below them.

Mughal manuscripts often show the *mahout* and a single fighting-man in armour. The fighting-man sits astride the elephant's back with a harness around his thighs and a rack of arms in front of him. The elephant's armour is shown as of quilted fabric or leather and is rarely painted to represent mail and plates. One elephant in *The Book of Jenghiz Khan* is shown wearing chamfron and complete body armour of elaborate lamellae, but other elephants in the numerous battle scenes are unarmed (Fig. 58).

These elaborate iron equipments can never have been too common or more of them would surely have survived. Whilst in India I heard reports of portions of these armours preserved in state armouries, but unfortunately I was unable to verify them. Descriptions usually indicated chamfrons, and none reported complete armours.

The elephant armour in the Tower Armouries came from Powis Castle, where by tradition it was said to have been taken by Robert Lord Clive at the Battle of Plassey in 1757. It consists of a chamfron extending half-way down the elephant's trunk, with flaps for the ears and circular openings for the eyes and the bony projections on the top of the skull which are frequently struck by the *mahout* with his *ankus*, or goad, to direct the animal's progress. This is entirely constructed of vertical columns of horizontal lamellae connected with mail, with brass-edged bosses on the ears and at the termination of the trunkguard. In the centre of the face a heavy brass-rimmed shield-shaped plate is riveted with a threaded hole in the centre. Romantic fancy suggests that this was for securing a large and formidable spike, but Mughal miniatures show large hair tassels fitted like fly-wisks in this exact position on leather chamfrons. There is a section of the same construction for the tender throat of the elephant and two large panels cut away to fit round either side of the neck, fastening with rings and ties at the centre of the front. These, and two large side-panels of rectangular shape, reach to the front of the elephant's hind legs. The side-panels attach to the breast sections with ties and rings, and a series of heavy straps secure them over the back. Two missing sections would have covered the animal's hind-quarters, their existence being indicated by the presence of rings on the rear edges of the side-panels.

The sections of body armour are built up of the usual vertical rows of lamellae and mail, but with square-framed plates breaking pairs of rows at intervals, with unbroken rows between. These square plates are embossed with elephants, peacocks, pairs of fish, and conventional flowers. A lining of coarse fabric padded with cotton wool prevented the armour from chafing the elephant's tough but sensitive hide. This armour was possibly an exception rather than the rule and may have been made for the war elephant of a prince. It weighs four hundred and forty-eight pounds and was probably made in the seventeenth century.

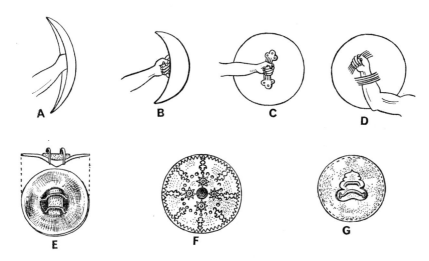

FIG. 59 Sinhalese shields
A Shield from a seventeenth-century fresco at Ridi Vihare, Kuru-
negala
B Shield from a seventeenth-century fresco at Käbal-ā-lena
C Shield with single grip
D Shield with double grip
E Inner side of a hide shield of the last King of Ceylon's bodyguard
and a section of the same above
F The silver shield donated by Levuké Dissava to the Maha Saman
Devale, Ratnapura
G Hide shield with copper studs and double grip. Colombo
Museum, after Deraniyagola

Ceylon

Armour was never widely used in Ceylon, and then mainly for ceremonial. Mr Deraniyagola, in his study of *Sinhala Weapons and Armour*,[7] the only work on the subject, states that Sinhalese warriors throughout history have generally relied almost completely on the shield (Fig. 59). This is borne out by such writers as de Queyroz (1688), who states:

'In war they do not use purely defensive armour, rather they consider it a proof of fear and weakness.'

The Mahavamsa chronicles describe the early use of shields and
large ones of hide set up in boats for the defence of landing-
parties when King Parakrama Bahu I invaded India. War
elephants were protected with coats of buffalo hide in 200 B.C.
Gaja Bahu's elephants had armour and King Parakrama Bahu's
soldiers wore coats 'wrought of iron and skins of deer' in the
twelfth century A.D.

Ancient sculptures show warriors with chains crossed on their
naked torsos and bracelets on forearms and upper arms, but these
are not protective—merely ornaments. Some seventeenth-century
frescoes show, in addition, a fold of chain hanging to the
shoulders at either side of the head, with metal discs at the sides
of the neck—but again, these may be ornaments and not for
defence. Greaves are also worn, secured by one or two straps
which may, like the Roman gladiator's equipment of shield and
greaves, have served to protect the limbs from a sweeping cut
below the shield. Mail (*palidal*) may have had a limited use, but
most armour appears to have been in the nature of a rich parade
costume such as that made for the last king (1815) which was sold
by auction in London in 1820. It consisted of a richly embossed
golden cuirass reaching from neck to waist, ornamented with
rubies and emeralds; greaves; a skirt of mail; a plaited gold collar
for neck and shoulders; handguards—more likely vambraces—
studded with diamonds, rubies, and emeralds; and a massive
golden girdle set with rubies and sapphires, etc.

Large shields were called *palanga* and smaller ones *palisa* or
paliha. Sculptures at Anuradhapura show heart-shaped as well as
circular bucklers. Large, standing shields reaching shoulder height
are shown on a fifteenth-century stone slab from Horana. Sixteenth-
century stone and ivory carvings commonly show small rectangular targets. Shields were equipped with single or double grips.

The usual material for shields was *gadumba* wood with outer
and inner coverings of elephant, or buffalo hide (*sambhur*), treated
with glue and decorated with lacquer, lead, steel, and silver. Bark
shields were also made and at times coated with lead, which was
apt to retain an opponent's sword which cut into it. A bark shield
of elliptical form, four feet by three feet, is in the Kandy Museum.
It belonged to Arauvevela Nilame, *c.* 1815. Shields of bark and
wicker were normally used for fencing, but occasionally in battle.
Silver ones were favoured for parade.

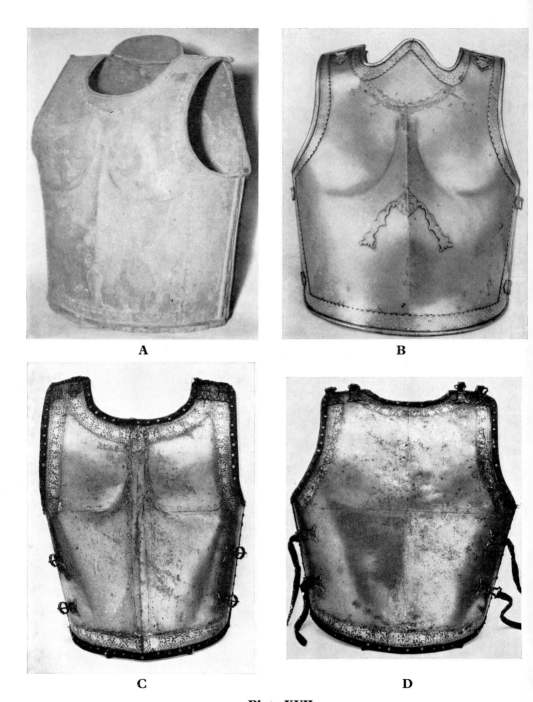

Plate XVII
Indian Cuirasses Inspired by Foreign Models

A Joined by hinges, eighteenth century. *Museum für Völkerkunde, Vienna*
B Breastplate with applied ornament, Gujrat or Sailkot, early nineteenth century. *Wallace Collection, London*
C and D Cuirass, Hyderabad, Deccan, late eighteenth century. *Tower of London Armouries*

Plate XVIII

Fabric Armour
A Helmet and cuirass (*peti*) built up of
many layers of cotton fabric faced
with velvet, of Tippoo Sultan of
Mysore, late eighteenth century.
Victoria and Albert Museum

B Quilted helmet and belt of crimson
velvet embroidered with gold orris
thread, of Tippoo Sultan of Mysore,
late eighteenth century. *Tower of
London Armouries* (*Not to scale*)

A

B

C

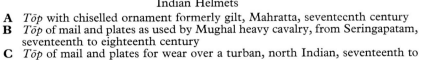

D

Plate XIX
Indian Helmets

A *Tōp* with chiselled ornament formerly gilt, Mahratta, seventeenth century
B *Tōp* of mail and plates as used by Mughal heavy cavalry, from Seringapatam, seventeenth to eighteenth century
C *Tōp* of mail and plates for wear over a turban, north Indian, seventeenth to eighteenth century
D *Tōp* of mail for wear over a turban, Lahore, eighteenth century
Tower of London Armouries (Not to scale)

A

B

C

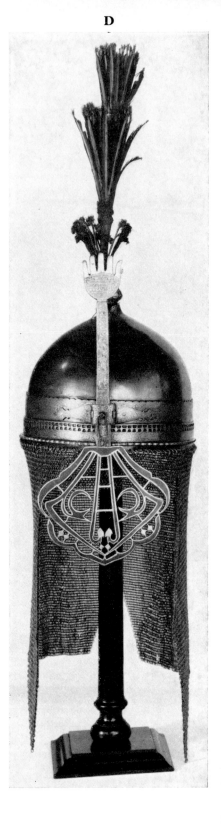

D

Plate XX Indian Helmets

A *Tōp* early Indo-Persian, north Indian, seventeenth century. *Museum für Völkerkunde, Vienna*

B *Tōp* with plumes of tinsel and feathers, Lahore, eighteenth century. *Tower of London Armouries*

C *Tōp* of Sikh type, Lahore, eighteenth century. *Tower of London Armouries*

D *Tōp* with deep oval bowl with *Qur'anic* inscription on upper terminal of the nasal, north Indian, nineteenth century. *Wallace Collection (Not to scale)*

Philippines

The inhabitants of the Philippine Islands—particularly those engaged in piracy, such as the Moros—used armour of various kinds ranging from the primitive bark hide and sinnet to the more sophisticated made of horn and metal.

The Philippines were taken by the Spaniards in 1565, but the Arabs had been there a long time before and converted many of the inhabitants to the Muslim faith. They also impressed the Moros with their armour, for the better-equipped warrior had copies made in horn and brass.

The Moro coats of mail and plate have frequently been classified as Indian, Chinese, and even Japanese. They are, however, quite distinctive in that the materials used are brass mail and kabau horn plates or brass alone. In the same fashion as the other armours of mail and plate construction already discussed, the plates are arranged in vertical columns from the waist upwards, to the chest in front, and well on to the shoulders at the back. There is a collar and short sleeves and a deep waist section, all of mail, with further plates forming the skirt. The coats open at the front and fasten above the waist with two swivel-hooks which lock through pierced eyes riveted in the opposite side.

The plates vary in size and those of metal are generally larger than those of horn, with applied ornaments in silver or white metal. The larger plates are tapering rectangles, set above the waist at front and sides. Some horn coats are made in a similar manner, but usually have smaller plates which fit the form of the torso more comfortably. All the mail is butted and made from a stout brass wire.

Probably the oldest pattern of helmet constructed with plates and mail is the simple rounded cap with the crown in segments of horn, resembling some western Indian specimens. The neck is guarded by square plates and mail, sometimes vandyked at the lower edge. Spanish influence caused many of these helmets to be fitted with a curved point at the apex in imitation of the stalk-like finial on morions.

Most Moro helmets were made in imitation of Spanish morions and burgonets, the latter being the more popular model. One type of horn helmet is made of sheets laced to a rawhide shape. The skulls are inclined to the conical, with a large curved finial, often pierced, and with a peak in front and neckguard behind. The binding of the segments is done with rattan, and in some places bamboo dowels help to keep the plates in alignment on the thick rawhide. Closer imitation of Spanish armour was achieved in the Moro brass helmets, which were frequently cast in sections and joined together by brazing. The burgonet-type helmets have the correct hinged cheekpieces, although a little shorter than the European originals and not joined under the wearer's chin. The Moros attached a plume to the side in front, perhaps in accordance with Oriental custom rather than following the Spaniards and wearing one at the back.

Morions with curved brims and a curved stalk at the point of the crown were a common form of sixteenth-century open helmet which developed their form in the fifteenth century, particularly in Spain under the name of *cabacete*. When armed, the officers, at least, of Spanish ships would have worn them—so that, apart from the alternative burgonet, the Moros must have seen many of them. They do not seem to have had quite the same appeal, for only one specimen of true morion shape is known to the author— a splendid one in the Horniman Museum at Forest Hill, London. It is of excellent shape, made with recessed panels on either side of the crown in imitation of areas normally outlined by etched decoration on European examples.

A horn helmet, in the collection of Major A. D. F. White, although having a peak and neckguard inspired by those of a burgonet, has the skull of a morion. But, as is usually the case, the stalk at the top is very exaggerated and elaborate.

The more primitive types of armour used by the Moros, and other tribes of the Malay Archipelago, are in the form of jackets and waistcoats of hide, bark, and woven cord; and the simplest of helmets are made like a low cone, from hide, with a chin-cord. Stone[8] illustrates a good series of Moro armour of all types.

CHAPTER FIVE

[1] It was always the accepted belief that Gandhara sculpture, and in general the art of N.W. India and Bactria, was under the influence of Hellenistic culture brought to the area by Alexander, who left Greek governors and settlements to hold his newly acquired domains. Apart from a series of coins struck by these early Bactrian Greeks, there is no sound evidence to back the theory. Modern scholarship believes that the Hellenistic domination of arts in this area is largely due to the close contact maintained with Rome through the trade routes of Asia by the Scytho-Parthians and, especially, the Kushans who succeeded them.

[2] M. N. Deshpande, 'The Rockcut Caves of Pitalkhora in the Deccan', *Ancient India*, No. 15, 1959, Plate LI, A and B.

[3] A fairly full description of Hindu armies is given by A. L. Basham, *The Wonder that was India*, Ch. IV, pp. 128–36, London, 1954.

[4] Wilbraham Egerton, *An Illustrated Handbook of Indian Arms*, p. 125, London, 1880. This work will long remain the standard reference for Indian arms and armour—being compiled, as it was, in an age when the old crafts were still alive and the old armouries and their inventories were still intact.

[5] C. Purdon Clarke, *Catalogue of the Arms and Armour at Sandringham*, London, 1910. This contains the gifts of arms and armour made to King Edward VII when, as Prince of Wales, he visited India in 1875–6. Many of the items described have the name of the princely donor and his State, so providing a useful guide for the identification of some of the more distinctive forms of armour and weapons.

[6] J. Marek and H. Knizkova, *The Jenghiz Khan Miniatures from the Court of Akbar the Great*, London, 1963.

[7] P. E. P. Deraniyagola, 'Sinhala Weapons and Armour', *Journal of the Ceylon Branch of the Royal Asiatic Society*, Vol. XXXV, No. 95, Part III, Dec. 1942.

[8] G. C. Stone, *A Glossary on the Construction, Decoration and use of Arms and Armour*, Portland, Maine, U.S.A., 1934. (Reprinted New York, 1961.)

China, Korea, Tibet, Bhutan

Armour of Hide

The earliest armour to be used in China, according to literary sources, was made of hide. From the Shang Dynasty (1558–1050 B.C.) bronze helmets have survived. These were found in tombs of men of high rank and are no doubt exceptions rather than the rule. They are of deep bowl form with a semicircular cut-away at the front, to fit round the face, and with another at the occiput. The edges have a turned or moulded finish and a loop is attached at the top of the bowl.

The Chou, who overthrew the Shang in 1050 B.C., laid down strict regulations to be followed by their court officials. This handbook of rules, known as the *Chou-li*,[1] refers to the court armourers as *han jên*—'men who envelop the body with a protective contrivance'. There were also instructions which the *han jên* were to follow when making armour of hide. There were two kinds of hide armour: that cut like a coat, called *kia*; and that of scales, called *kiai*.

The *kia* made from the hide of the two-horned rhinoceros (*si*) consisted of seven layers; that made from the hide of the single-horned rhinoceros (*se*) consisted of six layers; and that made from a combination of both types of hide, consisted of five layers. As the two-horned rhinoceros was thought to live for a hundred years and the one-horned variety for two hundred years, armour from their hides was said to last for similar periods. Therefore, an armour made from a mixture of both would be expected to last three hundred years.

To make a cuirass, a dummy torso was prepared and the hides weighed. Two piles equal in weight were allocated, one for the upper half and one for the lower. The hides were then cut and fitted to the dummy and the various layers placed on each other and then sewn at the edges. As far as one can judge, the finished cuirass was like a sleeveless coat opening at the front—the upper half from neck to loins and the lower, forming a skirt, reaching to the knees. These *kia* could be rolled up when not in use and stored in a case termed *kao*.

FIG. 60 Mongol troops wearing leather armour, late thirteenth century, from the *Moko Shurai Ekotoba Emaki*; Japanese Imperial Collection

Thomas of Spalato,[2] a thirteenth-century historian, and Marco Polo[3] both refer to the Mongols as wearing armour of ox-hide in several layers pressed together, and very strong. These leather armours are well illustrated in the *Moko Shurai Ekotoba Emaki* in the Japanese Imperial Collection, the picture scroll of the Mongol invasion of Japan in the thirteenth century, which shows the coats longer in the skirt, with wrist-length sleeves (Fig. 61). Some are drawn as if they are stitched across horizontally at frequent intervals. The helmets are rounded, with hoods attached. At the sides of the warriors' faces are sprays of feathers or hair— a not uncommon feature on Chinese helmets.

The North American Indians,[4] of Mongol stock, used armour of hides. The moose or caribou skins were sewn or glued together with from two to six thicknesses and wrapped around the body from the left side, with ties over the shoulders and at the right side. The surface was strengthened with sand mixed with glue.

FIG. 61 Chinese soldier in leather armour, clay figurine of the Northern Wei Dynasty (A.D. 385– 535); Faculty of Letters, Kyoto University

Many of the tribes of the West Coast, and also the Shoshone and Algonquin Blackfoot in the Rocky Mountain region, used such armour. When trade guns were introduced, in the late eighteenth century, armour went out of use.

The Chinese continued to use armour of rhinoceros hide down to the T'ang Dynasty.[5] The *Tso chuan* of the Chu'un-ts'iu Period (722–481 B.C.) frequently refers to red-lacquered hide armours, a type that continued for many hundreds of years. When the rhinoceros became scarce, armour was made from buffalo hide. The most important Chinese book on arms and armour, the *Wu pei chi* (80 volumes), written by Mao Yuan-i and published in 1621, discusses a statement by Siun King that sharkskin armour was every bit as good as that made of rhinoceros hide and therefore should

be called *shui si* ('water-rhinoceros').[6] It is also said to have been
used by the Mongols. Shark or rayskin, originally used in China
and neighbouring countries for many purposes, including the
adornment of military equipment, was usually too thin and brittle
for armour. One can only suggest that it was used as a veneer over

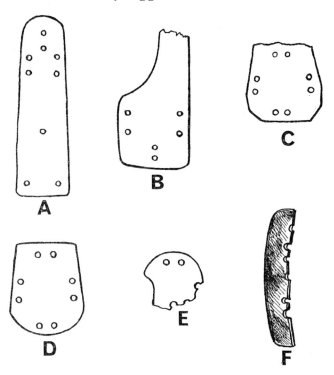

FIG. 62 Lamellae found in the excavations at Etsin-gol after Hedin
          A Sung or Yuan Dynasty   A–E Iron
          B–F Han Dynasty   F Lacquered leather

a stronger substance to enhance its appearance—a not uncommon
practice in Japan for portions of an armour in the Momoyama
and Edo Periods.

Lamellar Armour
Excavation of the fortified *limes*, or watch towers, of the Han
Dynasty at Etsin-gol in south-west Mongolia by Sven Hedin's
expedition in the spring of 1931 produced several lamellae
(Fig. 62) of iron and a fragment of a lacquered leather one.[7] The
sites were dated to the period 100 B.C. to A.D. 100, and the lamellae

most likely belonging to the latter century under the Later Han (A.D. 25–220). Wooden record tablets also found on these sites record the equipment issued for the use of the frontier guards. As well as the old type of leather *kia*, a new form of armour under the name of *k'ai* is listed. The term means 'metal leaf' and could refer to either scale or lamellar construction. Berthold Laufer is of the opinion that scale armour was intended, a development from armour of leather scales.[8] As, however, rectangular lamellae were predominant amongst the armour fragments found in these Central Asian sites, it is likely that the frontier scribes were referring to armours of lamellae, later referred to as *t'ie cha*.

The Iranian fashion of arming, and a modified form of their cavalry tactics—influencing the warlike, restless Hiung-nu (Huns) in Central Asia—had eventually passed to China, and with the reforming and rearming of her army on this 'new model' China was able to strike back at her troublesome neighbours as never before.

Before Later Han times the Chinese army had consisted of chariots (Fig. 63): a thousand in the regular army, each containing three men, a driver, a spearman, and an archer. With each chariot was one hundred men, seventy-two of whom were fully equipped foot soldiers.[9] The wearing of armour was restricted to the men in the chariots, and the infantry had only a shield for defence.

Some Chinese cavalry had existed before Later Han times—but only, it would appear, to be disbanded when they had routed a frontier attack and their leaders saw no need to keep them in training at considerable expense. The Emperor Wu (140–87 B.C.), who is regarded as the reformer of Chinese cavalry, was simply copying the methods employed by his nomadic enemies.[10]

Several Han generals, including Ch'ao Ts'o, were great soldiers who took their duties very seriously. As tacticians some were brilliant, and with brutal discipline they forged a unit capable of destroying the most cunning and daring Turkish and Hunnic armies. The cavalry had to operate as one at all times. The Asiatic tribesmen had overcome their habit of fighting as loose groups of individuals and, with ruthless commanders, often very gifted in the arts of war, they had swept away the old Chinese armies one after another. By copying their enemies, the Chinese generals were able to turn the tide—at least, when they had the ability and the money to support and equip the right sort of army.

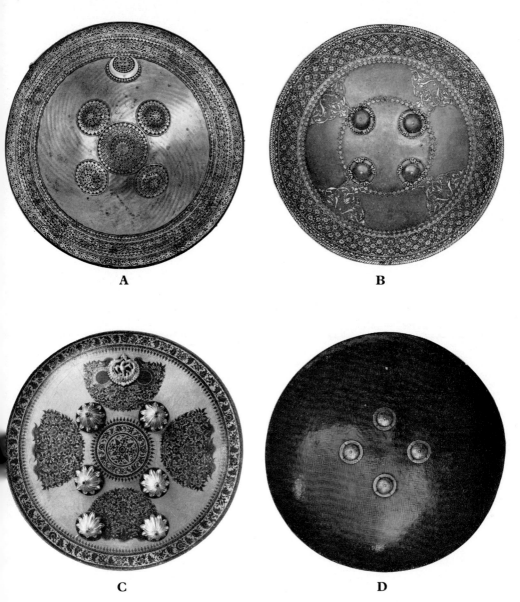

A

B

C

D

Plate XXI
Indian Shields

A Fluted steel with applied copper-gilt ornament, Hyderabad, Deccan, late eighteenth century
B Grey watered steel with chiselled and gilded decoration, north-west India, late eighteenth century
C Painted buffalo hide with gilded bosses, Sind, nineteenth century
D Black buffalo hide with damascened steel bosses, Mahratta, eighteenth century

A, B and D *Tower of London Armouries*
C *Wallace Collection, London (Not to scale)*

A

B

C

Plate XXII
Chinese Armour

A *Ting kia* worn at Court by military officials, mid nineteenth century. *Wallace Collection, London*

B *T'ie cha* of lacquered leather lamellae laced with doeskin, Na-khi, south-west China, seventeenth to nineteenth century. *Tower of London Armouries*

C *Kiai* of copper scales, Ch'eng-tu, Sze-ch'uan, eighteenth to nineteenth century. *Field Museum of Natural History, Chicago (Not to scale)*

The clay figurines placed in tombs as guardians in the first centuries of our era convey to us a fair picture of the Chinese cavalry and infantry at the time of their change-over from armour of hide to scale and lamellar. The helmets are frequently hoodlike and suggest leather rather than metal, though some are without doubt meant to represent a metal bowl with neck- and earguards of quilted fabric or scale armour. There are also helmets shaped

FIG. 63 Eighteenth-century Chinese reconstruction of an ancient war chariot, after Werner

like Phrygian caps, built up of vertical segments or lamellae. Cuirasses are clearly shown as reaching from shoulder to waist, joined over the shoulders by narrow straps. The surface of both breast and back are covered with horizontal rows of scales or lamellae, generally placed so that the plates in each row come immediately beneath each other, overlapping upwards—not imbricated, as the scales of a fish. There are also quite often raised lines running up the centre of each plate for some two-thirds of its length, which could either represent connecting laces between rows of lamellae or an embossed rib to strengthen the flat metal scales. We are faced here with the problem of a convention which can never be definitely solved without the unlikely event of a complete example of an armour being found in a Chinese tomb or other archaeological excavation. This form of cuirass is represented as worn over a skirted garment and full breeches gartered at the knee as in Protohistoric Japan (Fig. 64).

A   **B**

FIG. 64 Soldiers of the Wu-Tai (Five Dynasties, A.D. 907–60)
A With leather helmet and short lamellar cuirass, Collection of
Mr M. Sorimachi, Tokyo
B With helmet of splints and skirted lamellar cuirass; Metropolitan
Museum of Art, New York

A little figurine of a cavalryman of the Northern Wei Dynasty (A.D. 385–535), in the British Museum (Fig. 65A) illustrates clearly a Chinese version of the 'cataphractus'. The man wears a rounded helmet cusped over his eyes and surmounted by a short central spike. A napeguard and earguards, probably a quilted fabric, are attached to the lower edge of the bowl. His body and thighs are painted with a pattern of scales lapping upwards in vertical rows, while covering his shoulders and upper arms is a large cloak. The warrior's thigh defences are very like those made

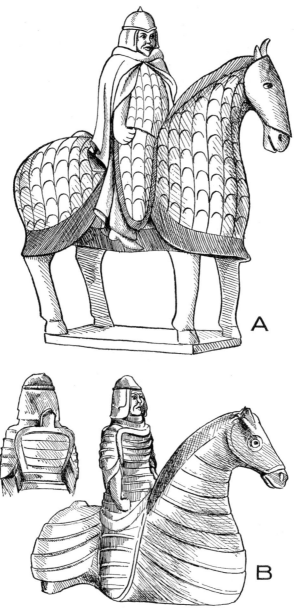

FIG. 65 Clay figurines of fully armed horsemen of the Northern Wei
Dynasty (A.D. 385–535)
  A British Museum
  B Musée Cernuschi, Paris. Compare the standing neckguard of this
     backplate with that on the leather cuirass from Indore in Fig. 51

of leather lamellae found in Tower 19 at Dura Europos. His horse
is completely covered with the same scaled armour to below its
knees—with the exception of its head, which is protected by a
rigid chamron. Like the scale horse bards from Dura, this Chinese
armour for man and horse is bordered with red. As these clay

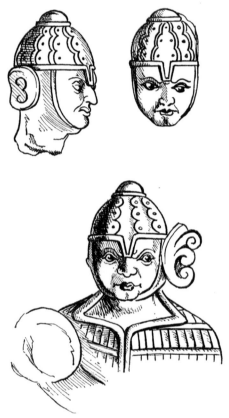

FIG. 66 Stucco heads of warriors from Mingoi, Chinese Turkestan,
eighth to tenth century; British Museum

figures are painted with a flat colour, which does not always
stand up to burial as does that of glazed pottery, we cannot
always be sure of their interpretation. In the case of the mounted
figure in the British Museum, described above, the armour is
white with black detail and may well represent polished iron.

The fact that the plates of the armours on these little figures are
not imbricated, and in many instances lap upwards, suggests very
strongly that they represent lamellar armour. Lamellar armour

reached Japan with the horse in the fifth century A.D. from China, a point which proves conclusively its wide use in conjunction with equestrian warfare in the Empire.[11] Although complete horse armours do not appear to have been used in Protohistoric Japan, some simple chamfrons have been found in burial mounds.[12]

Another similar Wei horseman, in the Musée Cernuschi, Paris, shows clearly the armour for man and horse almost entirely of lamellar. The man wears no cloak in this example and his

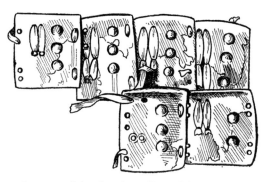

FIG. 67 Large lacquered leather lamellae with the remains of doeskin lacing from the Tibetan fort site at Mīrān, Central Asia, third or fourth century A.D. British Museum

shoulderguards are shown attached to a collar worn beneath the cuirass and under the shoulder-straps (Fig. 65B).

Chinese Turkestan, which provided the first real evidence for the use of lamellar armour in China, also provided many paintings and stucco figures of men wearing such armour. Sir Oral Stein, during his excavations at Mingoi, found finely executed figures wearing long coats of lamellar and built-up rounded helmets surmounted by a large boss, like an inverted cup (Fig. 66). This last feature is frequently to be seen on the leather helmets of Chinese figurines and later Chinese and Korean helmets. It can also be found on Japanese helmets of the sixth to eighth centuries and is there called Mongolian (Fig. 95, 4). This may be, in fact, the source from whence this shape of helmet originated, the purpose of the projection being to house a bun of hair worn on top of the head.

The Mingoi armoured figures which date from the eighth to tenth centuries A.D. wear lamellar of double-lobed outline like

that seen on two fighting warriors on a Sāssānian silver bowl in
the Hermitage at Leningrad, dating from about the sixth century.
Stein's expedition also found rectangular red-lacquered leather
plates at Mirān (Fig. 67), dating from the third to fourth centuries and at Niya, a group of third-century 'green' hide lamellar,
also of rectangular shape.

Raw or green hide was strong, light, and easy to prepare, and

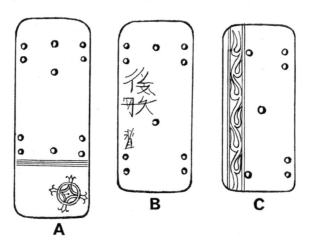

FIG. 68 Lamellae of red lacquered hide from the Na-khi armour in the
Tower of London Armouries
  A Originally positioned in the lower edge; with engraved border
  B Lamellae now positioned in the centre of the back; with engraved
     inscription
  C From the edges of the front opening; with engraved border, now
     scattered throughout the armour

it may have been much more common than armour of iron
lamellae, particularly amongst the more primitive societies on
China's borders. A rawhide lamellar armour from the Na-khi of
south-west China (Fig. 68), now in the Tower Armouries,
London (XXVI–106ᴬ), is of a type illustrated in early Persian
manuscripts and described by thirteenth- and fourteenth-century
Europeans visiting Asia. It is an example of the unchanging
fashions of Asia—for as well as the construction and shape of the
garment being the same, the plates are lacquered red and gold,
with those at the borders engraved with scroll designs. This
lacquering and engraving of hide lamellae would seem to be of
very great antiquity, for not only is it seen on the Mirān lamellae

found by Stein, now in the British Museum, but is also suggested by the patterns painted on the conventionally treated lamellar armours worn by warriors in early Persian miniatures—such as the Mongols in Rashidu'd-Din's *History of the World*, painted at Tabriz, 1306–12 (Fig. 15).

This Na-khi armour is of considerable age and has been remade,

FIG. 69 Armed Lokapāla painted on a silk banner from cave of 'Thousand Buddhas', Tun-Huang, Tang Dynasty (A.D. 618–905) after Stein

probably several times. The helmet, of rounded conical form, is built up of vertical plates, each with a central rib and cusped edges, laced together with thongs. It is surmounted by a plume-tube and edged with leopard fur and may be of Tibetan origin. The plates bear traces of gilding and have been relaced and repaired many times. Similar armours were made in Sze-ch'uan, to the east of Tibet, differing from the iron Tibetan ones only in the system of lacing. Whereas the lace connecting the rows of lamellae on a Tibetan armour passes from plate to plate horizontally across a garment, the southern Chinese ran their connecting lace from top to bottom, joining the upper projecting corner of each lamellae—a system which makes this connecting lace more vulnerable to the cutting weapons of the enemy.

Johannes de Plano Carpini[13] gives an account of his journey to the court of the Great Khan at Karakorum in 1246 and describes in some detail the making of Mongol lamellar armour:

像軍將周

FIG. 70 Eighteenth-century representation of a Chou General armed in the Tang fashion, after Werner

'The upper part of their helmet is of iron or steel, while that part guarding the neck and throat is of leather (see figures from Mingoi, Fig. 66). Whereas the majority wear leather armour (lamellar?), some have their harness completely wrought from iron, which is made in the following manner. They beat out in large numbers thin iron plates a finger broad and a full hand long. In each they bore eight small holes, through which they pull three straight leather thongs. Thereupon they arrange these plates one above another, as it were, ascending by degrees, and tie the plates to the thongs mentioned by means of other small and tender thongs drawn through the holes. And in the upper part they fasten a single, small thong, doubled on each side, and sewn on to another, that the plates may be well and tightly knit together. Thus a uniform protection is effected by these plates, and such like armour is made for their horses as well as for their men. It is so highly polished that a man may mirror his face in it.'

Another Western observer of the Mongols, Friar William of Rubruck (1253), records:

'I saw two who had come to present themselves before Mangu, armed with jackets of convex pieces of hard leather, which were most unfit and unwieldly.'[14]

The Mongolian influence not only spread to China but also westward to the nomadic Russian tribes, thus a typical Mongol helmet—with rounded boss at the apex and cusped brow-plate

FIG. 71 Relief of a warrior on a stone panel from the mausoleum of the Emperor T'ai Tsung at Li Ch'üan erected in A.D. 637, from a cast in the British Museum

and nasal—was found at Kertsch, in the Crimea, in what was believed to be an Avarian grave of the second half of the fifth century A.D. The plates are joined by lacing—a system common in many early Asiatic societies, including Japan. Accurate Chinese representations of lamellar are rare, probably because the conventions used to illustrate the different forms of armour are vague and frequently hard to define.

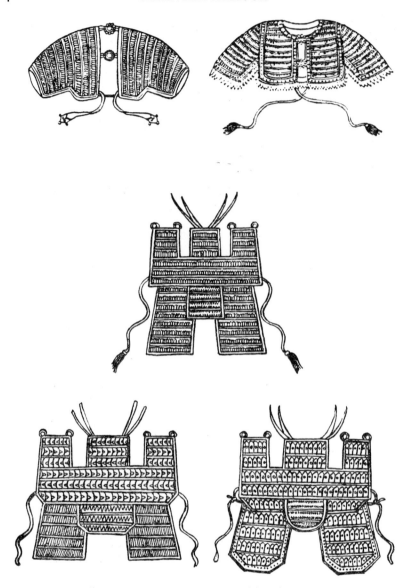

FIG. 72 Lamellar cuirasses with two shoulder defences in the Tang fashion still being made in the Ming Period (1368–1628), from the *T'u shu tsi ch'êng* and *Wu pei chi*

In paintings of the T'ang Dynasty (618–905) armours are often a combination of several forms, such as scale, leather, and lamellar —the last being used for the defences for the thighs (Fig. 69). Many T'ang figurines of warriors who appear to be wearing

頭鍪頓項圖

頭鍪頓項圖

FIG. 73 Helmets with crests of hair, feathers, and small flags in the Tang fashion still being made in the Ming Period (1368–1628), from the *T'u shu tsi ch'êng* and *Wu pei chi*

simple loose clothes may actually represent armed men with their armour covered by fabric. A stone relief panel from the Mausoleum of the Emperor T'ai Tsung at Li Ch'üan,[15] erected in A.D. 637, shows a warrior with his horse (Fig. 71). He wears a close cap, long loose coat, trousers and boots. At his right side hangs his quiver of arrows and, where the front skirts of his coat turn back, the lower part of a long coat of lamellar armour is exposed.

The practice of covering armour in this way may have been more common than we know and could have eventually led to the manufacture of the armours which survive from the late eighteenth and nineteenth centuries, discussed later under the heading of Brigandines. Lamellar armour remained in use for a long period of time in China. In the *Wu pei chi* of 1621 three

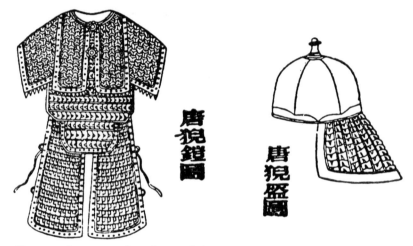

Fig. 74 Armour of scales and lamellar construction called 'Lion Armour', from the *T'u shu tsi ch'êng*

examples of lamellar armour are illustrated (Fig. 72). They take the form of all Chinese armour made from the T'ang period onwards and consist of cuirass, fastening down the centre of the back and over the shoulders, with extensions over the thighs and a shorter central panel for the privates. Over this was worn a short cape or bodice which fastened on the chest and was provided with sleevelike extensions for the shoulders and upper arms. This bodice, which would have tended to rise up and strike the chin in action, was held in position with two long ties which passed from the centre of the front, crossed at the back and returned to the front, where the ends were tied. These ties terminated in ornamental tags or tassels.

In the seventh year of Hung Wu (A.D. 1374), all armour was

ordered to be laced with leather thongs instead of cords. In the sixteenth year (A.D. 1383), the Emperor ordered armour to be made with thirty sections in the neckguard, two hundred and ninety for the body portion, seventeen for the 'heart' portion (plastron), and twenty for each shoulder portion. All of these were made from leather cured with lime.[16] These armours were obviously of rawhide lamellae and—judging by the number of pieces allowed for each portion of the body—they must have been

FIG. 75 Painted stucco figurine of a warrior in armour and helmet of lamellar construction, from Toyuk near Turfan, T'ang Dynasty (618–905) after Stein

of large rectangular type, similar to those found by Stein at Mirān.

Amongst the helmets illustrated in the *Wu pei chi* (Fig. 73) and the later work *T'u shu tsi ch'êng*, largely redrawn from the former, are numerous helmets with neckguards of lamellar. Also, both works show what is termed 'Lion Armour' (Fig. 74), which is similar to the armours described above, but only part lamellar— the body and thighs—with an overcape and shoulder defences of elaborately embossed scales.

The paintings and stucco figurines of the T'ang Dynasty found by Stein in Chinese Turkestan show helmets built up of lamellar. Though usually rounded in the paintings, the figurines wear helmets of distinctly conical form, cusped over the warrior's eyes and descending to the shoulders at back and sides of the head

(Fig. 75). This form of helmet is but another variation of the type built up of laced segments such as have been found in Avarian graves at Kertsch in the Crimea and which were still in use in Tibet in the nineteenth century. The more rounded helmets represented on the figurines from Kara-shar are perhaps of Iranian fashion. The edges of the vertical plates are cusped in a similar manner to those of the early Sāssānian helmet in the British Museum (Pl. I, A).

Scale Armour

Scale armour (*kiai*) was in use from archaic times, when the scales

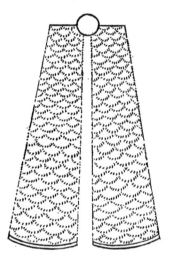

FIG. 76 Coat of paper armour from the *Wu pei chi*

were of leather fastened to a fabric or soft leather body. By the time of the Anterior Han (179 B.C.–A.D. 23) scales of copper and bronze (*k'ai*) were in common use; and although lamellar armour was introduced from Central Asia at this period, scale armour held its own until the nineteenth century, when armour was finally abandoned.[17]

As stated in the previous section, scales were used for part or all of an armour—including, sometimes, the complete helmet. Scales were forged from iron in Later Han (A.D. 25–220) times and were quite general under the succeeding dynasties, though even as late as the nineteenth century copper-scale armours could still be resorted to. One example in the Field Museum of Natural History, Chicago, collected in Ch'eng-tu, Sze-ch'uan, bears signs of actual use in action (Pl. XXII, C). The *T'ang leu tien*[18] ('Six Statutels of the T'ang Dynasty') lists and describes the types of armour then in use. Amongst them are the following: *si lin kia* ('armour of thin scales'), which is classified under armours of iron; *Shan wen kia* ('armour with mountain pattern'), probably a zigzag line of pointed scale heads which could, in fact, be a variety of lamellar armour similar to those made in Japan in the sixteenth century, the pattern of the small plates being termed *'yamamichi-gashira'* (mountain-path head).

What may also have been scale armour is alluded to in the *Lan p'ei lu* under the name of *jung kia*.[19] *Jung* is the soft core of young deer's antlers, and Laufer interprets the meaning as a hide cuirass strengthened with shavings of horn. *Jung kia* may simply be an armour of horn scales.

Mail

Mail has no real place in Chinese military history. It was certainly known to the Scythians—but then, possibly, only acquired through trade or raids in eastern Europe. Any mail used by Central Asian nomads, and perhaps through these brought to China, would have been of Persian manufacture. When first mentioned in Chinese annals, it comes as tribute from K'ang (Samarkand) in the K'ai-yüan period (713–741) and is termed *so tse k'ai*.[20] Mail is listed as one of the thirteen types of armour made in the Imperial Armoury under the T'ang Dynasty and almost certainly copied from foreign models. Its production was restricted and only important military officers would be issued with it.

The General Hau Shi-chung (d. 1151) is credited in his biography with having invented *lien so kia* ('chain-connected armour') capable of resisting arrows.[21] Laufer suggests that this is not true mail, but rings or chains sewn on a foundation—a form of armour which is only known from the Eskimo and primitive tribes of north-east Asia,[22] who used Chinese and Japanese pierced coins or large iron washers sewn upon leather, which could never be claimed as proof against arrows. Therefore, it is more likely another name for mail of interlocked rings.

The military regulations of the Ming Dynasty make no mention of mail, although it would appear to be illustrated in the *Wu pei chi*, where it is shown as a typical Chinese armour of scales (Fig. 77). This convention for mail is, however, common to Persian and Mughal Indian miniatures where we know with certainty that mail is represented. A very careful drawing of a short mail coat and breeches, with every ring delineated, is given in the *Huang ch'ao li k'i t'u shi* (Ch. 13, p. 53), where it is described as a *so-tse kia* from Turkestan and a spoil of war kept in the treasury.

The skill, time, and cost involved in the manufacture of mail in

鋼絲連鐶甲

Fig. 77 Armour of mail as represented in the *Wu pei chi*

quantity, and the lack of interest in military matters, obviously deterred any Chinese government from equipping large bodies of troops with it.

Brigandine (ting kia, 'armour with nails')
Most of the Chinese armour met with today comes under the category of what was termed in Europe 'brigandine', and it will be so classified here. This is armour of fabric with plates secured on the inside—sometimes with an internal lining, but frequently without. The plates are attached with round-headed rivets (*ting*), usually gilt, which are visible on the outer fabric and no doubt

A

B

C

Plate XXIII
Chinese and Korean Armour

A Helmet of a high court official with applied gilt ornament including the repeated
   Buddhist inscription *Om mani padme hum*, mid nineteenth century
B *Po* or large infantry shield of cane painted with a tiger's face, mid nineteenth century
C Korean court officials helmet with neck and ear guards of red cloth edged with otter
   fur, mid nineteenth century

A and C *Bernisches Historisches Museum*
B *Tower of London Armouries* (*Not to scale*)

A   B

Plate XXIV
Chinese Armour
A Armour of an emperor with plates in breast, back and thigh defences,
  taken by the French from the Summer Palace in 1861
B Armour of a military court official taken with the above. The breast, back
  and thigh defences contain plates whilst that in Plate XXIIA contains none
  Musée de l'Armee, Paris

were favoured for the richness they afforded to even a garment of plain cotton stuff (Fig. 79).

As suggested above, this form of armour may have been devised in China through the habit of military men wearing rich coats over the practical but not particularly beautiful lamellar armour.

The President of the Board of War under the Emperor T'ai-

鎌子甲

FIG. 78 Coat and breeches of mail from Turkestan from the *Huang ch'ao li k'i t'u shi*

tsung of the T'ang Dynasty was a certain Ma Sui, who died in A.D. 796.[23] He devised a combination of armour and uniform (*k'ai i*, 'armour clothing') to be made in three different lengths, and men so equipped were able to move freely and even run in comfort. The *Ch'u hio ki*,[24] compiled by Sü Kien in the early part of the eighth century, gives the names of some parts of the armour derived from clothing, such as the skirt of the armour—*shang* ('clothes for the lower part of the body'). The inner side of an armour, *lei*, and the coat of an armour, *kia i*, together are termed *kao*. The general term for clothing, *i-shang*, is here applied to armour, and the word *kao* clearly indicates that a textile robe enveloped the entire armour. These passages could well establish the date of origin for the brigandine in China.

Brigandines may be looked upon as a simplification of lamellar in so far as the rectangular plates are of similar size, but do not require the tedious process of drilling up to fourteen holes in each one. Three or, more often, two holes in one edge were all that was required. The plates were laid in rows overlapping the row beneath and each other on one side by about one-third of their width. This was sometimes increased to half the plates' width to produce a double thickness throughout.

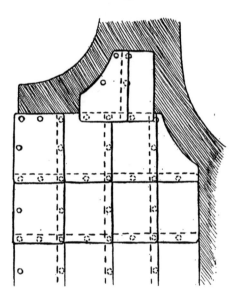

FIG. 79 Detail of Chinese and Korean brigandine construction. All rivets are obscured by the overlapping plates, except those on the extreme left-hand edge

Iron, copper and leather were employed for these plates, varying in part with the purpose for which the armour was required, but primarily with quality. Iron used in them varied considerably from very thin soft sheet in a common soldier's coat to thin, tough, elastic steel in an officer's armour.

The usual form taken by these armours is a basic jacket, with or without sleeves; an underskirt, like a divided apron, of ankle length; and a pair of high boots. Over the jacket are buttoned, or fastened with flat cords and buckles, certain reinforces, such as semicircular shoulderpieces, deep crescent-shaped gussets beneath the arms, and rectangular pieces below these and across the front opening over the privates. In some, the sleeves are dispensed with or built up of hundreds of narrow horizontal splints attached to fabric, which can be fastened to the shoulders by buttons or strap and buckle in a similar manner to the *kote* of Japanese armour. Sometimes, splinted 'vambraces' are provided to tie round the forearm. Each of these sections is lined with its rows of plates, and in several instances some external reinforces are applied, such as circular silvered copper mirrors on breast and back, or a border of three or four overlapping splints on the upper edges of the shoulderpieces. These metal fittings are frequently gilded or, on armours of high court officials, of copper gilt, pierced and engraved, principally with designs of dragons. The divided skirts of horsemen's armours have rows of exposed narrow lamellae secured by rivets within a broad frame of fabric. This may be due to tradition—for in the T'ang period paintings of armed men frequently show the thigh armour of lamellar construction even if the rest of the armour is of scale. Sometimes, these have circular external knee-plates with rows of horizontal lamellae below them, which can be tied closely round the leg. Above the knees the plates are secured behind the fabric.

Armours dating from the K'ien-lung period (1736–95) at Chicago, amongst the earliest known in the Western hemisphere, have portions which are studded, but not backed by plates. This was the beginning of the end for armour in China and shows that it was fast becoming a uniform and little else. Several military court officials' uniforms in Britain, such as that in the Wallace Collection, are made of rich blue and gold brocade, woven in a conventional scale pattern, and carry an external powdering of gilt nail-heads, but no internal plates. The helmets are silvered copper with applied fittings of pierced and engraved copper-gilt, sometimes set with corals and turquoise. Dragons and waves dominate the theme of decoration. Crests of red hair, stiff tails of sable-like bulrushes, feathers and netting are mounted in a slender crest-tube surmounting the crown—a decadent form never seen on real Chinese helmets. Anciently, a tassel of yak or pony hair dyed red, or a spray of feathers, would be the limit of helmet ornament. The Persian fashion for wearing little pennants attached to the slender, rodlike apex of their helmets probably dates from the Mongol invasion of China in the thirteenth century.

Although the rounded helmets of T'ang fashion persist

throughout the succeeding dynasties of Chinese history, particularly in art and military books, the Mongolian conical bowl,
with its inverted cup at the apex and cusped brow-plate, survived
and eventually became the dominant form of helmet in China and
Korea. In the Military Museum, Istanbul, is a Persian helmet with
a skull greatly influenced by the Mongolian fashion (Fig. 16ᶜ). It is
dated to the late fourteenth century. From the late sixteenth century, when Toyotomi Hideyoshi invaded Korea, the Mongolian
helmet was in fairly general use, to be occasionally copied by Japanese armourers in the seventeenth century, as were also Korean and
Chinese civilian hats. The average conical helmet of Mongol form
has concave sides, with a small peak set high on the brow-plate,
which is cusped over the eyes. The cheek flaps, with or without a
lining of plates, fasten with buttons across the throat, while a
third flap is attached over the nape of the neck at the back. Linings
take the form of a quilted conical cap with chin-cords, and further
ties are supplied inside the helmet for the same purpose.

'Banded' Armour

'At the Court of the Emperors of the Kin Dynasty (1115–1234)
in Peking the guards were all clad in armour.[25] The guards on
the left were all wearing banded cuirasses coloured blue (*ts'ing
t'ao kia*) holding flags bearing yellow dragons. On the right the
guards were wearing banded cuirasses coloured red (*hung t'ao
kia*) holding flags bearing red dragons.'

The presence of the word *kia* defines an armour of hide, and the
word 'banded' (*t'ao*) may simply imply that the colours were
applied in bands.

There are, however, instances where armour represented by
Chinese artists was quite definitely built up of horizontal bands or
plates and suggests a similar construction to the *lorica segmentata*
of the Roman legionaries. It also compares with Japanese armour,
of the sixteenth century and later, constructed with plates of
leather or iron (*ita mono*) laced together vertically with pairs of
braids.

Amongst the painted banners found by the Stein Expedition in
a cave near Tun-Huang was one painted with armed gods, several
of whom wear an armour of the usual T'ang pattern; but instead
of scales or lamellar covering the various parts, they are built
up of horizontal segments or plates (Fig. 80). There are no indica-

tions of lacing to hold the plates together and it is therefore possible that they are either laced internally or attached to a soft leather or fabric base.

Protohistoric Japanese armour of laminated iron plates was laced internally—as also is the neckguard of a Japanese helmet of the late seventeenth century made in the Mongolian fashion now in the Tower of London Armouries (XXVI–94ᴬ).

FIG. 80 'Banded Armour' from a painted silk banner of Lokapāla Vaiśravana with the divine host, from Tun-Huang, cave of 'Thousand Buddhas' after Stein

Another method of construction for this form of armour is a variation of brigandine or 'coat of plates', as used in Europe in the fourteenth century, where horizontal plates are attached by their upper edges to the inside of a fabric or leather garment.[26] As the fabric derives a stepped surface from the upper edges of the plates, European artists drew such armour as if the plates were on the outside, and it is not impossible that a similar convention was employed here. Only by seeing the colours of the original could one decide, and then not with any degree of certainty.

Paper Armour

In the T'ang period, a certain Shang Sui-ting was credited with the invention of paper armour. It was then used as a protection by ordinary people, but under the Sung Dynasty it was officially recognized as a cheap but practical defence. In the year 1040 the troops stationed at Kiang-nan and Huai-nan, in Au-hui Province, were ordered to make thirty thousand suits of paper armour for distribution amongst the garrisons of Shen-si Province. The localities mentioned were noted for their paper production.[27]

FIG. 81 Horse with scale chamfron and neck armour and peytral of lamellar, after L. P. Cibot

Paper armour was particularly favoured in southern China in Ming times by the garrisons defending the coast against Japanese raiders. The best papers were those from Korea—much prized in China and Japan for their toughness and durability. Ten to fifteen thicknesses sewn together were considered best for military use. It is said to have been proof against musket balls.

The illustration of paper armour in the *Wu pei chi* of 1621 shows a sleeveless coat of imbricated scales opening down the front (Fig. 76). Whether each scale was from ten to fifteen layers thick we are not told.

The *T'ang shu Hsü shang chuan*[28] relates that the General Hsü Shang, when commander at Ho Chung, organized the equipping of a thousand soldiers with *k'ai* of paper. Even strong arrows could not pierce it.

Horse Armour

Horse armour (*kiai*) of leather was used for chariot horses in archaic China. From the use of the term *kiai* it would imply an armour of leather scales. The earliest use of *ma k'ai*, or metal horse armour, dates from the early third century A.D., but this reference is regarded by Laufer with considerable suspicion.[29] In A.D. 519 there was a more reliable reference to metal horse armour, when King A-na-kuai of the Jwen-jwen presented to the Emperor Su-tsung of the Wei Dynasty one set of brilliant armour, complete for man and horse (*jên ma k'ai*), and six sets of iron armour for man and horse.[30]

Mention has already been made of the northern Wei figurine of an armoured horseman, in the British Museum, painted with large scales, and of another in the Musée Cernuschi, in Paris, which clearly represents lamellar armour. These illustrate the type of armour used in the sixth century and show how closely related it was to that of Iran and Central Asia.

Under the T'ang Dynasty, horse armour was used considerably, whole cavalry units being thus equipped. This is borne out by the existence of numerous clay figurines of warriors mounted on barded horses and by many contemporary literary references.

The rebel Kao K'ai-tao, who took over Yü-yang Province in 618 and called himself Prince of Yen, possessed several thousand armoured horses and ten thousand men.[31]

Laufer gives many references to the continued use of horse armour, and the numerous references to its use by the Mongols by the European visitors to Asia in the thirteenth century—particularly to China under the Great Khan—proves its wide use up to that time.

The *Wu pei chi* of 1621 illustrates portions of a horse armour of lamellar construction (Fig. 82), and a fully armed horse given by Cibot[32] shows both lamellar and scale armour (Fig. 81). (Compare with the Tibetan horse armour in Pl. XXVI, C.) The back of this animal may only be covered with fabric and, as no saddle is shown, it could represent a horse used for drawing siege engines.

In the Metropolitan Museum, New York, are two pieces of imitation brigandine horse armour (*ma ting kia*) of silk, studded with gilt nails, which date from the late eighteenth century or first half of the nineteenth century. They consist of a hood for the head and neck of the horse, and a crupper—and no doubt originally included a peytral or breastpiece.

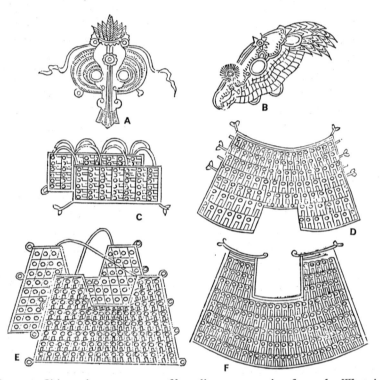

FIG. 82 Chinese horse armour of lamellar construction from the *Wu pei chi*

A and B   Chamfrons   E   Flanchards
C   Neck armour   F   Crupper
D   Peytral

The Shield

In archaic China the shield was of considerable importance, for with the majority of soldiers it was their sole defence—and for the infantry this may also be said of the Han and even the T'ang dynasty.

Wooden shields of rectangular form, with a marked medial ridge, were used in the early chariots. These are mentioned in a Han dictionary, the *Shi ming* by Liu Hi,[33] which describes the infantry shields (*pu tun*) as long and narrow and a shorter narrow shield (*kie tun*) for use in chariots. The materials from which they

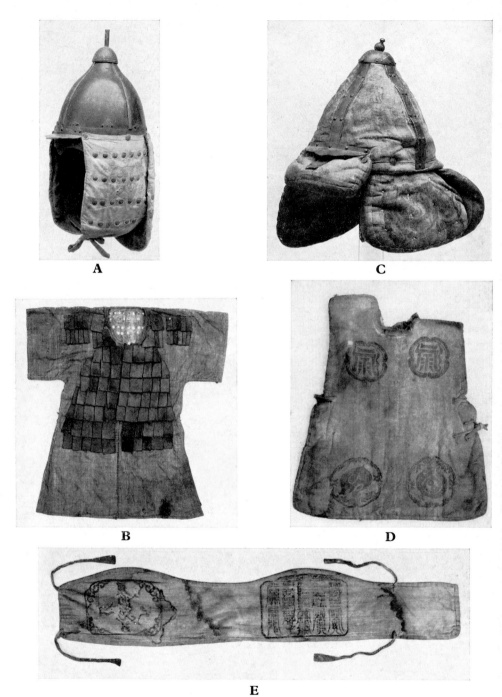

Plate XXV
Korean Armour

A and B Armour of a cavalryman of hemp cloth lined with plates. The coat is shown
inside out, nineteenth century

C, D and E Helmet, cuirass and belt of a foot soldier of quilted hemp cloth printed
with characters and devices, nineteenth century

Metropolitan Museum of Art, New York (Not to scale)

A

B

C

Plate XXVI

Tibetan Armour
A   Model of a lamellar armour
    brought from Tibet in 1904
B   Back of same
C   Armour for man and horse of
    lamellar and leather brought
    from Tibet in 1904 by the
    Younghusband Expedition
    Tower of London Armouries
    C on loan from the *Victoria
    and Albert Museum*
    (*Not to scale*)

Plate XXVII

Basic Types of Oriental
Armour
A Lamellar, Tibet
B Mail, Mamlūk

C Scale, Punjab, India
D Mail and plates, India.
Detail of construction of
an elephant armour
*Tower of London
Armouries (Not to scale)*

A

B

C

D

A

B

C

D

Plate XXVIII
Japanese Lamellar Armour

A Red laced *ō-yoroi*, second half twelfth century. *Tokyo National Museum*
B Red laced *ō-yoroi*, second half fourteenth century. *Kasuga-jinsha, Nara*
C Blue-black leather laced *dō maru*, mid fourteenth century. *Kasuga-jinsha, Nara*
D Red-and-white-laced *haramaki*, late fifteenth century. *Oyamazumi-jinsha, Omishima*
(*Not to scale*)

were made were either boards or rhinoceros hide. Those made of boards (*feng pien*) were called *mu lo*; those made from rhinoceros hide were called *si tun*. Some were also made of grass or bamboo and, often being extremely light, could 'float in blood or water'.

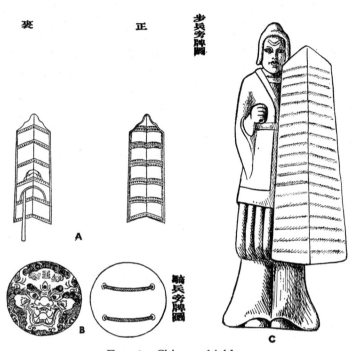

FIG. 83 Chinese shields
A Infantry shield, inside showing support
B Cavalry shield painted with dragon's face and inside showing
    double enarmes
C Figurine of foot soldier with long shield, A.D. 500; British
    Museum
A and B from the *T'u shu tsi ch'êng*

All shields were lacquered—red being the most popular colour, though black was sometimes used. Red, the colour of blood, was widely used as the colour for war. In China it was largely used because it was believed to terrify one's enemy. Lacquer also preserved leather and wood and prevented warping and distortion in changing climatic conditions.

The *pei k'uei* was a round shield of hide, lacquered red, which 'shone like the sun'.[34] Liu Hi also describes other forms of shield, such as: a large flat one called *Wu k'uei* ('Generals of Wu') which,

as its name implies, was said to be used by the generals of the
country of Wu; and the *sü tun*, a tall shield from the country of
Shu (Sze-ch'uan). The latter was also called 'shield of the K'iang
(Tibetans)'.

When T'ai Tsung (A.D. 976–98) of the Sung dynasty heard
that southerners were using the *piao ch'iang* and *p'ang p'ai*, he
ordered his own troops to be trained in their use. The infantry
used a cowhide shield about eight feet long, the cavalry a circular
red lacquered one (Fig. 83). *P'ang* means side, so that, in fact, both
of the above mean a defence at the side.

Shields of wicker or rattan were used in many countries of the
East, and China was no exception. One form, the *li p'ai*, made
from either bamboo or wood, was used primarily for siege
purposes as a defence against stones and arrows cast from the
walls of forts and cities. It was the Chinese equivalent of the
European mantlet, and measured five feet in height and three feet
in width. Another shield used in siege warfare on the defensive
side was called *lang ya pai*, made of elm with nails fixed in the top
and blades on the four edges.[35] Ropes were attached to rings on
the front and back so that it could be suspended from city walls
in order to strike an enemy attempting to scale them.

The shield in China would appear to be related closely to the
use of the sword, just as in England 'sword and buckler' were
popular in the sixteenth and seventeenth centuries. The famous
Han relief known as 'The Battle of the Bridge' shows warriors
armed with short single-edged, ring-pommelled swords, and
rectangular shields with double-lobed outline at top and bottom
and transverse convex curve at the centre. They would have been
approximately three feet in length. A round shield is also shown
in this relief.

The *T'u shu tsi ch'êng* shows the tall, ridged infantry shield with
supporting prop, so that a defensive wall could be made from
shields as with the European pavise and the Japanese *tate*. Also in
this work is an illustration of the circular cavalry shield, painted
with a dragon's face and equipped with double enarmes for the
left arm.

Large, circular, convex shields called *po* survive from the nineteenth century. They are of wicker, with a cane loop for the forearm and a straight wooden grip. All are painted with a traditional
tiger face and have a brass boss in the centre. An example of one

of these is shown in Pl. XXIII, B in the Tower of London Armouries (XXVI–56ᴬ). They may have been carried by the Tiger Soldiers, who wore striped uniforms.

The circular hide shields carried by Chinese cavalry may have resembled the circular convex shields such as were used in north India, Tibet, and Bhutan. One of the stucco figures from Mingoi,

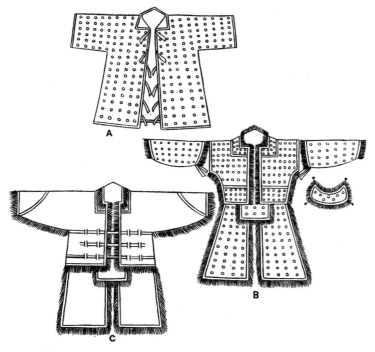

FIG. 84 Three armours from the '*Five Ceremonies*', Korean, eighteenth century. A and B are probably 'Iron Studded Armour', A the blue cloth and B the red cloth one with separate sleeves. D cannot be identified

now in the British Museum, has a circular shield of convex section with a raised rim and five bosses. This model is of the eighth to tenth centuries.

Korea

The close proximity of Korea to China, frequent warfare, and an overall similarity of culture, has meant that Korean armour tended to follow Chinese fashions rather than those of her other, more isolated, neighbour Japan.

Korean armour only differs from the Chinese in detail and,

without further evidence, we must assume that the development followed a similar progression from hide to scale and lamellar and, eventually, to brigandine. It is also probable that since the Chinese imported special paper from Korea for making munition armours, the Koreans also made such armours themselves.

Gilt bronze lamellae, measuring one and a quarter inches wide and nine and a half inches long, and drilled for lacing in the conventional manner, were found in a tomb believed to be fourth to fifth century A.D. at Kyungju. Also found in the same grave were two pieces of a gilt-bronze breastplate, such as we see on Chinese figurines of the Wei and T'ang dynasties, and in such frescoes as those found at Kizil in Chinese Turkestan of the seventh to eighth centuries, worn over coats of lamellar.

Military textbooks seldom mention armour, and it is only such works as *The Five Ceremonies*, described by Boots,[36] which give any details of armours, and then only those in use in the eighteenth and nineteenth centuries (Fig. 84).

Two helmets illustrated by Boots from his own collection, and another in a Japanese collection, are of considerable age—possibly of the sixteenth or early seventeenth centuries—and these illustrate striking archaic features (Fig. 85). The rounded conical bowls are built up of four main segments joined by other plates riveted on the outside, the edges of which are cusped between the riveting points—exactly as in the early Sāssānian helmet at the British Museum and, as pointed out in Chapter II, to be seen in nineteenth-century Tibetan helmets. Some seventeenth-century Japanese helmets based upon Korean models also have narrow external plates which are an elaboration of this construction. They are mostly the work of the Kaga schools of armourers. The Boots helmets are perhaps typical of the older Korean models— one with a flat crescentic peak, the other with a down-turned concave brim. The helmet in the Japanese collection is like the Boots peaked example, but retains a neck and two ear flaps of lamellar. As with other neighbours of the Chinese Empire, Korea may have retained lamellar armour in its old simple form for very much longer than China herself.

An early example of a Mongolian helmet, probably made in Korea and certainly used there, is now in the Genkō Memorial Hall at Hakata, which commemorates the defeat of the Mongol invasions of Japan in 1274 and 1281. The bowl is conical, of four segments joined by narrow strips with a medial rib, and at the apex is riveted a wide crest-tube. The peak is large, like the other helmet described above, and below this is a deep brow-plate with two eye-holes breaking the bottom edge.

The later armours follow the typical Chinese pattern, consisting of a fabric coat with an underskirt, divided like an apron, reaching to below the knees. Separate shoulder defences of Chinese

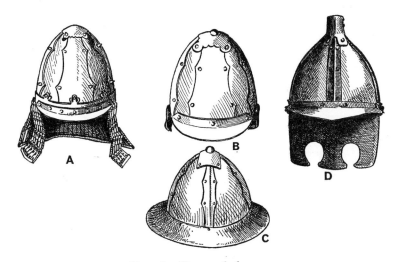

FIG. 85 Korean helmets
A With neck- and earguards of lamellar, late sixteenth century, in a
   Japanese collection
B Late sixteenth century; Boots collection
C Brimmed helmet, late sixteenth century; Boots collection
D Mongolian style, late sixteenth century; Genkō Memorial Hall,
   Hakata, Japan

form or separate sleeves were occasionally used, but the majority are made as a square-cut coat with full half-length sleeves. For high officials the edges were trimmed with otter fur, and most armours had a broad belt of a distinctive colour and quality to denote rank.

The late helmets of Mongolian pattern are much less angular than Chinese examples. The three fabric flaps for neck and sides of the head are lined with small rawhide plates, and the coats are more likely to contain plates than not.

The materials used for armour are seldom as rich as those employed in China—cotton or hemp fabrics being the most usual, coloured or printed with symbols with wood blocks. The uniforms of officials which survive are mostly of European woollen cloth, either bright red or dark blue.

In the G. C. Stone Collection in the Metropolitan Museum of Art, New York, are two interesting examples of nineteenth-century munition armours. One, for a cavalryman, consists of a black lacquered leather helmet, reinforced with russet iron, decorated with silver. The cheek- and neckguards are lined with leather plates, as also is the simple hemp cloth coat at the front and back and on the shoulders. The other armour, for a foot soldier, is entirely of padded hemp cloth with printed devices. The helmet, of Mongolian shape, is strengthened with strips of iron and the usual peak; and the body armour is a sleeveless padded cuirass with a wide overbelt. The helmets were generally crested with the traditional tassel of hair, in Korea, of red horse-hair.

Helmets of officials are frequently black lacquered and richly mounted with embossed, pierced and engraved gilded copper fittings. This decoration is usually superior to Chinese work and shows better taste.

The armours described in *The Five Ceremonies* are as follows:

'Mercury Armour': made of iron plates woven together with leather thongs (lamellar) and painted silver-white with mercury.[37]
'Willow Leaf Armour': of raw pigskin pieces instead of iron, painted black.[38]
'Paper Armour': made of twisted paper strings, painted black.[39]
'Iron Ring Armour': of small iron rings linked together (mail).
'Mirror Flag Armour': of iron plates and rings woven in alternating rows (mail and plates).
'Iron Studded Armour': with iron plates studded like stars on a blue cloth or on a red cloth. The red suit had separate sleeves tied with a cord. The sleeves were copper studded. The coat was lined with deerskin and had a wide red belt.[40]

Tibet

Through the unchanging character of Tibetan culture, many aspects of early Central Asian life are preserved to us. One of these aspects—of immense value to the student of arms and armour—is the preservation of a complete military equipment which has remained unchanged since the fourth or fifth century, except for the introduction of firearms at some time after the sixteenth century.

From Chinese records of the Han and T'ang dynasties, and from Sir Aurel Stein's excavations at Mīrān in Chinese Turkestan, we know that the K'iang—as the Chinese called them—were a strong and warlike people. They were not then shut away in their mountain fortress, but played an active part in Central Asian affairs.

The fort site at Mīrān, dating from the third or fourth century A.D., yielded portions of lacquered hide lamellar armours, both red and black, with engraved patterns. The largest of these are two and a half inches by three and a half inches and are laced with double vertical doeskin laces. The later iron lamellae are half this width and only single vertical laces connect each plate to its neighbours above and below.

Johannes de Plano Carpini's description of a Mongol lamellar armour and its manufacture in the thirteenth century fits exactly the armours for man and horse taken by the Younghusband expedition to Lhasa in 1904.

The helmets are rounded in form, built up of eight radial segments laced together with leather thongs. The plates are arranged so that half their number are inside and half outside, the external ones overlapping an internal one on each side. The external plates each have a medial rib and are cusped between the lacing holes. A moulded iron plume-tube is laced to the centre by its base-plate, and the lower edge is finished with a band of lamellae to which in turn are laced neck and cheek defences, each constructed of three rows of lamellae.

The normal body armour was in the form of a long coat, entirely constructed of horizontal rows of iron lamellae laced together with doeskin. It was customary for all iron to be polished bright and the hide to be its natural cream colour. The coat of lamellar opened down the front, and the long skirt had two further openings provided towards the rear of each hip—so that when the wearer was upon horseback the rear portion of the skirt was spread over the horse's crupper. The coat was joined over the shoulders by straps constructed of small lamellae—usually older, large ones cut down, laced together and lined with leather. To these straps the flaplike shoulder defences were laced permanently. They varied in length according to the number of laminations, but in some instances were made to wrist length and laced up on the inside. To the bottom edge of the skirt it was customary to lace irregular pieces of buckskin or leather fringes.

A fine specimen of this type of armour in the Royal Scottish Museum, Edinburgh (1909–406), has leather extensions from elbow to hand, laced to the shoulder defences and closely studded with embossed circular washers. A model lamellar armour in the Tower Armouries, London, has panels of brocade mounted upon leather attached to the sections of the skirt and to the edges of the shoulders. Another example, on loan from the Indian Section of the Victoria and Albert Museum, is a leather coat with old lamellae laced to the surface, and panels of leather faced with printed cotton fabric fastened to the edges of the skirt. The helmet with this armour has neck and cheek flaps of the same materials, and the general crudeness suggests that the owner of it was making do with old scraps.

Persian, Indian, and Bhutanese mail is known to have been acquired by Tibetans, just as Chinese armours were obtained, in trade or as diplomatic gifts. A heavy Chinese helmet of Mongolian shape acquired from Tibet is in the Museum für Völkerkunde, Vienna. Fine-quality mounts of gilded copper, pierced and engraved, have been added, and large gold Bhuddist symbols applied to the russet surface of the bowl. The neck and cheek flaps are of Chinese brocade and are lined with iron plates held by gilt-headed nails, and could be the originals.

A simple form of lamellar body armour, possibly made for the better-armed foot soldier in Tibet, was constructed of two panels, joined over the shoulders and open at the sides. It would be secured round the body with a belt and would have reached to about mid-thigh. The lower edge was extended with additional flaps of buckskin. There is a specimen of this type in the State Ethnographical Museum, Stockholm.

Shields were not generally used in Tibet, but examples found there are small, slightly convex, and made of lacquered buffalo hide. They have four brass bosses covering the hand-loop rivets and a fifth which is purely ornamental. They may have been acquired from Bhutan, where this defence was more generally used.

Horse Armour

Tibetan horse armour, like that for the man, is of very great antiquity. The chamfrons, made of leather and covered with small square plates each with a tall central boss, resemble the studded leather chamfrons from the Roman fort at Newstead, now in the National Museum of Antiquities, Edinburgh. Tibetan examples, however, usually have a wide strip of iron down the centre of the face, with pierced brass finials hinged at top and bottom—one to lay on the horse's nose and the other to lay between its ears.

The neck armour, when present, consisted of two panels—one for each side of the neck, and reaching from throat to shoulders. They were made of stiff tooled and lacquered leather set with rows of iron studs. The peytral, or breast defence, was of long iron lamellae laced in the regular manner, but mounted on panels of fabric or leather, and usually with a lower border of stiff lacquered leather edged with studs and a fringe of red-dyed yak hair and strips of brocade.

Similar pieces were provided for either side of the crupper, with another section to fill the space left beneath the tail. Flanchards of lacquered leather of oval shape were supported on either side of the horse's body by leather ties from the saddle.

Any gaps left between the peytral and crupper sections were provided with lacquered leather panels—and if movement was required, hinges were added. Fastenings were by leather tie or small tinned buckles and plaited narrow buckskin straps.

Bhutan

The armour of the Bhutanese falls between that of north India and Tibet, deriving most of its characteristics from the former and only details from the latter and from China to the north-east. For all this, the Bhutanese equipment has a character of its own.

From India came the short-sleeved mail shirt, generally of large riveted rings and not of the later Indo-Persian butted variety. Also from the Indian side of the Himalayas came the large helmet-bowl forged from one piece of iron, a solid defence to which the Bhutanese added a small Mongolian-type peak with deeply flanged edge and three neck flaps—one at the back and another at each side, of fabric. When action was not expected, these flaps were worn tied up over the crown. It was usual to have an ornamental finial of brass, riveted to the centre of the helmet-bowl, which took the form of a clawlike terminal of a Buddhist thunder-bolt; but some special troops carried large fanlike ornaments set transversely across the helmet and mounted in a tubular socket.[41] *Pagris* of twisted silks of diverse colours were sometimes tied around the helmet.

The mail shirt was reinforced with a form of *char aina* consisting of four circular convex iron plates, joined with narrow crossed straps of leather, with two longer straps for the shoulders, so that one came in the centre of the breast, one at the back, and one at each side. Around the waist was tied a belt—deeper in the centre, which was worn to the front, and tapering towards the ends—built up of narrow lamellae riveted to a leather backing.

Almost identical armours were used in Sikkim and Nepal; and the Tibetans also acquired pieces of Bhutanese equipment—particularly the one-piece helmets.

Lighter, quilted helmets made like typical Asiatic winter caps, with ear and neck flaps, were reinforced with strips of iron.

Shields were circular and of buffalo hide, lacquered black with a red rim. The brass bosses were copied from Indian models, as in the crescent-and-star motif. A central boss, engraved and pierced, generally carried the mask of a grotesque Buddhist guardian to drive away evil spirits.

The Bhutanese do not appear to have used horse armour.

CHAPTER SIX

[1] Berthold Laufer, *Chinese Clay Figures*, Part I, *Prolegomena on the History of Defensive Armor*, Field Museum of Natural History, Publication 177, Vol. XIII, No. 2, Chicago, 1914, Part II, p. 175.

[2] G. Strakosch-Grossman, *Der Einfall der Mongolen in Mitteleuropa*, p. 28, Innsbruck, 1893.

[3] Ed. of Yule and Cordier, Vol. I, p. 260.

[4] W. Hough, *Primitive American Armor*, Report U.S. National Museum, 1893, pp. 641–7.

[5] Berthold Laufer, op. cit., Part II, p. 189.

[6] Chavannes, *Les Memoires historiques de Se-ma Ts'ien*, Vol. III, p. 217.

[7] Folke Bergman, 'A note on ancient laminae armour in China', *Ethnos*, Vol. I, No. 5, Sept. 1936.

[8] Berthold Laufer, op. cit., Part III, pp. 209–14.

[9] Legge, *Chinese Classics*, Vol. IV, p. 626.

[10] Berthold Laufer, op. cit., Part III, p. 230.

[11] Yamagami Hachiro, *Japan's Ancient Armour*, Japanese Government Tourist Library, No. 31, Tokyo, 1940.

[12] Suenaga Masao, *Nippon Jodai no Katchu*, Tokyo, 1934.

[13] C. R. Beazley, *The Texts and Versions of John de Plano Carpini*, pp. 89, 124, London, Hakluyt Society, 1903.

[14] W. W. Rockhill, *The Journal of William of Rubruck*, p. 261, London, Hakluyt Society, 1900.

[15] This is now in the University Museum, Philadelphia. A cast is in the British Museum.

[16] E. T. C. Werner, *Chinese Weapons*, p. 34. Royal Asiatic Society North China Branch (Extra Vol.), Shanghai, 1932.

[17] Berthold Laufer, op. cit., Part III, p. 213.

[18] 'Six Statutes of the T'ang Dynasty', quoted in both *Ko chi king yüan*, Ch. 41, p. 3, and *P'ei wên yün fu*, Ch. 106, p. 73, early eighth century. See Laufer.

[19] Quoted in *P'ei wên yün fu*, Ch. 106, p. 74. See Laufer.

[20] Bretschneider, *China Review*, Vol. V, p. 123.

21 Giles, *Biographical Dictionary*, p. 251. His complete biography is in *Sung shi*, Ch. 364, p. 1.

22 W. Hough, ibid., p. 643. Also illustrated in G. C. Stone, *Glossary of the Construction, Decoration and Use of Arms and Armor*, New York, 1934 and 1961, p. 22, Fig. 29.

23 Giles, *Biographical Dictionary*, p. 569.

24 Bretschneider, *Botanicon Sinicum*, Part I, p. 143, No. 76.

25 M. Chavannes, *Toung Pao*, 1904, pp. 163–92.

26 Bengt Thordeman, *Armour from the Battle of Wisby 1361*, 2 vols, Stockholm, 1939. History of the Coat of Plates, Ch. VIII, pp. 285–328.

27 Berthold Laufer, op. cit., Ch. VI, p. 292.

28 E. T. C. Werner, op. cit., p. 33.

29 Berthold Laufer, op. cit., Ch. VII, pp. 306–7.

30 *Pei shi*, Ch. 98, p. 6. 'Brilliant armour' possibly refers to one of iron highly polished.

31 *T'ang shu*, Ch. 86, p. 4B.

32 L. P. Cibot, *Lettre sur les caractères chinois*, Brussels, 1773.

33 Berthold Laufer, op. cit., Ch. II, p. 187. Werner also quotes from this source.

34 E. T. C. Werner, op. cit., Shields, p. 39.

35 E. T. C. Werner, op. cit., Shields, p. 40.

36 J. L. Boots, 'Korean Arms and Armour', *Transactions of the Royal Asiatic Society, Korean Branch*, Vol. XXIII, Part 2, Seoul, 1937.

37 This may have been a common practice in ancient China as well and the reason why white paint was used to represent armour on Wei and T'ang figurines.

38 This rawhide lamellar armour is one of the oldest forms. Unlacquered hide lamellae of the third century were found by Stein at Niya in Chinese Turkestan.

39 One presumes that this was a coat woven or plaited from paper cord.

40 This is a rather misleading description and obviously means that the starlike studs held the plates on the inside of the coat.

41 A fully armed Bhutanese warrior wearing a large crest is shown in the last plate of the *Chung Kuo Ping C'hi Shih Kao*, Peking, 1957.

Japan

Plate Armour and Early Lamellar

Japan is the only country in the Orient with an unbroken history of her arms and armour. Influence from the Asiatic continent was controlled; for although there were periods when Chinese, Korean, and eventually European art and culture were anxiously sought and digested, there were also long periods in Japan's history when she cut herself off and forcefully ejected all attempts at contact from outside. Whatever Japan borrowed from abroad was eventually absorbed into her own culture, taking on national characteristics and becoming an almost indistinguishable part of the whole.

The Protohistoric Japanese—the Yamato people, as they are called—who inhabited the western part of the islands, had developed the knowledge of casting in bronze and working in iron. As their culture grew, they improved their ability to work iron to a very high degree, so that by the fourth and fifth centuries A.D.—the period from which their remarkable burial mounds begin to contain arms and armour—we find helmets and cuirasses, with their accessories, of no mean order.[1]

The earliest of these armours, probably a development in iron from primitive helmets and cuirasses of bamboo and hide, were more advanced than any armour being made elsewhere in the contemporary world.

These armours were called *tankō* and consisted of a beaked rounded helmet of horizontal iron plates joined by rivets or leather lacing, with a laminated neckguard of plates laced together internally (Fig. 86). Today, we call this shape *shōkakufu no hachi* or 'battering-ram bowl' because of the sharply ridged beak in the front (see also Fig. 95, 1 & 2).

The cuirass was shaped to the body and was built up of horizontal plates within a frame, riveted or laced together. The opening was at the centre of the front, and the right half of the breast—
or both halves—would be hinged at the side to admit the body.
One example was found with no hinges, so that it must have been
sprung on to the body in a similar manner to ancient Greek

FIG. 86 Reconstruction of a
Protohistoric Japanese plate
armour (*tankō*), fourth to seventh
century A.D., after Suenaga

bronze greaves. Cotton fabric ties secured the cuirass over the
shoulders, and leather laces fastened the front opening.

Neck and shoulders were provided with a two-piece collar
joined with ties at the centre of the chest and back, and permanently laced to these were the laminated defences for the upper
arm. These were curved iron strips fitted to the outside of the
shoulder and arm and had much the same appearance as those
used with the Roman legionary *lorica segmentata*. This collar,
termed *uwa-manchira*, with its shoulderguards, was worn over the
shoulder-straps of the cuirass—hence the word *uwa*, meaning
'outside' or 'over the top of'.

The forearms were protected with tubular *kote*, like Indian and

Persian vambraces, with short rows of laced lamellae for the back
of the hands. Over the pronounced flange of the cuirass, at the
waist, was tied a large hooplike skirt in two sections: one at the
front and one at the back, consisting of a series of narrow curved
laminations laced, like the neck- and shoulderpieces, on the inside.

It has been possible to reconstruct the Protohistoric Japanese
armour completely, for evidence has survived for every con-
structional detail—including fabric and leather laces, and plaited
and wrapped bindings to the edges of solid plates. Even the type
of feathers attached to the crest-holders laced on the top of some
helmets have been identified by the remaining quills. The crest-
holders were like three pronged forks pointing to the back of the
helmet, with pheasant-tail feathers tied to the prongs.

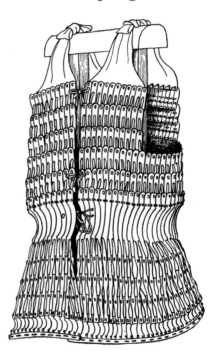

FIG. 87 Reconstruction of a
Protohistoric Japanese coat of
lamellar (*keikō*), fifth to eighth
century, after Suenaga

With the flow of Chinese and Korean culture in the fifth and
sixth centuries the horse and lamellar armour were introduced
into Japan. This lamellar armour, called *keikō*, quickly took on a
Japanese character, being adapted to the form of the earlier *tankō*
as far as the new method of construction would permit (Fig. 87).

From the continent there came a new form of helmet with a

rounded bowl and a broad flat peak. These helmet-bowls were built up of horizontal rings alternating with rows made up of triangular segments, a form of construction also adapted to the older helmets and solid cuirasses. To the top of the round bowl was fastened an inverted cup surmounted by a stem and another shallow cup having the appearance of a modern champagne glass. The upper cup was pierced around its circumference with pairs of small holes for attaching hair or feather crests as worn in China.

The neckguards were similar to those on the earlier helmets, and it may be that the Japanese preferred their own kind to the continental pattern of lamellar or fabric.

The body armour consisted of a sleeveless jacket opening at the front, with a skirt reaching to the upper part of the thighs. A very marked waist was produced by using narrow concave lamellae, and a row of shorter concave plates was used for the bottom edge of the skirt to give it rigidity. Cotton shoulder-straps were laced to the upper rows of lamellae at front and back and the ends tied on the shoulders.

Neck armour with shoulderguards attached were reproduced completely with laced lamellae, the plates varying in size and shape according to the position they occupied. The vambraces were built up of splints shaped to fit the forearm closely and without handguards, or they were of the old tubular type as described above.

Japanese history really begins in the seventh century with the capital in the city of Nara. The Nara Period, as it is called, lasted from 646–793, and was a time of expansion and enlightenment.

Both plate and lamellar armours were being used, some being an admixture of both fashions. Not only do we have the actual armours recovered from the *dolmens*, or burial mounds, but we have a remarkable series of *haniwa*, or large clay figures, representing people, animals, and houses of the period, which were buried around the earth-covered stone burial chambers to prevent soil erosion. Amongst the *haniwa* are a splendid group of warriors, both part and fully armed, showing us just how the armour was worn and the clothing and arms used with it.

Some armoured *haniwa* wear the old beaked helmet with neck-guard and large cheekpieces of lamellar construction, as we have seen were used in Tibet and Korea. With this the warrior might wear a complete lamellar armour, including defences for his legs, or simply a coat and a pair of vambraces. One *tankō* found quite recently had a skirt of large round-headed lamellae attached to the flange of the cuirass with straps and buckles, while a very complete *keikō*, now in the University Museum, Kyoto, has an old beaked helmet with a laminated plate neckguard. This armour also has splinted vambraces and shinguards.[2]

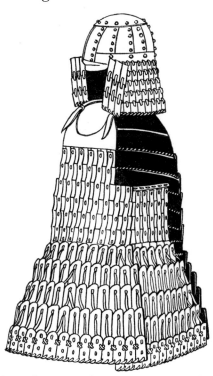

FIG. 88 Reconstruction of a later *keikō* from which *ō-yoroi* was developed, eighth to tenth century, after Sasama

In the Early Heian Period (794–896) which follows, changes are only seen in details of construction. Helmets were made up of horizontal bands with overlapping vertical plates between, and several examples found have their plates heavily gilded and decorated with punched ornament (Fig. 89). Some lamellae were also gilded, a number of which are to be seen in the Metropolitan Museum of Art, New York.

A great variety of plates and methods of lacing were tried out in this period, but in the later years the average mounted warrior began to use a new form of lamellar armour of a distinctly Japanese type built up of rectangular lamellae in two sections— one for the front and one for the back, connected over the

shoulders. The sides were open and were therefore filled with
two separate pieces, tied under the arms, before the cuirass
proper was put on. To begin with, the older collar with attached
shoulderguards was used with this; but as time went on the
shoulder-straps were stiffened and padded to carry the considerable weight of the iron lamellar and the collar was discarded.
The shoulderguards were then made separate and fastened to the
shoulder-straps by cords, so becoming more like the true *sode*
(lit. sleeve) of later Japanese armour.[3]

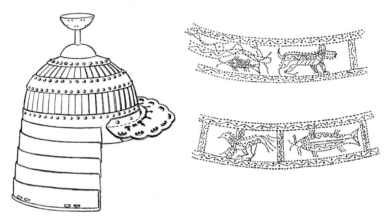

FIG. 89 *Mabezashi-tsuke-hachi* or *maru no hachi* as worn with *keikō*, fifth
to eighth century; Tokyo National Museum
  A The complete helmet
  B Punched decoration on the bands of the skull which are wrapped
     in gilded copper

From the last of the burial mounds there survive a number of
late-eighth- and early-ninth-century helmets which are chiefly
constructed with vertical plates, but most of them retaining the
forward crest. One of these, the typical helmet of the ninth century, approaches the conical in form and is capped by an inverted
cup shape. The brim-plate encircling the lower edge is cusped over
the eyes and its modern appellation *moko-hachi-gyo* (Mongolian
bowl shape) bears out its true provenance. Except that the helmet
is joined by rivets and has a bowl of only eight plates, it is of the
same form as the helmet from Kertsch, in the Crimea, found in an
Avarian grave. The Avarian helmet had a neckguard of mail,
while the Japanese had one of small round-headed lamellae.
    In the ninth and tenth centuries, in what is called the Middle

Heian Period, the armour tended to become two distinct styles. That for the foot soldier evolved from the lamellar cuirass of coat form, and the horseman's armour developed from the later lamellar armour with separate side-plates.

All early Japanese armour was lacquered against the wet, usually black, and so far all lacing was carried out with strips of leather. The shapes of lamellae and some methods of lacing are shown in Figure 90.

Later Lamellar Armour

The transition from the early lamellar armours to the distinctive Japanese armour familiar to most people took place in the Middle and Later Heian Period, when the noble warrior-families were becoming powerful and privileged. Their lust for power led Japan into several hundreds of years of internal warfare and bloody strife, with an ever-growing demand on the armourer's skill.

Before Middle Heian times the lamellae of an armour were lacquered before lacing and, when joined together into laminations, had a certain flexibility. The new technique was to lace them into strips first and then lacquer them heavily to make them both rigid and waterproof. This practice probably came about through an increase in the use of tough rawhide (*neri-gawa*) for parts of the armour—for to prevent softening with long exposure to the wet a thorough sealing with lacquer was found to be necessary.

Armour lacing became a distinctive feature of Japanese armour from this time, for the use of dyed and stencilled doeskin, cut into strips and used for joining the laminations together, added rich colouring to the armours.[4] Because leather was difficult to wash and hardened after wetting, substitutes were sought and heavy plaited silk braids were tried as well as strips of folded silk fabrics. The lacing braids or strips of leather were called *odoshige* and the completed lacing of an armour *odoshi*. Lamellae were called *sane* (scales) and the lacing which secured them to each other in laminations *shita-toji* (lower binding).

By Late Heian times, the armour of the wealthy warrior (*bushi* or *samurai*) had developed into the fully fledged *yoroi* or, as we call it today, *ō-yoroi* (great armour) because all of its main features are large (Fig. 91). The helmet bowl (*hachi*), with the inverted cup removed from the top, was low and rounded with a large

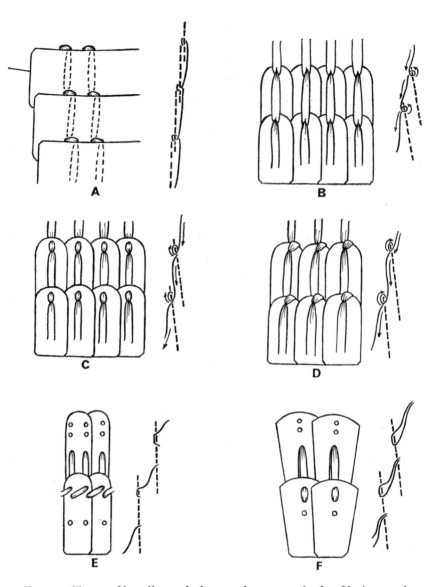

FIG. 90 Types of lamellae and plates and some methods of lacing used in the construction of Japanese *tankō* and *keikō*

A The lacing of solid laminations

B to F Types of *kedate* (erect lacing) used in *keikō*, fifth to tenth centuries

G to I Types of *kedate* used for *keikō*

J Heavy plaited silk lacing of an early *ō-yoroi*, early eleventh century

K *Ō-arame* (large scales and wide lacing) of a late-eleventh-century *ō-yoroi*

L *Shita-toji* (lower binding) of lamellae from an early *keikō*, fifth to sixth centuries

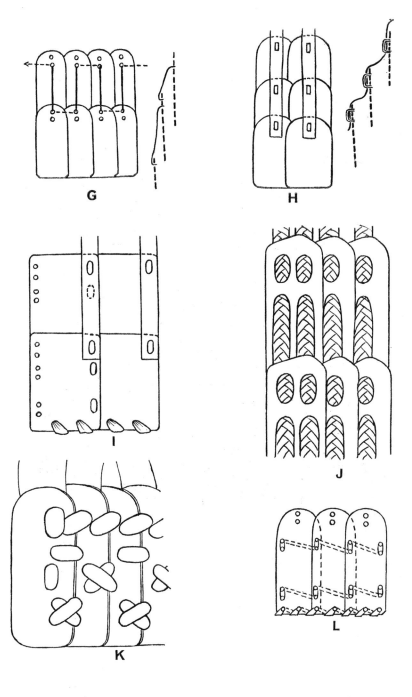

G

H

I

J

K

L

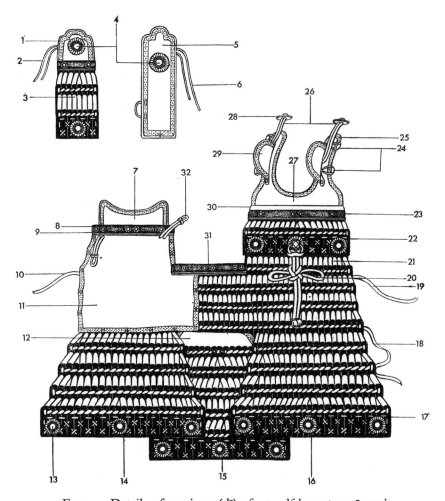

FIG. 91 Details of a cuirass (dō) of a twelfth-century ō-yoroi

1 Kamuri-ita	14 Mae no kusazuri	26 Takihimo
2 Tsuke-o	15 Imuke no kusazuri	27 Oshitsuke
3 Sendan no ita	16 Hikishiki no kusazuri	28 Kohaze
4 Kiku no maru	17 Hishinui no ita	29 Shōji no ita
5 Kyūbi no ita	18 Dō-saki no o	30 Ichimonji
6 Tsuke-o	19 Hikiawase no o	31 Waki-ita
7 Muna-ita	20 Agemaki	32 Takahimo
8 Keshō no ita	21 Dō-saki	33 Tsubo-ita
9 Mizu-hiki	22 Saka-ita	34 Kōmori-tsuke
10 Hikiawase no o	23 Hassō-kanamono	35 Waidate no kusazuri
11 Tsurubashiri	24 Sode-tsuke no kuda	36 Koshi no o
12 Kōmori-tsuke	25 Watagami	37 Tsubo no o
13 Suso-kanamono		

hole in the centre (*tehen*) for the wearer's short queue of hair to pass through.[5] This hole was finished with an ornamental gilded copper rim. The rivets of the bowl had large conical heads (*hoshi*, lit. stars) and simple broad spatulate ornamental gilt strips were laid over the front plate—and sometimes the back plate—secured with large gilt rivets. A gilt ring was fastened to the centre of the back and carried a tasselled cord bow called *agemaki*. To the lower edge, over the face, an iron convex peak was fastened with

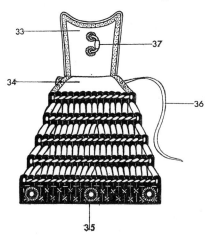

three rivets. It was covered with stencilled doeskin, with a gilt rim (*fukurin*) at the lower edge. A neckguard (*shikoro*) of five curved laminations, with the ends of the upper four turned outwards on either side of the face, prevented a sword from entering between the edges of the laminations and cutting the lacing. These turn-backs, called *fukigayeshi*, were covered with stencilled leather with a chrysanthemum-shaped gilt ornament attached through the upper corner (*kiku no maru*).

Linings were flush fitting and of stencilled leather, with silk cords, for tying the helmet beneath the chin, knotted through holes in the plates on either side of the front plate.

Warriors often protected the face with a brow- and cheekguard (*happuri*), tied behind the head beneath the helmet (*kabuto*), lacquered black outside and red within, or covered with stencilled leather.

The cuirass (*dō*) was made to wrap around the body from the left side, leaving the right side exposed. A separate right side-plate, with its pendent section of laminated skirt, was put on before the rest of the cuirass. The three remaining sections of the skirt were permanently attached to the cuirass at front, back, and left side—the last connected by a strip of stencilled doeskin, as also was that on the right side-section. The right side-piece was a solid iron plate, covered within and without with leather and edged with a gilt rim. Cords, passed through eyeletted holes in the centre of the plate, were tied around the body. The whole section, with its pendent skirt section (*kusazuri*), was called *waidate*.

At the top of the breast section was a solid iron strip attached to the upper row of lamellar with chrysanthemum-headed rivets. This was called *muna-ita* (breastplate) and cords fastened through it, connected with toggles attached by cords to the shoulder straps of padded rawhide on the backplate. Toggles were frequently used for fastening pieces of Japanese armour to each other and were termed *kohaze*. The shoulder-straps (*watagami*) carried loops (*gumi*), for the tying cords of the shoulderguards at the front and centre, and also crescent-shaped standing-plates (*shōji-ita*) to prevent the iron cap-plate of the shoulderpieces from striking the neck.

An apron of stencilled leather covered the front of the cuirass from below the upper breastplate to the waist, and on the backplate a large tasselled bow (*agemaki*) was tied through a gilt ring. Cords from the rear edge of the shoulderguards were tied to the loops of the bow to prevent them from swinging forward.

Guards of different patterns were hung over the shoulder-strap fastenings: at the right, three laminated short plates with a leather-covered iron cap-plate (*sendan*); at the left, a solid iron plate of rectangular shape with a scalloped upper edge (*kyūbi*).

Shoulderguards (Fig. 92) were large and rectangular (*ō-sode*), made with seven rows of lamellae and a transversely curved iron cap-plate (*kamuri-ita*). Cords were fastened to rings inside the upper edge, for tying with special knots to the loops on the shoulder-straps of the cuirass and to the neck of the bow on the backplate. A fourth cord was attached to a ring on the inside of the back edge of the third plate from the top, and these were tied to the loops of the *agemaki* bow.

The older vambraces were discarded, and in the tenth century a close fabric sleeve was worn on the left arm only, with a rounded plate for the back of the hand. In the eleventh century a

Plate XXIX
Japanese Lamellar Armour

A White-and-maroon-laced *ō-yoroi*, *c.* 1400, restored for use *c.* 1800
  Victoria and Albert Museum
B White-leather-laced *ō-yoroi* with solid iron laminations made by
  Myōchin Ki no Munechika between 1779–80. *Collection of the author*
C White-twill-laced *ō-yoroi* made *c.* 1850 in imitation of a late fourteenth-
  century one. *Collection of the author*
D Pink-, green- and white-laced *ō-yoroi* made by Masuda Myōchin Ki no
  Muneharu in 1860 for presentation by the last Tokugawa Shōgun to
  Queen Victoria. *Victoria and Albert Museum* (*Not to scale*)

A

B

C

D

Plate XXX
Japanese 'Modern' Armour

A *Haramaki* of solid iron laminations made for a Christian *daimyō*, Naitō Yukiyasu *c.* 1570. *Tower of London Armouries*

B Red-lacquered *ni-mai-dō* with helmet in the form of a Nichiren monk's cap by Nagasone Masanori, the rest by Myōchin

C Laminated *yokohagi-dō* probably by the Unkai School, late seventeenth century. *Tower of London Armouries*

D *Sendai-dō* laced with helmet signed Myōchin Toshiyuki, eighteenth century. *Collection of L. J. Anderson (Not to scale)*

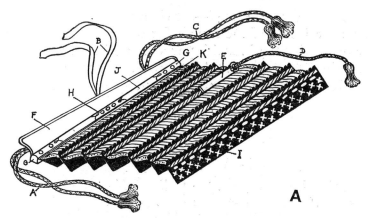

FIG. 92 Types of shoulderguard
A *Ō-sode*

A Kake-o (suspending cord) tied to the fore loop of the cuirass shoulder-strap
B Shōzoku no o (dress cord) tied to the rear loop
C Uke-o (securing cord) tied to the loops of the Agemaki bow on the backplate
D Midzu-nomi no o (water-drinking cord) passed through the loops of the Agemaki and tied to the Agemaki no kwan (large ring on the backplate)

E Kōgai-kanamono
F Kamuri-ita
G Kiūshō-kanamono
H Aida-kanamono
I Hishi-nui no ita

J Keshō no ita (strip of wood covered with leather)
K Mizu-hiki or Ryūmon (double piping of red and white twill)

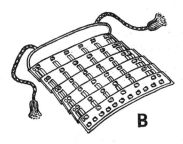

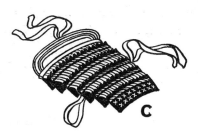

B *Mogami-sode*   C *Tsubo-sode*

second plate was added to the forearm and a small one at the point of the elbow; and soon after another larger one was attached on the part above the elbow. The right arm went unprotected, except for the shoulderpiece—the sleeve of the armour robe being tied in at the wrist. Soft doeskin gloves were worn at all times by *samurai*—the right one having an additional pad on the inside of the thumb for drawing the bowstring, in place of the ring used for this purpose in other Asian countries.

The shins were protected by well-shaped greaves (*suneate*) of three black lacquered iron plates joined by hinges and secured by

FIG. 93 Foot soldier wearing *dō-maru*, late thirteenth century, from the *Moko Shurai Ekotoba Emaki*, Imperial Household Collection

two ties over fabric leggings (*habaki* or *kiahan*). Bear or sealskin boots covered the feet.

The *samurai* was first and foremost a mounted bowman, and his armour was designed for this purpose. At this early date his swords, a long one and a dirk, were but secondary arms.

Infantry were few, being largely made up of lesser *samurai*, their servants (*chugen*), and other poor retainers. Their armour consisted of a simple close-fitting cuirass of lamellar construction, fastening at the right side (*dō-maru*) (Fig. 93). The shoulder-straps were leather covered, as were the upper plates of breast and back; and the skirt was divided into seven sections—three at the front, and four at sides and back. Shoulderguards were small, leather-covered, iron, leaf-shaped plates (*gyōyō*) with gilt rims.

Generals (*taishō*) and other eminent warriors wore crests on the front of their helmets. In their early form they were straight, slender horns with bifurcated ends, springing from a deep crescent-shaped plate bearing a demon's head (*onigashira*), or a dragon (*ryū*) and clouds, etc. In the twelfth century the demon's head was embossed.

The Kamakura Period (1185–1367) saw little change in both forms of armour, except in details and decoration. Helmet-bowls were built up of a greater number of plates and the rivet-heads were slightly smaller. The shape of the *hachi*, or bowl, was more rounded (*zaru-nari*; basket shape) and larger chrysanthemum ornaments were applied to the peak and turn-backs of the neck-guard. These metal fittings were also attached to the shoulder-strap guards, and not infrequently to the lowest plates of shoulderguards and skirt of the cuirass. Bars of silver or copper gilt were also applied across the plates of sleeves or shinguards.

The infantry equipment improved little. Some wore brow- and cheekguards and some plated sleeves in pairs, while the poorer samurai wore a helmet, sometimes shoulderguards, or even full *ō-yoroi*: in fact, lacking nothing but a horse. The infantry *dō-maru* ('round the body') was occasionally copied for men of rank, and one fine early example is preserved at Ōyamazumi-jinsha Shrine. It dates from the second half of the twelfth century and is associated with Minamoto no Yoshitsune (1159–1189), the most famous of leaders in the wars between the Minamoto and Taira clans. It has many features in common with the *ō-yoroi*, having large shoulderguards, the *sendan* and *kyūbi* to guard the shoulder-strap fastenings, and the leather apron on the breast (*tsuru-bashiri*, 'bow string path').

Early in the twelfth century a solid iron plate was added to the cuirass of *ō-yoroi* beneath the left arm, because the armpit had been so exposed when a man was shooting with the bow. This *waki-ita* (side-plate) was, like the other solid portions of the armour (*kanagu-mawari*), covered with leather and edged with a gilded rim.

Armour for the thighs was not introduced before the first half of the thirteenth century. This was called *hiza-yoroi* (knee armour) and later *haidate* (girt shield), several examples being shown in the picture scrolls of the *Heiji Monogatari*,[6] painted in the mid-thirteenth century (Fig. 94). *Hiza-yoroi* was made in the form of a divided apron tied about the waist, with the lower sections, faced with plates of leather or iron, tied round the thighs.

A marked reduction in the size of lamellae, with a consequent increase in the number used for each part of an armour, is very noticeable in the late thirteenth and early fourteenth centuries.

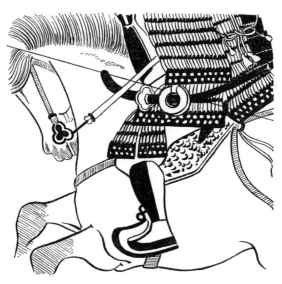

FIG. 94 Detail of a horseman wearing *hiza-yoroi* (knee armour) from the *Heiji Monogatari Emaki,* mid-thirteenth century; Museum of Fine Arts, Boston

As the lacing braid passed vertically through every lamellae, the reduction in their width required a narrower width of the braid.

The silk braid (*ito-odoshi*) was probably woven on a loom by the thirteenth century. A varied and colourful range of patterns had developed for the lacing of armour, and although leather—either plain or stencilled—continued to be used, silk braids, by their richness, were gaining favour.

Changes in tactics brought about many modifications in armour styles in the fourteenth century. Armies were increasing in size and much more fighting was done on foot with the sword and curved spear (*naginata*). The Kamakura Period lasted until 1367, but there is another name for the period bridging this and the next (Muromachi Period, 1368–1567) which is more apt—for from 1336 until 1392 Japan was torn by two factions, the South (*Nan-chō*) and North (*Hoku-chō*), supporting two imperial dynasties—namely, the Namboku-chō Period, when such loyalists as Kusunoki no Masashige and his sons gave their all for the old Emperor Go-Daigo.

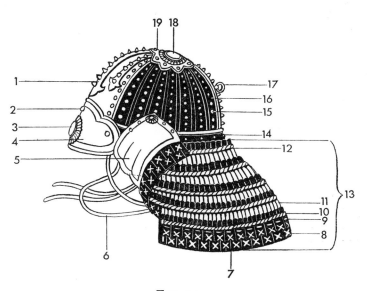

FIG. 95

A Details of the *gomai-kabuto* of the eleventh to thirteenth century

1	Shinodare	11	Kedate
2	Sankō no byō	12	Hachitsuke no ita
3	Kiku no maru	13	Shikoro
4	Mabezashi	14	Koshimaki
5	Fukigayeshi	15	Hoshi (rivets, lit. 'stars')
6	Kabuto no o	16	Hachi (helmet-bowl)
7	Katazuri	17	Kasa-jirushi no kwan
8	Hishinui no ita	18	Tehen
9	Uname	19	Tehen no kanamono
10	Karame		

A type of helmet was developed in the second quarter of the fourteenth century made without large rivet-heads, so that only the flanged edges (*suji*) of the plates stood up above the lacquered surface of the bowl. The old knobbed helmets were called *hoshi-kabuto* and the ridged bowls *suji-kabuto* (Fig. 95). The shape of the helmet-bowl was still low and rounded, but the hole in the crown was made smaller, for in the second half of the thirteenth century the warrior untied his queue when putting on his helmet

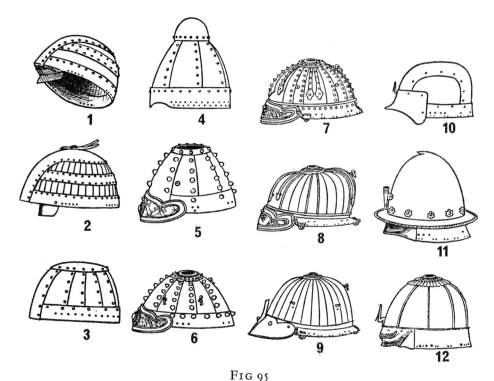

FIG 95

B Types of *hachi* (helmet-bowl)

1 *Shōkakufu-hachi* with horizontal plates, fourth to sixth century
2 *Shōkakufu-hachi* with intermediate rows of vertical plates, sixth to eighth century
3 *Shōkakufu-hachi* with vertical plates, eighth to tenth century
4 *Moko-hachi-gyo* (Mongol shape), eighth to ninth century
5 Early form of *hoshi-kabuto* with large *tehen*, late tenth to eleventh century
6 *Hoshi-kabuto*, twelfth to thirteenth century, later called *shii-nari*
7 *Hoshi-kabuto*, late thirteenth to early fifteenth century, called *Ō-boshi*
8 *Suji-kabuto*, fourteenth to early sixteenth century, later called *Akodanari*
9 *Suji-kabuto*, sixteenth to nineteenth century, later called *kōshōzan*
10 *Sanmai-kabuto* of Hineno type, sixteenth to nineteenth century
11 *Namban-kabuto* converted European morion mounted back to front, late sixteenth century and seventeenh century
12 Heavy shotproof helmet of Haruta School type, late sixteenth century and early seventeenth century

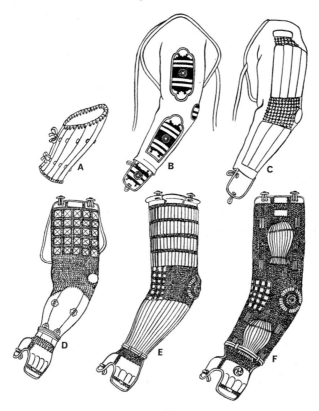

FIG. 96 Types of *kote* (armour sleeve)
A Protohistoric vambrace of laced splints, fifth to seventh century
B *Yoshitsune-gote* as worn with *ō-yoroi,* eleventh to thirteenth
   century
C Early *shino-gote* as worn with *dō-maru,* thirteenth to fifteenth
   century
D *Tsutsu-gote,* late fifteenth century to nineteenth century
E Later *shino-gote,* sixteenth century to nineteenth century
F *Oda-gote,* sixteenth century to nineteenth century

and the hole, with its decorative rim, remained simply as an ornament. The neckguard was made broader and the turn-backs at either side were folded right back so that they almost laid upon it.

Two new additions to the armour were the mask for chin and cheeks which left the eyes and nose uncovered, called *hōate,* usually with a pendent throatguard of iron lamellae attached. In addition to this, many wore an independent throatguard attached to a ring tied at the back of the neck (*nodowa,* lit. 'throat ring'). It covered the exposed upper part of chest and throat and was worn either beneath or over the breastplate (*muna-ita*).

Mail (*kusari*) first makes its appearance in the fourteenth century. This was constructed of round and elliptical rings, the latter sometimes doubled. It was at first used to connect the plates of the sleeves (*kote*) (Fig. 96); but whatever part of the armour it was used for, at any date, it was always mounted upon fabric.

Splints were used on sleeves instead of solid plates and plate extensions were attached to the shinguards to protect the knees (*tateage-suneate*).[7] (Fig. 107[1].)

The wearing of foot soldiers' *dō-maru* (Fig. 97) by men of all ranks began in the first half of the fourteenth century, and the fashion steadily gained in popularity as more and more actions were fought on foot. The ridged helmet was that usually found with *dō-maru*, and as the century proceeded the shape of the neck-guard became flatter and the turn-backs were halved in size. With the lighter armour, the neckguard was sometimes reduced to three plates (*san-mai-kabuto*, 'three-plate helmet')—the older five-plate type (*go-mai-kabuto*, 'five-plate helmet') continuing to be used with *ō-yoroi*. *Ō-yoroi* reached a high standard of richness and beauty in the second half of the century. Large pierced, engraved, and chiselled mounts of copper gilt (*kanamono*) were applied to helmets, shoulderguards, and the lowest plates of the pendent skirt sections. Fine mounts were also applied to sleeve-plates, and a magnificent pair of these is preserved at Kasuga Shrine, Nara. Stencilled leather, with patterns of lions, blossoms and foliage, and brilliant lacings gave to Japanese armour a richness never attained before or since and a standard of craftsmanship which the great smiths of later years tried in vain to imitate (see Pl. XXVIII, B). Most of these armours were made in Nara.

Another light, close-fitting cuirass, similar to the *dō-maru*, was the *haramaki* (Fig. 98), which opened at the centre of the back instead of at the right side. This, primarily designed for footmen, was soon equipped with shoulderguards, helmet, and all other additional pieces worn by the *samurai*. In many instances a narrow backplate (*se-ita*) was made to cover the back opening, but was regarded by many as a 'coward's plate'. A smaller version still was the *hara-ate*, or bellyguard, for breast and sides only, with a single short tasset or *kusazuri* over the privates. It was fastened across

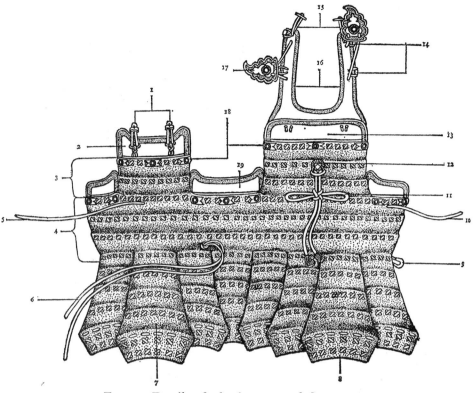

FIG. 97 Details of a leather-covered *dō-maru, c.* 1400

1	Takahimo no kohaze	11	Agemaki
2	Muna-ita	12	Agemaki-tsuke no kwan
3	Tate-age	13	Oshitsuke no ita
4	Nagagawa	14	Sodetsuke no kuda
5	Hikiawase no o	15	Takahimo
6	Kurijime no o	16	Watagami
7	Kusazuri	17	Gyōyō
8	Hishinui no ita	18	Hassō-kanamono
9	Kurijime no kwan	19	Waki-ita
10	Hikiawase no o		

the back with crossed braces and the oversash or belt (*uwa-obi*) through which the dirk was thrust. When introduced in the Nanboku-chō period, it was worn by the infantry.

The horns on the front of the helmet became more common. They were curved and much broader than older ones when put on *ō-yoroi*, some reaching extreme proportions (*ō-kuwagata*). But with *dō-maru* and *haramaki* they were smaller and more restrained in most cases. It was also customary in the late fourteenth and

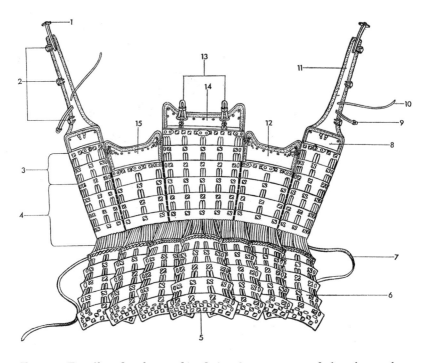

Fig. 98 Details of a *haramaki* of the first quarter of the sixteenth
century

1 Takahimo no kohaze	9 Sei-ita-tsuke no o
2 Sode-tsuke no kuda	10 Hikiawase no o
3 Tate-age	11 Watagami
4 Nagagawa	12 Waki-ita
5 Hishinui no ita	13 Takahimo
6 Kusazuri	14 Muna-ita
7 Dō-saki no o	15 Waki-ita
8 Oshitsuke	

fifteenth centuries to wear a central crest in the form of a classical
sword blade (*ken*), the horns and central crest being termed *mitsu-
kuwagata*.

From the footmen, again, the *samurai* copied the custom of
wearing a pair of sleeves (*kote*)—for with the increase in fighting
with sword and spear both arms needed protection.[8]

For the greater part of the fifteenth century and the first quarter
of the sixteenth century the knobbed helmet was out of favour
and the ridged bowl steadily increased in height at the back,
creating quite a balloonlike appearance when viewed from
behind. In its earlier development, about 1400, it was called

FIG. 99 Types of *shikoro* (neckguard)

A Tenth century to early fourteenth century, to the left a single
 lamellae from the upper plate attached to the helmet-bowl
B *Ō-manjū-jikoro* (large rounded), fourteenth century and fifteenth
 century
C *Kasa-jikoro* (spreading like a hat), fourteenth and fifteenth cen-
 turies
D *Komanjū-jikoro* (small rounded) sixteenth to nineteenth century
E *Ichimanjū-jikoro* (one rounded) or *Hineno-manjū*, sixteenth to nine-
 teenth century
F *Hineno-jikoro*, sixteenth to nineteenth century

akoda-nari; and by 1500, in its more developed form, *dzu-nari* or
'head shape' (Fig. 95, 8). The neckguards with these helmets were
very flat and, by their name *kasa-jikoro*, likened to the Japanese
hat (*kasa*) (Fig. 99ᶜ).

Later Plate Armour

The *Ōnin no ran*, or War of Ōnin, which lasted throughout the
whole Ōnin era from 1467 until 1477, had much to do with the
great changes in armour styles which began in the second half of
the fifteenth century and continued throughout the sixteenth.
Through ambitious retainers turning on and overthrowing their
lords, many new *samurai* families came into being. This was a
common happening in the Muromachi and Momoyama Periods,
and many a name to be heard today in aristocratic Japanese circles
(where titles are now abolished) began their rise to power in this
period of violence and sweeping change.

Amongst the developments in armour styles was the substitu-
tion of solid plates for lamellar construction. This does not mean
that lamellar went out altogether, but it was used less. The solid
plates, or *ita-mono*, were of iron or tough rawhide and were
frequently cut along the top edge and moulded on the face side
with lacquer to represent rows of lamellae. The old *ō-yoroi*
vanished from the battlefields of Japan because it was unsuitable
for the changing warfare. Large shoulderguards were replaced
with smaller types: one close fitting at the top and wider at the
bottom (*chu-sode*), and the other—usually made with *haramaki*—
rounded to the shoulder and arm and tapered towards the bottom
(*tsubo-sode*).

The plates of both *dō-maru* and *haramaki* were made of iron,
with each section of the cuirass hinged in four places so that they
could be open to admit the body and closed in the usual way.
Although the old close lacing continued to be used for solid plate
armours, it was soon realized that the large number of holes that
had to be made in a plate were a very real source of weakness—
and so the wide-spaced pairs of braids were introduced to reduce
this to the minimum. The old lacing was called *kebiki* ('hair
spread over') and the new fashion *sugake* ('sparse pointed').[9]

Reduction of weight was—until the introduction of firearms—
the prime consideration of the *samurai*, and so the neckguards of
helmets were made close fitting (*Hineno-jikoro*), shoulderguards

were replaced by small close-fitting defences attached to the upper sleeve (*Bishamon-gote*), and cuirasses were made in two sections—hinged at the left and tying at the right. The tassets, or skirt sections over the hips and upper thighs, were of seven to eleven parts, each of five plates. The *agemaki* bow on the backplate was no longer required, but the ring at the back of the helmet to which streamerlike badges (*kasa-jirushi*) were attached was generally retained. The bow was said to stop the ring from rattling.

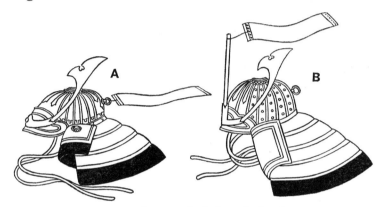

FIG. 100 *Kasajirushi* (helmet badges)
A Attached to the *Kasajirushi* no kwan
B Attached to a stick mounted in the fore-crest socket, from the *Gun-yō-ki*

The thigh armour was faced with leather or iron small plates or lamellae and mail. Some *samurai* preferred breeches with mail and plates sewn to the front, which were less cumbersome to wear. Splints mounted upon fabric, or mail and fabric, formed comfortable shinguards, and socks and straw sandals replaced the old horseman's fur boots.

Cuirasses were greatly simplified and made to fit the torso better. Solid lames of iron, sometimes made to represent lamellae of various sizes, were joined with close, wide-spaced or crossed laces (*hishi-nui*) and even riveted solidly together (*okegawa-dō*). This last type was made with horizontal plates (*yokohagi-dō*) or with vertical plates (*tatehagi-dō*).

In 1542–3 the Portuguese arrived at the island of Tanegeshima and introduced the matchlock musket to the governor. Under their guidance the first Japanese muskets were made, and before

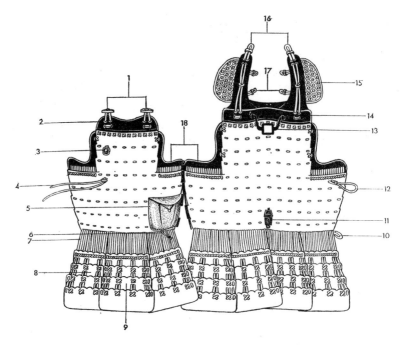

FIG. 101 Details of the *dō* of a *tosei-gusoku* (modern armour)

1 Aibiki no kohaze	10 Kurijime no Kwan
2 Muna-ita	11 Machiuke
3 Saihai no kwan	12 Takahimo
4 Takahimo	13 Gattari
5 Tsuru-bukuro	14 Watagami no yoko-ita
6 Kurijime no neo	15 Kohire or Kata-ate
7 Yurugi-ito	16 Aibiki no o
8 Kusazuri or Gesan	17 Kote-tsuke no neo
9 Kinkakushi	18 Waki-ita or Kanagu no mawari

very long their manufacture spread to other centres where sword-smiths and armourers tried their hand at improving this new weapon.

Most armourers were more concerned with producing armour that would withstand the new threat, and the answer was probably found by the leading school—the Myōchin family, who had risen to eminence in the first years of the sixteenth century.[10]

The best armour was made from plates of soft iron faced with hard steel, the two welded together to make a sound defence against most known weapons. It could be made of any thickness required by the armourer's patron and stood up well to tests made with bullets fired at close range. Test-marks (*tameshi*) are not uncommon on pieces made in the late sixteenth and early seventeenth centuries.

A new type of helmet with deep sides was developed in the first half of the sixteenth century, built up of from eight to seventy-two plates, usually made with a flange on the exposed edges. This was the *kōshōzan*, or 'high victory mountain', type. Some makes were taller than others, just as some had rather flattened tops to the crowns and others—particularly those by *Myōchin Nobuiye* and his pupils—were more rounded. The hole in the top (*tehen*) was now very much smaller and the ornamental fittings reduced in size. The helmet peak was no longer covered and had a flanged edge. Gilt rims were out of favour for most parts of the armour they were formerly applied to.

All iron not lacquered was given a russet finish—a practice adhered to in later years by smiths who wished to display the high standard of their work. Flaws and fire scars could be obscured with lacquer, and Sakakibara Kōzan recommended his readers to inspect all armour made for them before it was lacquered, for this very reason.

The half-mask (*mempō*) with a nosepiece was in use in the second half of the fifteenth century. It was made with a detachable nose for converting it into a *hōate*. Some whole masks were made in the late Muromachi Period, but were not popular, for they restricted vision. The most popular of all masks was the *hambō*— a very small guard for the chin and lower part of the cheeks. Its prime purpose was to enable the helmet to be tied more tightly about the face.

The helmet-lining was of leather or closely stitched fabric, attached to the edge of the bowl with strengthening crossed straps above it. The helmet-cord was attached to three, four, or five rings or cord loops on the helmet-brim. Its length was from about six to nine feet, varying with the method employed for securing the helmet to the head. There were many different ideas on the subject and pegs, hooks, and loops had to be fastened to the masks to assist the operation. As the helmet-bowl was somewhat larger than the small, ancient ones, a headcloth (*hachimaki*) was put around the head to act as a shock-absorber.[11]

Hoshi-kabuto, or knobbed helmets, were reintroduced in the late Muromachi Period, built up from thirty-two to seventy-two plates, with as many as thirty small conical rivet-heads on each plate, carefully graded in size, with the largest at the bottom and the smallest at the top. Each rivet passed through two overlapping plates, so that these high-sided *hoshi-kabuto* were of very great strength and, if the number of those surviving is anything to judge by, extremely popular.

As well as the remarkable multiplate helmets, there were those

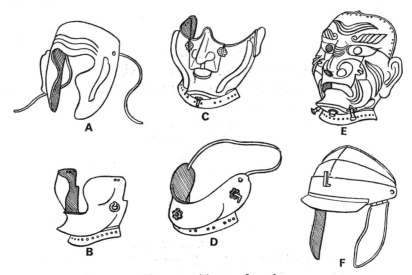

FIG. 102 Types of mask
A *Happuri*, tenth to fourteenth century
B *Hōate*, fourteenth to sixteenth century
C *Mempō*, late fifteenth century to nineteenth century
D *Hambō*, second half of sixteenth century to nineteenth century
E *Sōmen*, late fifteenth century to nineteenth century
F *Hanburi*, a substitute for a helmet, sixteenth century to nineteenth century

made from only three or four plates. Both the Hineno and Haruta schools specialized in such helmets, which, although made in large numbers for munition armours, were also used by men of rank, who had them disguised with fanciful applied shapes in paper, wood, leather, and lacquer.

The Hineno helmet consisted of two side-plates joined by a broad one running from front to back. A brim-plate (*koshimaki*, lit. loin-wrap) was applied round the lower edge and a concave peak (*mabesashi*) over this in front, rising high on the brow like a reinforce (Fig. 95, 10). The neckguard normally found on these helmets, and many others of contemporary fashion, were also a

Plate XXXI

Japanese 'Modern' Armour

A *Yokohagi-dō* by Myōchin O-Sumi no Kami Fujiwara no Munesada in 1653. *Tower of London Armouries*

B *Uchidashi* (embossed) armour by Myōchin Ki no Muneakira in 1727. *Wade Collection, Snowshill Manor, Gloucestershire*

C Purple-laced *ni-mai-dō* with helmet signed Yamato no Kami Fujiwara Ietsugu, c. 1850–60. *Collection of L. J. Anderson*

D *Tatami-gusoku* (folding armour) with helmet by Saotome Iesada the remainder by Myōchin Muneyasu in 1837. *Maidstone Museum, Kent (Not to scale)*

A

B

C   D

Plate XXXII

Japanese 'Modern' Armour

A Yellow-laced *dō-maru* made for an Ito Daimyō of Okada
probably by the Hōjō School, *c.* 1800. *Collection of L. J. Anderson*
B Light-blue-laced *nuinobe-dō* mounted for a Kobayakawa Daimyō,
c. 1725. *Manchester University Museum*
C Dark-blue-laced *haramaki* with helmet bowl by Saotome Ietada,
c. 1850. *Victoria and Albert Museum*
D Flame-red laced leather armour decorated with hares gambolling
over waves made for one of the Mori Daimyō of Saiki, *c.* 1850.
Collection of L. J. Anderson (*Not to scale*)

Hineno invention. They were concave and close fitting, of from five to seven plates, laced with close or widely spaced lacing.

Helmets of the second half of the sixteenth century—of the 'Age of Battles', as it was called—tend to be of the simplest construction, for it was in this period that those shaped like tall *samurai* caps (*eboshi-nari*), peach-shaped (*momo-nari*), plum-shaped

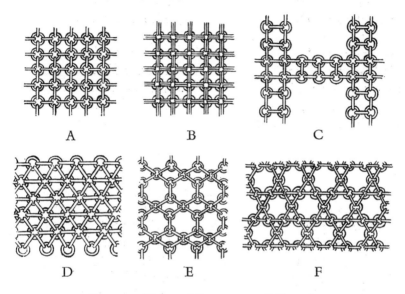

A   B   C

D   E   F

FIG. 103 Types of Japanese mail (*kusari*)
A *Hitoye-gusari* or *fusa-gusari*
B *Futaye-gusari*
C *Kaushi-gusari*
D *Hana-gusari* or *asa no ha-gusari*
E *Kame-kō-gusari*
F *Kagome-gata-gusari*

(*uma-nari*), nut-shaped (*shii-nari*), etc., were introduced. All were simple in make and seldom displayed a high standard of craftsmanship. Armour was wanted in large quantities—and providing it had defensive qualities, the interior finish did not matter.

Mail and splints were used widely for sleeves, thigh armour and shinguards; also, mail shirts (*kusari-katabira*) and hoods, or folding armours built up of small plates and mail (*tatami-gusoku*), were issued to bodies of infantry. Many of the foot soldiers were issued with a conical iron or leather lacquered hat (*jingasa*) and a simple iron cuirass of *okegawa* type. These infantry armours were called *kachi-gusoku* (infantry armour); *ashigaru-gusoku* (common soldier armour); or, if they opened at the back like a *haramaki*, they were termed *hata-ashigara-gusoku*. Some consisted of helmet or war-hat and cuirass, while others were more or less complete armours. It all depended on the wearer's status as a warrior.[12]

Portuguese and Spanish visitors became quite common in the second half of the sixteenth century and these were followed by the Protestant Dutch and English, who came solely for trade without interest in politics or religion.

With these 'southern barbarians'—as the Europeans were called—came pieces of European armour, which were acquired as gifts or by trade. Those that survive are either of Dutch or Italian make and, it would seem, largely consist of morion, collar, and cuirass. The morions are of the type called Spanish, with back-turned stalk at the apex of the crown and with either flat or up-curved brim. The cuirasses, like that incorporated in an armour of the Shōgun Ieyasu at Tōshō-gū Shrine, Nikkō, and another in the Metropolitan Museum, New York, are of deep peascod form. Later in the seventeenth century short-waisted cuirasses were altered and copied. The European gorget or collar was made into an *uwa-manchira* and worn over the cuirass, not beneath as was originally intended.

Japanese neckguards and peaks were added to these helmets, and pendent *kusazuri* attached to the cuirasses. Many *namban-gusoku* were entirely of Japanese make and several features of foreign origin were reproduced until armour was finally discarded.

From *namban-dō*, with their medial ridge to the breastplate, was evolved the *hatomune-dō* or pigeon-breasted cuirass, which was a solid iron cuirass of typical Japanese character with a medial ridge to the breast—either *nimai-dō* (two-piece cuirass, with hinge at the left) or *gomai-dō* (five-plate, with four hinges). Other cuirasses were made like these without the ridged breastplate, the most outstanding being the *Yukinoshita-dō* invented by Myōchin Hisaiye of Yukinoshita, in Sagami Province. This was a five-piece cuirass of hard steel-faced iron, rather straight sided, with iron shoulder-straps with hinged extensions for the points of the shoulders (*kohire*), and guards for the cord fastenings to the breastplate (*gyōyō*). The pendent *kusazuri* were all of plain iron plates with flanged edges. A cuirass by this maker, dated 1592, is in the collection of Mr L. J. Anderson of London. A series of sixteenth-century cuirasses are given in Fig. 105.

Very few armours made after about 1570 have shoulderguards, except for a classical form of *dō-maru* which it would seem were made especially for presentation. Two such armours were sent to King James I of England and VI of Scotland in 1613 and are now in the Tower of London. Another is in the Armeria Reale, Turin,

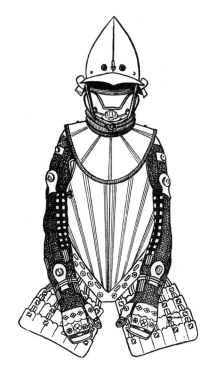

FIG. 104 *Namban-gusoku* of Tokugawa no Ieyasu containing morion, gorget, and cuirass of European make, late sixteenth century, Toshō-gu Shrine, Nikkō

and three more are in the Musée de l'Armée in Paris. They are all in the fashion of about 1500 and fitted with large shoulderguards. The Tower armours are both by Iwai Yozaemon of Nambu. The Iwai, like the Haruta, are first recorded as armour-makers in the Muromachi Period.

The Momoyama Period (1568–1614)—or the Middle Period, as Japanese historians call it—would have been rather colourless as far as the armour is concerned if it had not been for the elaborate crests and flags which became so popular with the simplification of armour.

Armour lacing was made of the durable dark and medium blue

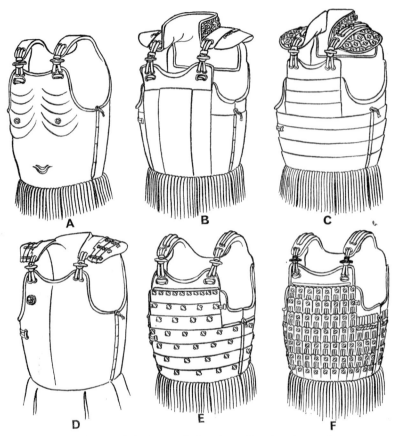

FIG. 105 Types of *dō* (cuirass) developed in the sixteenth century

A *Niwa-dō*   D *Hatomune-dō*
B *Tate-hagi-dō*   E *Hishinui-dō*
C *Yoko-hagi-dō*   F *Nuinobe-dō*

silk braids or of dyed leather in similar shades. Green, brown, white or black were also favoured. Purple was used for the armour of men of rank, such as *daimyō*, but as with black and rotted leaf colour—a shade of brown—the dyes rotted the silk rather quickly.

The backplate of the cuirass, freed of the large *agemaki* bow of earlier days, was fitted with a bracket at the back of the shoulders and a socket at the waist, into which a tube was put for inserting a bamboo shaft with right-angle bracket for a small flag (*sashi-mono*). This *sashimono* carried the wearer's badge (*mon*) or, if he were an ordinary soldier, that of his lord.

Helmet-crests were more personal devices—and although frequently only a simple gilt or silvered sun or moon disc attached to a bracket in front (*mayedate-mono*), some were quite elaborate and fastened to the top of the helmet (*kashira-date*), at the sides (*waki-date*), or at the back (*ushiro-date*). Amongst the more popular forms of side-crests were stag antlers and buffalo horns made of lacquered wood or leather. Dragons' and demons' heads were favoured for the front; and after Toyotomi Hideyoshi's campaigns in Korea in 1592 and 1597, the Chinese type of hair or feather crest was sometimes worn in the *tehen* as a *kashira-date*.

Internal peace was finally established in Japan by Tokugawa Ieyasu in 1603, and there followed about two hundred and fifty years of unbroken peace. The last battle, the largest ever fought in Japan, took place at Sekigahara in October 1600. Tokugawa Ieyasu brought eighty thousand men into the field against the forces supporting Toyotomi Hideyori, which consisted of a hundred and thirty thousand men. When the slaughter finished, Hideyori's army was routed, leaving thirty thousand dead behind and hundreds of heads to be inspected by Ieyasu and his command. This was the famous occasion when he put on his helmet —a converted morion—and created the Japanese proverb 'After victory tighten the cords of the helmet'.

Ancient and Modern

Ancient armour was called *yoroi* and modern armour *gusoku* (a complete set or equipment). Modern (*tosei*) is used to denote armour made after 1568, although many later armours were made in the ancient fashion and were simply classified as *sane-yoroi* as opposed to armour of plate.

The loyal supporters of Ieyasu were rewarded with large estates and, in turn, assisted in the organization and administration of the country. It was a feudal state ruled over by the Shōgun, supposedly appointed by the Emperor. But in Ieyasu's case he was self-appointed, and until 1867 the Emperor lived in seclusion without any authority.

The *samurai* were, in most cases, better off than they had ever been and their prosperity is reflected in the quality of their arms and armour made during the Edo Period (1603–1867).

Quite early in the seventeenth century certain ancient features were revived. These were low rounded helmet-bowls, shoulder-guards, close lacing, and metal fittings of silver or copper gilt or soft metal alloys, such as the blue-black *shakudō*. Wide-spreading rounded neckguards and *agemaki* bows on backplates were re-introduced, both conflicting with the *sashimono* staff and brackets.

In spite of the fact that presentation armours had been made with shoulderguards in the sixteenth century, when revived for use with ordinary armours the makers made extraordinary mis-

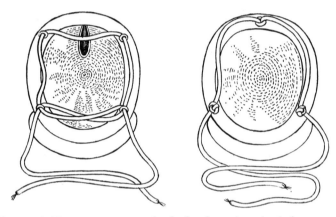

FIG. 106 Two common methods for fastening the helmet cord
A *Yotsu-tsuke* (four-loop fastening)
B *Mitsu-tsuke* (three-loop fastening)

takes in the provision of loops for their attachment.[13] The mistakes were, in fact, many—for, in spite of the large numbers of early armours resting in temples and shrines all over the country, where they had been deposited as votive offerings, the armourers and their patrons do not appear to have made any attempt to examine them, relying almost completely on poor illustrations in historical works and paintings.

The Myōchin school, above all others, gained fame as metal-workers of the highest order, receiving the patronage of the wealthiest in the land. The Haruta, the Iwai, and other lesser armourers, turned their hand to the mounting and tailoring of armour produced by the Myōchin, who were thus able to con-centrate on the all-important smithwork. Unfortunately, Myōchin Kunimichi (1624–43) and his successors, Munesuke (1688–1735) and Muneakira (1673–1745), turned to the production of ugly and impracticable embossed (*uchidashi*) armour. The work of these

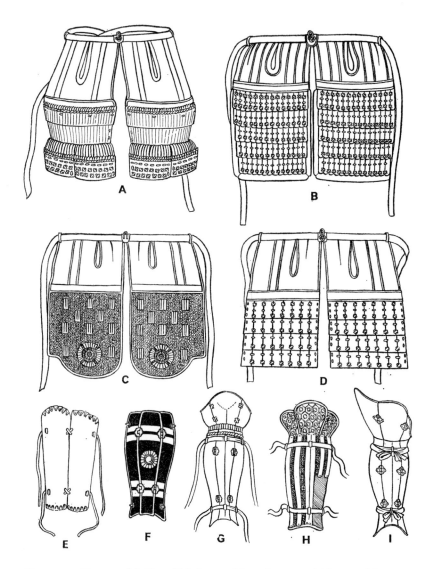

Fig. 107 Types of *haidate* (thighguards) and *suneate* (shinguards)
A *Hiza-yoroi*, thirteenth century and fourteenth century
B *Kawara-haidate*, sixteenth century to nineteenth century
C *Etchū-haidate* or *kusari-haidate*, sixteenth to nineteenth century
D *Iyo-haidate* or *ita-haidate*, fifteenth to nineteenth century
E Protohistoric shinguard
F *Tsutsu-suneate*, eleventh to fourteenth century
G *Tsutsu-suneate* or *Bishamon-suneate*, fifteenth to nineteenth century
H *Shino-suneate*, fifteenth to nineteenth century
I *Ō-tateage no suneate*, fourteenth to fifteenth century and
late seventeenth to nineteenth century

smiths, if not beautiful, is in many instances remarkable. Although famous for artistic ironwork, the armours of Munesuke would not be so outstanding without the splendid metal fittings (*kana-mono*) of Haruta Tamba. Muneakira left several splendid helmets and cuirasses. One of his specialities was helmets in the form of seashells, and a fine specimen—a large conical wreath shell—is on an armour by him in the Wade Collection at Snowshill Manor, Gloucestershire.

The embossed ornamentation of cuirasses was confined, usually, to the centre of the breastplate. This decoration took the form of figures of deities—Shinto or Buddhist—dragons, and other mythical creatures attributed with some remarkable power, and protective *bonji*: debased Sanskrit characters, each used to symbolize the name of a Buddhist divinity.

The publication of the *Honchō Gunkikō* by Arai Hakuseki in the early eighteenth century gave the *samurai* an added interest in the early military equipment. This, the first history of arms and armour in Japanese, illustrated and described many of the armours preserved in shrines and temples. For the first time, the *samurai* were aware of *ō-yoroi*, *dō-maru*, *haramaki*, and *hara-ate*. To begin with, the desire for *dō-maru* seems to have been far greater than for other kinds, perhaps because it was closer in style to the armour they were most familiar with, and also because there were no problems involved in its manufacture.

Dō-maru of the first half of the eighteenth century had the wrong fastening for the shoulderguards, but were otherwise handsome and very wearable armours. The helmet-bowls were usually of sixteenth-century multiplate high-sided type, although some had early attempts at ancient low rounded bowls, with or without knobs.

Kote, or sleeves, were of fifteenth-century *tsutsu-gote* pattern, with three hinged fitted plates on the forearm. Shoulderguards

FIG. 108 Japanese helmet shapes
A Ko-yui-eboshi (small tied cap)
B Mukō-shika (stag's face)
C Jōtō (military head)
D Tsubo-nari (jar shape)
E Kaburi-ya no kabuto (whistling arrow helmet)
F Waku-ito (spool of thread)
G Kasshiki-gashira (Zen novice's head)
H Ni-Ō-tō (legendary divinity's head)

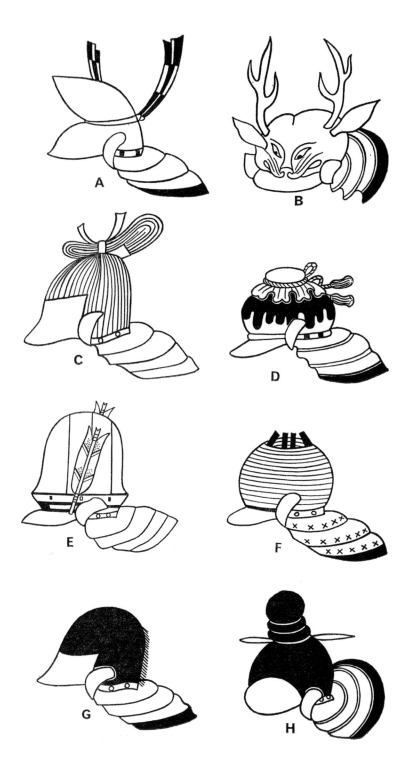

A

B

C

D

E

F

G

H

were either the large rectangular *ō-sode*, the broad-based medium *chu-sode*, or the tapering *tsubo-sode* generally associated with *hara-maki* in the Muromachi Period.

Masks were almost always the half-masks with nosepiece (*mempō*), and *sendan* and *kyūbi* of *ō-yoroi* were often used on *dō-maru* in place of the leaf-shaped *gyōyō* to cover the shoulder-strap fastenings. Thighguards (*haidate*) were of closely laced rigid laminations of lamellae construction (*odoshi-haidate*) or of iron or leather rectangular plates in five rows. These were either flat plates or of 'S' section, like roof tiles (*kawara-haidate*). Plate shin-guards were preferred to the plainer splinted and mail ones. They were of three well-fitted sections, joined with hinges, and with extensions to cover the front of the knee. These were called *tsutsu* (tubular) or *Bishamon-suneate* (after the God of Felicity) or had very large kneeguards, *ō-tateage no suneate*.

The ordinary *samurai* seldom aspired to rich *sane-yoroi*, being content with good, serviceable armours in the Momoyama style with shoulderguards added. He achieved his individuality by having one of the many different helmet shapes available or by wearing a striking crest on a strong multiplate helmet.

Kaga Provincial armourers specialized in fine armour of russet iron, inlaid with patterns in gold and silver (*zōgan*, damascene), engraved and overlaid patterns, also in gold and silver, and applied and pierced ornament generally splashed with white bronze (*sawari*). Borders and ribs on helmet-bowls were roped in the European manner.

The Kaga helmet could be of quite orthodox shape, but many were of a form of *namban-bachi* (foreign bowl) which would appear to be a confusion of Chinese, Korean, and European hats and helmets. Some of these were quite obviously taken from the European copotain hat of the late sixteenth and early seventeenth centuries, and others were a combination of copotain hat and morion. Korean hats and brimmed helmets frequently had applied cusped ribs in imitation of the plates of Korean helmets, but they were here only slender ornamental overlays.

Sleeves from Kaga were distinctive and very common. Having been a popular type, they were copied in all parts of the country. Their main features were large, fluted, gourd-shaped plates on fore and upper arm, set into the mail and surrounded with little ribbed rectangular plates called, for obvious reasons, rafts (*ikada*).

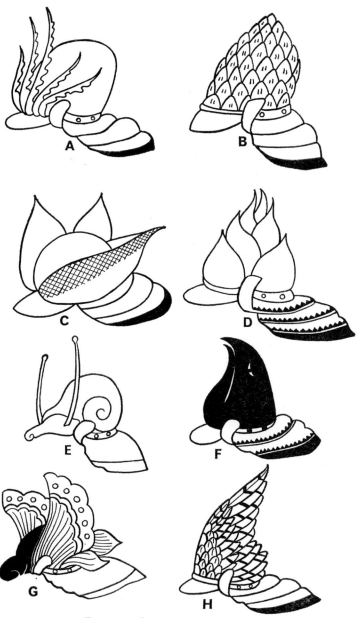

FIG. 109 Japanese helmet shapes
A Taku no kabuto (octopus helmet)
B Matsu-fuguki or Matsu-kasa (pine cone)
C Hōzuki (ground chestnut)
D Shijiyui or Murasaki-takenoko (purple bamboo shoot)
E Katasumuri (snail)
F Tobi-gashira (kite head)
G Chō no kabuto (butterfly helmet)
H Toriwa no kabuto (bird-wing helmet)

Their handguards were rather broad and squat, with embossed ridges on the knuckles. *Kaga-kote* with splints on the forearms, and also splinted shinguards, frequently had circular plates pierced with flower designs between the splints.

In the second half of the eighteenth century the *daimyō* and wealthier *samurai* indulged more and more in the acquiring of 'ancient' armours, paying large sums in gold for genuine pieces to be combined in the *ensemble*. Genuine helmet-bowls from before the sixteenth century were hard to find and, in consequence, fakes were produced and aged by artificial means.

An *ō-yoroi* in the Victoria and Albert Museum and a *dō-maru* in the Museum für Völkerkunde at Vienna are examples of old armours completely relacquered, relaced, and restored for use. They may have been ancestral armours or—like another in the Metropolitan Museum—acquired by exchange from a temple for a piece of land and restored to their present condition.[14]

Hybrids, such as the *ō-yoroi* in the author's collection, were not uncommon. This armour, by Myōchin Munechika in 1779–80, is constructed like a solid-plate transitional *dō-maru* of the late Muromachi Period, with hinges in the plates of the cuirass and widely spaced white leather lacing. It has the form of a lamellar armour combined with the simplicity of an armour of the 'Age of Battles' (Pl. XXIX, B).

The numerous books written for the education and guidance of *samurai*, dealing with arms and armour and their use, rules, and etiquette governing military behaviour, etc., led to the revival of many ancient fashions and customs. Most of this knowledge had no place in Edo times, for it had died long before or with the War of Ōnin, and the whole manner of conducting war had changed. It was, however, a time of peace, and the more elaborate the ceremony of parades became the greater the appeal they had to the tradition-worshipping *samurai*.

Gorgeously mounted and laced *ō-yoroi* were the final attainment of the armourers of the Edo Period. They were inspired by the masterpieces of the second half of the fourteenth century, but with their structural faults they could never attain the functional perfection of the originals. Nor were the large, gilt mounts any more than poor imitations. They were parade armours, at best; and with the threat of foreign invasion and growing dissatisfaction with the Shōgunate, sensible *daimyō* and *samurai* had new

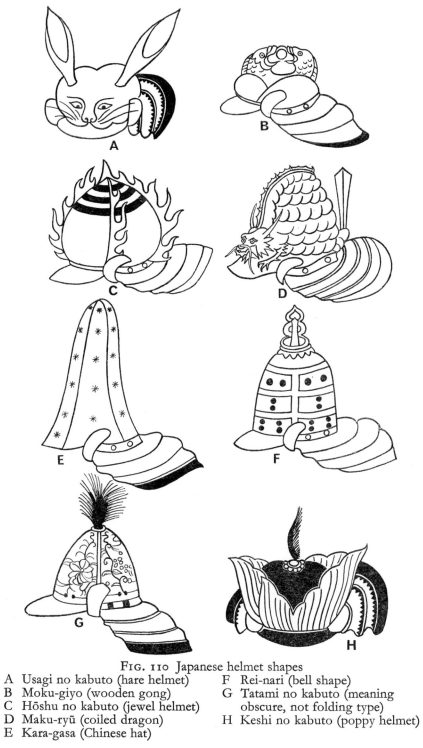

FIG. 110 Japanese helmet shapes

A   Usagi no kabuto (hare helmet)
B   Moku-giyo (wooden gong)
C   Hōshu no kabuto (jewel helmet)
D   Maku-ryū (coiled dragon)
E   Kara-gasa (Chinese hat)
F   Rei-nari (bell shape)
G   Tatami no kabuto (meaning
     obscure, not folding type)
H   Keshi no kabuto (poppy helmet)

armour made in the serviceable fashions of the Momoyama Period. A large gift of arms, horse harnesses, and lacquer, sent by the last Shōgun, Iemochi, to Queen Victoria in the early 1860s, included one of these very rich *ō-yoroi* made specially by Myōchin Muneharu in 1860 (Pl. XXIX, D).

Tough lacquered rawhide had always been a substitute for iron for Japanese armour, and in the third quarter of the nineteenth century a large number of armours—both of ancient and Momoyama fashion—were made entirely of leather, including the mask and the helmet-bowl. When first made, the leather would have been tough and resistant; but unfortunately, due to changing climates and frequent neglect, many surviving specimens have warped and shrunk, with a consequent blistering, cracking, and peeling of the lacquer.

Myōchin masters maintained their high standard to the very last, as we can observe in the surviving works of such smiths as Muretane, Muneyasu, and Munetomo. The crispness of detail and finish in the hard russet steel of their armours must always be a source of pleasure to the beholder.

The formation of a standing national army after the restoration of the Emperor Meiji, in 1868, led to the abandonment of armour. The carrying of two swords, the privilege of the *samurai* class, was banned in 1876. But when the Satsuma clan and their supporters revolted, in 1877, many *samurai* again brought out their armour and their swords for the last time.

Clothes Worn Under Armour

The Yamato warrior of the Protohistoric Period wore, as far as we can deduce, his everyday clothes beneath his armour. These consisted of a simple jacket (*kimono*), girded at the waist with a girdle (*obi*), straight full breeches (*hakama*) gartered below the knees, and boots of leather.

As the armour developed and became more colourful so were the clothes worn with it enriched. In Late Heian times silk court dress (*suikan*) was worn; but by the early Kamakura Period a special armour robe (*yoroi-hitatare*) (Fig. 111) with full matching breeches was customary. The robe was a short, full-sleeved *kimono*, adorned on breast, back, and sleeves with silk pompons (*kiku-toji*), and with cords at the wrists of the sleeves for gathering them close (*kukuri*). Breeches (*hakama*) were full and gathered into

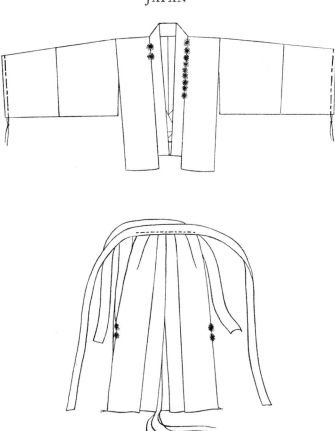

FIG. 111 *Yoroi-hitatare*. Robe (*hitatare*) with matching pleated breeches (*hakama*), worn under armour from the twelfth century to the fifteenth century and revived for use with early-style armours in the Edo Period

pleats at the front of the waist, with pompons at each side-seam and draw-cords at the bottom to gather the legs below the knees.

The infantry wore close simple *kimono* and knee-length breeches (*kobakama*), or full short breeches, or simply just a loincloth (*fundoshi*). All classes wore cloth leggings (*habaki* or *kiahan*) with double ties secured at the back of the calves, the ties of the shin-guards being at the front.

From the Ōnin era onwards a variant of the footmen's *koba-kama* was adapted by the *samurai*, and a small close-sleeved *kimono*, not necessarily of the same material, was worn with them. These shirts were called *sodeboso* or *kosode*, the close sleeves being more suitable for drawing the *kote* over the top.

This practice continued throughout the Edo Period until armour ceased to be worn, except in the case of the wealthier *samurai*, who chose to wear *dō-maru*, *haramaki*, and *ō-yoroi*, and who wore the appropriate *yoroi-hitatare* with them.

Storage and Transportation

The Ainu (Ezo) of the island of Hokkaido in northern Japan, who retained much of their ancient culture in the last century, still had some leather lamellar armours of similar make to the lamellar coats found in burial mounds in western Japan belonging to the Yamato people of the Protohistoric Period. The Ainu armours were stored in circular tublike boxes—for when not supported these armours would collapse within themselves, so that the container required no great depth.

Similar boxes may have been used by the Japanese, and it was probably not until the square-skirted *ō-yoroi* was devised that the armour chest of rectangular shape was used. The oldest armour chests were deep rectangular boxes standing on six legs: two on each of the long sides and one at each end, with a lid fitting over the outside of the upper edge. They were generally black lacquered and fitted with gilded copper corners and shoes to the legs. They were called *yoroi no karabitsu*, the name suggesting a Chinese origin.

This form of box was traditional for *ō-yoroi*, and therefore when these armours were reproduced in the Edo Period *karabitsu* were usually supplied with them.

Dō-maru and *haramaki* made for *samurai* in the Muromachi Period were also furnished with the six-legged chest; but with the simplification of equipment in the late fifteenth and early sixteenth centuries the smaller armour box was devised. The older box was secured with cords through which a pole could be passed, for transportation between two porters, while the new legless box was provided with iron loop handles with square extensions for a carrying-pole which projected above the lid when raised. Some had a square tube built in the depth of the lid, with the handle extensions corresponding to the openings on the outside. Clasps and locks were provided to the usually flush-fitting lids, and lacquered leather or paper and linen covers were provided. Some boxes had curved sides and others were deep, with padded leather carrying-loops at one side, so that they could be carried on the back of a single porter—or even by the soldier him-self.

Light boxes were made of wicker within a wooden frame, or of papiermâché; but most were of light wood, varnished or lacquered, and usually bore the owner's badge (*mon*).

These *gusoku-bitsu*, as they were called, were sometimes made in pairs for large, rich armours in the Edo Period.

Armours, when packed, were put into bags and wrappings specially designed for each part. The flat envelopes for shoulder-

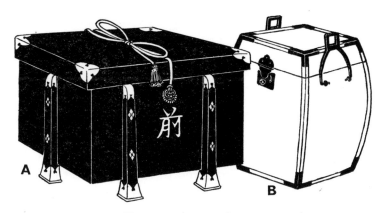

FIG. 112 Armour boxes
A *Kara-bitsu*, used up to the late fifteenth century
B *Gusoku-bitsu*, used from the late fifteenth century to the nineteenth century

guards, shinguards, etc., bore the name of the parts to be con-tained in them. Helmets and cuirasses were wrapped in cloths, large bags, or tubular pieces like pillow-cases with both ends open. Some bags were of stout cloth lined with paper, whilst others—like the wrappings—were of soft fabric. Yellow was a common colour for these.

The Shield
Flat, rectangular shields with pointed tops were used in Proto-historic Japan, but we are not certain of their size or the materials from which they were made.

Hand-shields (*te-date*) do not appear to have been used very much at any time in Japanese history, the more usual being a standing rectangular pavise (*tate*) supported by a hinged prop at the back. Shields of this type were used to form defensive walls on land, on the sides of boats, and on the walls of castles; and they did not alter in appearance from the eleventh century to the nineteenth century.

The Buki Nihiaku Dzu[15] illustrates several forms of shield, all pierced with square or triangular loops, including a small rectangular one to be held in the hand by a horseman (*bajō-date*). The others, including the normal wooden *tate*, are all for siege purposes and include a rack to support bundles of bamboos, a tall right-angled screen with loops made to fold (*biōbu-date*), and a long one on wheels, similar to mantlets used in Europe and called *kuruma-date*.

Ordinary standing shields were painted with black bars at the top and sometimes a *mon*. Some of these were made to fold at the centre, but they were generally solid and when transported were carried on the soldiers' backs.

An iron folding shield in the Tower Collection, London, is made of thirteen curved plates, like a large rectangular shoulder-guard, laced with heavy pairs of silk braids. It is made rigid by two vertical strips of iron secured to the upper and lower plates with turning-pins. An iron loop handle is provided on the fourth plate from the top, with a turning-pin and loop for the securing of an iron support. It is probably of the eighteenth century or later.

Horse Armour

Simple iron chamfrons with applied gilt-bronze borders have been found in Protohistoric burial mounds in western Japan, but there is no evidence of the use of horse armour of any other kind before the Edo Period. The large leather flanchards (*aori*), suspended from the saddle at the sides of the horse's body, were only defensive in the sense that they protected him from the heavy stirrups.

When first devised, probably in the eighteenth century, horse armour (*uma-yoroi*) consisted of grotesque moulded leather or papiermâché chamfrons, brightly lacquered to represent dragons or caricatures of horses' heads (*ba-men*). Crinets, or neck armour, were of small plates and mail, with large sections for throat and breast and for the crupper of fabric covered with small embossed square pieces of lacquered rawhide. Peytrals, or breastplates,

were sometimes made from small plates of iron or leather connected with mail, and cruppers were also made with large rawhide ribs attached to a foundation.

Complete horse armours are to be seen in the Museo Stibbert,
Florence, and in the Musée de l'Armée, Paris.

CHAPTER SEVEN

1 Sunaga Masao, *Nippon Jodai no Katchū*, Tokyo, 1934. This work illustrates a remarkable series of these excavated armours, with details of construction and comparative reconstructions.

2 J. Edward Kidder, *Japan*, Ancient Peoples and Places Series, London, 1959. An excellent guide to the history of ancient Japan, with good illustrations of actual armour and also of armoured *haniwa*.

3 Sasama Yoshihiko, *Nippon Katchū Zukan*, 3 vols, Tokyo, 1964. Volume I contains an excellent series of drawings showing the development of lamellar armours.

4 Sasama, ibid., Vol. I, Plates VI–IX. An interesting series of colours and patterns of armour lacing are given here, taken from eleventh- and twelfth-century paintings and actual specimens of armour.

5 Sakakibara Kōzan, *Chukō Katchū Seisakuben*, Edo, 1800. Translation edited by H. Russell Robinson, *The Manufacture of Armour and Helmets in 16th century Japan*, London, 1963, Ch. II, pp. 35–36.

6 Three scrolls make up this work, which is now divided between the Boston Museum of Fine Arts, the Tokyo National Museum, and the Seikado Foundation, Tokyo. Hundreds of armed men, both horse and foot, are illustrated in considerable detail.

7 A painting of Ashikaga Takauji (1305–58), bearing the cypher of his son Yoshiakira and formerly the property of the Moriya family, shows splinted arm defences and shinguards, with small standing knee pieces.

8 The *Moko Shurai Ekotoba Emaki*. Picture scroll of the Mongol Invasion of Japan, 1281, painted in the late thirteenth century; shows several footmen wearing pairs of *kote*, whilst the *samurai* only wear one on the left arm. The *Yuki Kassen Ekotoka Emaki*, which illustrates episodes in the civil war of 1440, shows almost all the *samurai* wearing pairs of *kote*.

9 Sakakibara, op. cit., Ch. XI, pp. 122–5.

10 Ibid., p. 20.

11 Matt. Garbutt, 'Japanese Armour from the Inside', *Transactions of the Japan Society of London*, Vol. XI, 1914.

12 The arming of soldiers according to rank is clearly shown in the manuscript *Yoroi-Chakuyo no Shidai* by Ountei Sadamasa, Edo, 1801, in the author's collection.

[13] Sakakibara, ibid., Ch. VIII, pp. 110–12.

[14] Thomas T. Hoopes, 'A Recent Acquisition of Japanese Arms and Armor', *Metropolitan Museum Studies*, Vol. II, 1929–30, pp. 221–35.

[15] Kobayashi Sukenori, *Buki Nihiaku Dzu*, Edo, 1846. This is a picture book of military equipment, fortification, and formations.

SELECT BIBLIOGRAPHY

Arai, Hakuseki, *The Armour Book in Honchō-Gunkikō*. Translation edited by H. Russell Robinson, London, 1964.

Boots, J. L., 'Korean Weapons and Armour', *Trans. Korean Branch Royal Asiatic Society*, XXIII, Pt. 2, pp. 1–37, Seoul, 1934.

Bullock, Randolph, 'Oriental Arms and Armor', *Bull. Metropolitan Museum of Art*, n.s. V, pp. 169–72, 1947.

Clarke, C. Purdon, *Arms and Armour at Sandringham*, London, 1910.

Dean, Bashford, 'Handbook of Arms and Armor, European and Oriental, Fourth edition', *Metropolitan Museum of Art*, Ch. XI, pp. 241–52, New York, 1930.

Egerton, Hon. Wilbraham, *An Illustrated Handbook of Indian Arms*, London, 1880.

Egerton of Tatton, Rt. Hon. Lord, *A Description of Indian and Oriental Armour*, London, 1896. A reprint of the former with much additional material.

Garbutt, Matt. 'Japanese Armour from the Inside', *Trans. Japan Society of London*, Vol. XI, 1914.

Grancsay, Stephen V., 'The Oriental Armor Gallery', *Bull. Metropolitan Museum of Art*, XV, pp. 87–88, 1920.

'A Loan Collection of Oriental Armor', *Bull. Metropolitan Museum of Art*, XXIII, pp. 127–9, 1928.

'The George C. Stone Bequest. Turkish, Balkan, Caucasian, and North African Arms and Armor', *Bull. Metropolitan Museum of Art*, XXXII, pp. 54–58, 1937.

'The George C. Stone Bequest. Indian and Persian Arms and Armor', *Bull. Metropolitan Museum of Art*, XXXII, pp. 167–72, 1937.

Hendley, Thomas Holbein, *Ulwar and its Art Treasures*, London, 1888. *Damascening on Steel or Iron, as practised in India*, London, 1892.

Hoopes, Thomas T., 'A Recent Acquisition of Japanese Arms and Armor', *Metropolitan Museum Studies*, II, pp. 221–35, 1929–30.

Arms and Armor, an elementary guide to the Collection in the City Art Museum of St. Louis, Missouri, U.S.A., 1954.

Kidder, J. Edward, *Japan*, Ancient Peoples and Places Series, London, 1959.

Laking, Guy Francis, 'Oriental Arms and Armour', *The Wallace Collection*, London, H.M.S.O., 1914, reprint 1964.

Laufer, Berthold, '*Chinese Clay Figures*, Part I, *Prolegomena on the History of Defensive Armor*, Field Museum of Natural History, Publication 177, Anthropological Series, XIII, No. 2, Chicago, 1914.

Mann, James G., 'The Influence of Art on Instruments of War', *Journal of the Royal Society of Arts*, LXXIX, pp. 740–84, London, 1941.

Mayer, L. A., 'Saracenic Arms and Armour', *Ars Islamica*, X, pp. 1–12, 1943.

Moser, H., 'Collection H. Moser-Charlottenfels', *Oriental Arms and Armour*, Leipzig, 1912.

Nesselrode, *Armes et Armures de la Collection du Comte de Nesselrode, au Château de Tzarevtchina*, Paris, 1904.

P(aul), F. V., 'Mohammedan Arms and Armour', *Museum of Fine Arts (Boston)*, Bull. XIV, pp. 18–21, 1916.

Robinson, H. Russell, *A Short History of Japanese Armour*, London, H.M.S.O., 1965.

Sakakibara, Kozan, *Chukō Katchū Seisakuben*, Edo, 1800. Translation edited by H. Russell Robinson, *The Manufacture of Armour and Helmets in 16th century Japan*, London, 1963.

Sasama Yoshihiko, *Nippon Katchū Zukan*, 3 vols, Tokyo, 1964.

Stöcklein, Hans, 'Die Waffenschätze im Topkapu Sarayi Müzesi zu Istanbul—Ein vorläufiger Bericht', *Ars Islamica*, I, pp. 200–18, 1934.

'Arms and armour', in Pope (A. U.), *Survey of Persian Art*, III, pp. 2555–85, 1939.

Stone, George Cameron, *A Glossary of the Construction, Decoration and Use of Arms and Armor in all Countries and in all Times, together with some closely related subjects*, Portland, Maine, 1934.

Suenaga Masao, *Nippon Jodai no Katchū*, Tokyo, 1934.

Thordeman, Bengt, *Armour from the Battle of Wisby 1361*, Vol. I, Ch. VII, pp. 245–84, Uppsala, 1939.

Werner, E. T. C., 'Chinese Weapons', *Royal Asiatic Society North China Branch* (Extra Vol.), Shanghai, 1932.

Yamagami Hachiro, *Japan's Ancient Armour*, Government Tourist Library, No. 31, Tokyo, 1940.

Zeller, Rudolf, and Rohrer, Ernst F., 'Orientalische Sammlung Henri Moser-Charlottenfels', *Catalogue of the Bernisches Historisches Museum*, Bern, 1955.

GLOSSARY OF TECHNICAL TERMS
USED IN THE TEXT

EUROPEAN TERMS USED THROUGHOUT THE TEXT

Aventail | The pendent mail defence attached to a helmet as generally used in Europe in the fourteenth and early fifteenth centuries.

Brigandine | A body defence made in the form of a coat or doublet of silk or velvet reinforced with canvas and lined with rows of plates secured by rivets. The rivet-heads were usually gilded to show up on the surface of the rich outer fabric and the plates were tinned to prevent rusting.

Cabacete | The Spanish name for a morion, a helmet with a narrow brim and a stalklike finial forged at the apex of the crown.

Cataphractus | The Greco-Roman term for a heavy armed cavalry-man. He might or might not ride on an armoured horse, but as the name implies he was originally protected with scale armour.

Chamfron | A defence for a horse's head.

Cingulum militare | The Roman military belt which supported the dagger (puggio) and sometimes the sword (gladius). Usually the sword was carried on a separate shoulder-belt.

Crest | An ornamental device surmounting a helmet and sometimes a horse chamfron.

Crupper | Armour for the hindquarters of a horse.

Cuirass | A defence for the body originally of leather, as the name implies, but now applied to any form of body armour.

Flanchard | A defence for a horse's flank generally suspended from the saddle.

Lamellae | The individual small plates employed in the construction of lamellar armour made from either metal, hide, bone, or wood.

Lamellar armour | Armour constructed with small rectangular plates each pierced with a regular series of holes and laced into horizontal rows with leather thongs or cords, the rows or laminations thus created then being connected to each other with vertical laces by various methods. The laminations generally overlap upwards, but in rare instances the order is reversed.

Laminations | Strips of metal or other strong material connected by various means to permit freedom of movement to body or limbs and at the same time provide a degree of protection.

Limes	Roman frontier forts or defences.
Lorica	Roman body armour.
Lorica hemata	A shirt of mail used by Roman soldiers probably derived from Celtic originals.
Lorica segmentata	A Roman legionary cuirass constructed with horizontal hoops of bronze or iron mounted upon internal leathers, hinged down the centre of the back and secured with clasps or straps and buckles at the front.
Lorica squamata	Roman scale body armour.
Machaira	A Greek and Persian sword developed from the Egyptian and Babylonian kopis. The blade curves forward from the hilt and has a concave cutting edge.
Mail	A defence constructed of rings or links of wire. The most usual construction for this defence is that made with circular rings, each one passing through four others, the joins being riveted, welded, or butted after linking up.
Nasal	A defence for the nose in the form of a strip or bar attached to the front of a helmet.
Peytral	Armour for the breast of a horse.
Phalerae	Medals and honours won by Roman soldiers worn attached to a harness of straps over the body armour.
Scale armour	A defence constructed with small plates of metal, hide, horn, or wood, secured by one edge to a foundation of leather or fabric placed in horizontal rows overlapping each other both sideways and downwards and usually imbricated like the tiles of a roof or the scales of a fish.
Spangenhelm	The modern German term for a conical helmet built up of segments of metal.
Targe or Target	A light shield or buckler usually of circular form.
Vambrace	A plate defence for the arm. When first introduced in Europe in the fourteenth century they only covered the forearm from wrist to elbow.
Zischägge	The German name for a seventeenth-century cavalryman's helmet evolved from the peaked Turkish *chichak*.

CHAPTER II PERSIA

Bazuband	A plate defence for the forearm with or without an extension for the hand.
Char-aina	'Four mirrors.' The name given to the Perso-Indian cuirass consisting of four circular or rectangular plates secured round the body with straps or hinges.
Clibanarius	A Persian cavalryman of the type called by the Romans *cataphractus*. Both rider and horse were completely armed.

Grīvpān	The Pahlavi name for the *kūiris* or pendent mail defence of a helmet.
Kūiris	The pendent mail defence attached to the lower edge of a helmet.
Kulah-khud	A helmet.
Ozan	An armourer.
Pagri	A turban or headcloth.
Rānapānō	A defence for the thigh with the kneeguard attached.
Shamsher	The Persian sword.
Sipar	A shield.
Zirih-baktah	A mail coat or shirt.

CHAPTER III   TURKEY

Chichak	A helmet.
Kilig	The Turkish sword.
Korazin	A cuirass of plates connected with mail.
Missiourka	A shallow skull-cap of iron with long pendent mail defence for head and neck for wear over a cap and headcloth. Although of Turkish origin it was more popular in eastern Europe.
Spahis	The Turkish cavalry.

CHAPTER IV   THE MIDDLE EAST

Daraka	A shield usually made of hide. See also *turs*.
Dībādj	Brocade used for rich coats worn over armour.
Dir	A mail shirt.
Djawshan	A coat of mail and plates combined.
Harba	A javelin.
Jibbah	A quilted coat worn beneath a mail shirt or as the sole body defence.
Karkal	A fabric coat lined with small plates. A brigandine.
Kawnas	A tall conical helmet.
Kazaghand	A mail shirt covered and lined with fabric.
Khawdha	A helmet.
Khuff	Riding-boots.
Mihmaz	Spurs.
Mudjaffaf	Heavy cavalry. A completely armed man and horse.
Muwa'ama	A helmet with a rounded skull of the type much used in Egypt and Turkey in the late fifteenth and sixteenth centuries.
Nimdja	A dagger. See also *sīkh*.
Rumh	A lance.
Saif	A sword, straight or curved.
Sāk al-mūza	Leg armour, probably for thigh and knee only.
Sīkh	A dagger. See also *nimdja*.
Tidjfaf	A horse armour of felt or quilted fabric.
Turs	A shield. See also *daraka*.

Chapter V   INDIA

Angirk'hah	A long rich fabric coat worn over the armour.
Ankus	An elephant goad.
Artak-i kajam	A quilted trapper for a horse usually forming a foundation for one of mail.
Bagta-kalghi	Plumes of heron feathers worn on the helmet.
Baktar-zillo	A scale armour.
Bhanjce	A defensive coat with a gorget (throatguard) attached.
Chakra	A steel quoit with sharpened outer edge, thrown as a missile. It was a great favourite of the Akali Sikhs, who were very skilled in its use.
Char-aina	A cuirass of four rectangular plates joined round the body with straps or hinges. The name is Persian in origin.
Chihal'ta	'Forty-fold coat.' A fabric coat of many layers worn by soldiers. See also *chiltah*.
Chihal'ta Hazar Māshā	'Coat of a thousand nails.' A coat of many layers of fabric faced with velvet and studded with thousands of small gilt nails arranged in patterns.
Chiltah	A corrupt form of *chihal'ta*.
Dastana	Plate defences for the forearm with or without extensions for the back of the hand.
Dhal	A shield.
Ganga-Jamni	Mail of iron rings with patterns worked in brass or copper rings likened to the meeting of the dark waters of the River Jamna with the muddy ones of the River Ganges.
Gardani	Armour for a horse's neck.
G'hug'hwah	A mail coat with a hood permanently attached.
Kajam	Horse armour of mail.
Kant'hah sobha	A gorget. Armour for the neck and throat.
Kashka	A chamfron or horse helmet.
Kincob	Brocade used extensively for lining armour.
Koftgari	The decoration of iron with patterns in gold and silver either inlaid or overlaid, commonly called damascening.
Kubega	A quilted coat worn under mail.
Kukri	The Nepalese sword.
Madu or Maru	A small parrying shield mounted in the centre of a pair of steel-tipped roebuck horns. In some instances the shield is absent, the horns being used to parry in a similar manner to the left-hand dagger of Europe.
Pagri	A turban.
Peti	A simple wrap-round cuirass of leather or fabric fastening at the front.
Sosun pattah	A sword with a forward-curving leaf-shaped blade with a concave cutting edge.
Tōp	A helmet whether a simple mail hood, one of mail and plates or of one piece of iron.
Zirih	A mail shirt or coat.

CEYLON

Gadumba	A wood used for shields.
Palanga	A large shield.
Palidal	Mail.
Paliha	A small shield.
Palisa	A small shield.
Sambhur	Buffalo hide used for facing shields.

CHAPTER VI   CHINA

Han-jên	Armourers at the court of the Chou Dynasty.
Hung t'ao kia	'Red-banded armour.' Probably a form of laminated armour.
Jên ma k'ai	'Brilliant horse armour.' Polished iron horse armour probably of lamellar construction.
Jung kia	Possibly an armour of horn scales.
K'ai	'Metal leaf.' An armour of metal scales or lamellae first recorded in Later Han times.
K'ai i	'Armour clothing.' Armour of fabric lined with plates.
Kao	The coat of a fabric armour.
Kia	An armour of hide, at first of rhinoceros but later of buffalo.
Kia i	The coat of an armour.
Kiai	An armour of hide scales. Also a horse armour of leather scales.
Kie tun	A shield for use in a chariot.
Lang ya pai	A large shield made of elm used in sieges.
Lei	The inner side of an armour.
Lien so kia	'Chain-connected armour.' Possibly an alternative name for mail or the Chinese equivalent of small plates connected with mail.
Li p'ai	A shield of bamboo or wood used in siege warfare.
Ma k'ai	Horse armour of metal, generally of lamellar construction.
Ma ting kia	'Horse armour with nails.' Horse armour of fabric with or without internal plates with gilt nail-heads on the outside.
Mu lo	A shield made of boards (*feng pien*).
P'ang p'ai	A circular red lacquered cavalry shield used in south China.
Pei k'uei	A round shield of red lacquered hide.
Piao ch'iang	An infantry shield of cowhide about eight feet long used in south China.
Po	A large circular convex cane shield generally painted with a conventional tiger's face and carried by infantry.
Pu tun	A long narrow infantry shield.
Shang	The skirt of a fabric armour.

Shan wen kia	'Armour with mountain pattern.' Probably an armour with pointed scale heads making rows of zigzag lines across the surface.
Si lin kia	'Armour of thin scales.' An armour constructed with thin iron scales.
Si tun	A shield made from rhinoceros hide.
So tse k'ai	Mail. Most mail in China was of foreign origin.
Sü tun	A tall shield originating in the country of the Shu (Sze-ch'uan).
T'ie cha	Lamellar armour.
Ting kia	'Armour with nails.' Armour of fabric lined with plates which were held in position with gilt-headed nails. Most late specimens contain no plates.
Ts'ing t'ao kia	'Blue-banded armour.' Probably a form of laminated armour.
Wu k'uei	'Generals of Wu.' A large flat shield.

Chapter VII   JAPAN

Agemaki	A symmetrical bow of cord attached to the back ring of a helmet or cuirass. It was also called *tombō-musubi* because it resembled the dragonfly in shape.
Akoda-nari	A type of ridged helmet-bowl likened to the shape of an Akoda incense-burner. It was low and rounded, with the back a little higher than the front.
Aori	Leather flanchards hung at the horse's sides attached to rings on the saddle.
Ashigaru-gusoku	Common soldier's armour.
Bajo-date	A horseman's shield.
Ba-men	A chamfron; a horse mask.
Biobu-date	A folding shield pierced with loop-holes.
Bishamon-gote	Sleeves with small shoulderguards permanently attached, likened to those worn by Bishamon-ten, one of the seven Gods of Felicity.
Bishamon-suneate	Tubular plate shinguards likened to those worn by Bishamon-ten, one of the seven Gods of Felicity.
Bonji	Debased Sanskrit characters put upon military equipment as protective charms.
Chu-sode	Medium-size shoulderguards.
Dō	Lit. 'body'. A cuirass; armour for the body complete with its pendent guards for the hips (*kusazuri*).
Dō-maru	A cuirass of lamellar construction wrapping round the body and fastening at the right side.
Dzu-nari	'Head shaped.' A type of ridged helmet with a high rounded back to the skull.
Eboshi-nari	'Cap shape.' A helmet shaped like a tall *samurai* cap.
Fukigayeshi	The earlike turned-back edges of a neckguard of a Japanese helmet.
Fukurin	Soft metal and alloy rims applied to the edges of leather-covered iron plates such as the peak of a helmet or the upper breastplate of a cuirass.

Fundoshi	The loincloth worn by all Japanese males.
Gomai-dō	A cuirass of five vertical sections joined with hinges.
Gomai-kabuto	A helmet with a neckguard of five plates.
Gumi	The loops on the shoulder-straps of a cuirass for the attachment of the shoulderguards.
Gusoku	A complete armour. A term generally employed to denote armour of Momoyama fashion.
Gusoku-bitsu	A light armour box with iron carrying-loops.
Gyōyō	'Apricot leaves.' Leaf-shaped leather-covered iron plates used as shoulderguards with *dō-maru* when worn by the infantry and later when adapted by the *samurai* and worn with large shoulderguards, the *gyōyō* were used to cover the shoulder-strap fastenings.
Habaki	Leggings worn beneath the shinguards. See also *kiahan*.
Hachi	Lit. 'bowl'. A helmet-bowl or crown.
Hachiman-za	'Seat of the God Hachiman.' The hole in the top of a helmet. This name was used in the Edo Period. See also *tehen*.
Hachimaki	A cloth tied about the head, frequently worn beneath the helmet.
Haidate	'Girt shield.' Armour for the thighs tied like an apron round the waist.
Hakama	Full pleated breeches worn by the Japanese male.
Hambō	A defence for the chin and lower cheeks.
Haniwa	Pottery models of people, animals, and objects planted around burial mounds in the Protohistoric Period.
Happuri	A guard for the brow and cheeks only.
Hara-ate	A light cuirass covering the front and sides of the body only.
Haramaki	A cuirass opening at the centre of the back.
Hata-ashigaru-gusoku	A cuirass for a common soldier opening at the back like a *haramaki*.
Hatomune-dō	'Pigeon-breasted cuirass.' A solid iron cuirass with a medial ridge to the breastplate.
Hineno-jikoro	A close-fitting helmet neckguard introduced by the Hineno school in the sixteenth century.
Hishinui	Crossed laces of leather or braid on the bottom plate of a piece of armour or used to join the plates of a cuirass.
Hiza-yoroi	'Knee armour.' An early form of thigh defence.
Hōate	A half-mask without a nosepiece.
Hoshi	Lit. 'stars'. The projecting rivet-heads on a helmet-bowl.
Hoshi-kabuto	A helmet with projecting rivet-heads on the bowl.
Ikada	'Rafts.' Small rectangular iron plates set into the mail of certain defensive sleeves and thighguards.
Ita-mono	Armour plates made from one piece of iron or rawhide, not built up of lamellae.

Ito-odoshi	The lacing of an armour with silk braid.
Jingasa	A war-hat of iron, copper, lacquered leather or paper.
Kabuto	A helmet complete with peak and neckguard.
Kachi-gusoku	Infantry armour.
Kaga-kote	Defensive sleeves of the type first made in Kaga Province.
Kamuri-ita	'Cap plate.' The upper plate of a shoulderguard or *sendan no ita* usually covered with leather.
Kanagu-mawari	The solid iron plates, generally covered with leather or lacquer, at breast, back, and sides of a lamellar cuirass.
Kanamono	Functional and ornamental soft metal fittings applied to an armour.
Kasa-jikoro	A neckguard of a helmet rather flat and spreading like a Japanese hat (*kasa*).
Kasa-jirushi	'Hat badge.' A streamer-like flag tied to the ring on the back of a helmet bearing the wearer's badge or that of his commander.
Kashira-date	A crest attached to the top of a helmet.
Kawara-haidate	Thighguards with plates shaped like roof tiles.
Kebiki	'Hair spread over.' Armour lacing with the braids set close together.
Keikō	The earliest Japanese lamellar armour introduced from Asia in about the fifth century A.D.
Ken	A straight sword of classical form introduced into Japan through Buddhist art.
Kiahan	Leggings worn beneath the shinguards. See also *habaki*.
Kiku no maru	Circular gilt rivet-heads on an armour in the form of chrysanthemums being both functional and ornamental.
Kiku-toji	'Chrysanthemum sewing.' Silk pompons worn on facings, sleeves, and back of an armour robe and on the side-seams of breeches.
Kimono	The ordinary robe or sleeved garment worn by Japanese men and women.
Kobakama	Small breeches worn by *samurai* and infantry from the late fifteenth century to the nineteenth century when wearing armour. They were closer fitting than *hakama*.
Kohaze	Long togglelike buttons used for fastening the shoulder-straps of cuirasses and such elements of modern armour as *kote*.
Kohire	'Little wings.' Solid or laminated guards for the point of the shoulder attached to the shoulder-straps of a cuirass.
Koshimaki	Lit. 'loin wrap'. The brim of a helmet-bowl to which the peak and neckguard are attached.
Kōshōzan	A name used in the Edo Period for the high-sided multiplate helmets of the sixteenth century.
Kosode	A *kimono* with small close sleeves. See also *sodeboso*.

Kote	Fabric sleeves with plates and mail attached to the outside, usually including an extension for the back of the hand.
Kukuri	Draw-cords at wrist and knee of *yoroi-hitatare*.
Kuruma-date	A large shield or mantlet on wheels.
Kusari	Mail.
Kusari-katabira	A mail coat lined with fabric.
Kusazuri	The pendent laminated guards for the hips and upper thighs attached to the waist of a cuirass.
Kyūbi or Kyūbi no ita	The solid iron plate for protecting the left shoulder-strap fastening on an *ō-yoroi* or late *dō-maru*.
Mayedate-mono	The front crest attached to a helmet.
Mempō	A half-mask with a nosepiece.
Mitsu-kuwagata	A pair of horns on the front of a helmet with a third straight one in the centre. This was a fashion of the Muromachi Period (1334–1572).
Moko-hachi-gyo	'Mongolian bowl shape.' A helmet of Asiatic origin used in Japan from about the ninth century to tenth century.
Momonari	'Peach shape.' A helmet shaped like a stylized peach with a pointed crown.
Mon	A family badge.
Muna-ita	'Breastplate.' The top plate of the breast section of a cuirass, usually a solid iron plate covered with stencilled leather.
Naginata	A spear with a single-edged curved blade.
Namban-bachi	'Foreign bowl.' A helmet-bowl of foreign make or design.
Namban-dō	A cuirass of foreign make or design.
Namban-gusoku	An armour containing foreign elements or one made under foreign influence.
Neri-gawa	'Hard leather.' Rawhide, usually buffalo hide, used for all parts of the armour as a substitute for iron.
Nimai-dō	A cuirass in two parts joined by a hinge at the left side.
Nodowa	'Throat ring.' A defence for the neck and chest; a gorget.
Obi	A sash or belt tied about the waist.
Odoshi	The complete lacing of an armour.
Odoshige	Strips of dyed doeskin or woven silk braid used for lacing the laminations of an armour together.
Odoshi-haidate	Thighguards with plates laced with braid as the rest of the armour.
Okegawa-dō	A cuirass introduced in the sixteenth century built up of horizontal or vertical plates riveted together.
Ō-kuwagata	Large flat metal horns attached to the front of a helmet.
Oni-gashira	A demon's head worn on the front of a helmet as a crest.
Ō-sode	Large shoulderguards.
Ō-tateage no suneate	Shinguards with large extensions to protect the knees.

Ō-yoroi	The lamellar armour worn by most horsemen up to the late fifteenth century, so called to distinguish it from later armours with smaller elements.
Sane	Large lamellae of hide or iron laced into horizontal strips to form the elements of an armour. Small lamellae were called *ko-zane*.
Sane-yoroi	An armour built up of lamellar.
Sanmai-kabuto	A helmet with a neckguard of three plates.
Sashimono	A flag or device carried on a bamboo shaft held in brackets on the backplate of an armour.
Sawari	'White bronze.' The splashing of russet-iron armour plates with white metal. A fashion of the Edo Period.
Se-ita	The narrow backplate of a *haramaki*.
Sendan or Sendan no ita	The laminated guard for the right shoulder-strap fastening of an *ō-yoroi* or late *dō-maru*.
Shakudō	A copper alloy containing a small percentage of gold which is patinated to a dark blue-black colour.
Shii-nari	'Nut shaped.' A helmet shaped like a nut, of rounded conical form of varying height.
Shikoro	The neckguard of a helmet.
Shita-toji	'Lower binding.' The lace securing the lamellae into rows to form the 'plates' of an armour.
Shōji-ita	'Screen plate.' Standing crescent-shaped plates attached to the shoulder-straps of a cuirass to prevent the upper edge of the shoulderguards from striking the neck when in action.
Shokakufu no hachi	'Battering-ram-shaped bowl.' A Protohistoric helmet with a projecting 'beaked' front.
Sode	Lit. 'sleeve'. A laminated defence for the shoulder and upper arm.
Sodeboso	A *kimono* with close-fitting sleeves. See also *kosode*.
Sugake	Lit. 'sparse pointed'. Armour lacing with the braids in widely spaced pairs.
Suikan	A court robe sometimes worn beneath armour in the eleventh and twelfth centuries.
Suji	Lit. 'line or stripe'. The standing flanges of the helmet plates.
Suji-kabuto	A helmet without projecting rivets on the bowl, but with standing flanges to each of the plates.
Suneate	Shinguards.
Tameshi	Tests made on armour with arrows or musket balls discharged at close range.
Tankō	A plate cuirass of the Protohistoric Period.
Tatami-gusoku	Folding armour. An armour which could be contained in a small box and easily transported by one person.
Tate	A rectangular standing shield of wood with a support.
Tateage-suneate	Shinguards with extensions to protect the knees.
Tatehagi-dō	An *okegawa-dō* with vertical plates.
Te-date	A shield for carrying in the hand.

Tehen	The hole in the top of a helmet. See also *Hachiman-za*.
Tsubo-sode	Shoulderguards of semicircular section tapering towards the lowest plate.
Tsuru-bashiri	'Bow-strings path.' The stencilled doeskin cover of a breastplate, usually a common feature of *ō-yoroi*.
Tsutsu-gote	Armoured sleeves with three large hinged plates on the forearms. The name likens them to a tube.
Uchidashi	'Embossed.' All parts of the armour were subjected to embossed ornament in the Edo Period.
Uma-nari	'Plum shaped.' A helmet shaped like a plum, of low rounded conical form.
Uma-yoroi	Horse armour.
Ushiro-date	A crest attached at the back of a helmet.
Uwa-manchira	Neck armour worn over the top of the cuirass.
Uwa-obi	The sash or belt tied over the cuirass.
Waidate	The separate right side-section of a cuirass of *ō-yoroi*.
Waki-date	Crest carried on either side of a helmet such as horns, ears or antlers.
Waki-ita	'Side-plate.' The iron plates beneath the arms on a cuirass.
Watagami	Lit. 'cotton chewing'. The shoulder-straps of a cuirass.
Yokohagi-dō	An *okegawa-dō* with horizontal plates.
Yoroi	An armour. The cuirass with its pendent skirt (*kusazuri*) and shoulderguards (*sode*).
Yoroi-hitatare	'Armour robe.' Clothing worn under armour.
Yoroi no karabitsu	A chest on six legs used for storage and transportation of armour in early times.
Yukinoshita-dō	A solid-plate cuirass of the type invented by Myōchin Hisaiye of Yukinoshita in Sagami Province.
Zaru-nari	'Basket shape.' A low rounded helmet-bowl.
Zōgan	Gold or silver damascene applied to iron armour plates. Kaga Province was famous for it.

INDEX

H